The Origins of Music Theory in the Age of Plato

Also available from Bloomsbury

*Aesthetic Themes in Pagan and Christian Neoplatonism:
From Plotinus to Gregory of Nyssa*, Daniele Iozzia
Anaximander: A Re-assessment, Andrew Gregory
Boethius' Consolation of Philosophy as a Product of Late Antiquity,
Antonio Donato

The Origins of Music Theory in the Age of Plato

Sean Alexander Gurd

BLOOMSBURY ACADEMIC
NEW YORK • LONDON • OXFORD • NEW DELHI • SYDNEY

BLOOMSBURY ACADEMIC
Bloomsbury Publishing Inc
1385 Broadway, New York, NY 10018, USA
50 Bedford Square, London, WC1B 3DP, UK
29 Earlsfort Terrace, Dublin 2, Ireland

BLOOMSBURY, BLOOMSBURY ACADEMIC and the Diana logo
are trademarks of Bloomsbury Publishing Plc

First published in Great Britain 2020
Paperback edition first published 2021

Copyright © Sean Alexander Gurd, 2020

For legal purposes the Acknowledgments on p. vii constitute
an extension of this copyright page.

Cover design: Terry Woodley
Cover image © Semiconductor, 20Hz (2011)

All rights reserved. No part of this publication may be reproduced or transmitted in any form or by any means, electronic or mechanical, including photocopying, recording, or any information storage or retrieval system, without prior permission in writing from the publishers.

Bloomsbury Publishing Inc does not have any control over, or responsibility for, any third-party websites referred to or in this book. All internet addresses given in this book were correct at the time of going to press. The author and publisher regret any inconvenience caused if addresses have changed or sites have ceased to exist, but can accept no responsibility for any such changes.

Library of Congress Control Number: 2019949426

ISBN: HB: 978-1-3500-7198-8
PB: 978-1-3501-9444-1
ePDF: 978-1-3500-7199-5
eBook: 978-1-3500-7200-8

Typeset by RefineCatch Limited, Bungay, Suffolk

To find out more about our authors and books visit
www.bloomsbury.com and sign up for our newsletters.

*Julija Šukys and Sebastian Šukys Gurd are
the heart of my being.*

*This book is dedicated to
the memory of Thomas Habinek.*

Contents

List of Figures	viii
Preface	ix
Introduction	1
Part One Plato	23
Chapter 1	25
Chapter 2	43
Chapter 3	59
Part Two Aristoxenus	91
Chapter 4	93
Chapter 5	125
Conclusion	157
Notes	163
Works Cited	193
Index	211

Figures

1. Basic format for the musical diagrams that follow — 15
2. Basic form of the tetrachord — 17
3. The central octave of the Greek tonal system, with note names — 18
4. Upper limits of movable notes in the three genera of tunings, according to Aristoxenus — 19
5. The Ratios corresponding to the musical intervals produced during the demiurge's construction of the world soul in Plato's *Timaeus* — 67
6. The completed world soul in Plato's *Timaeus* — 68
7. The first set of proportions, imagined as strips of material — 69
8. The first set of proportions imagined as marks on a single strip of material — 70
9. Two conjunct tetrachords in the enharmonic genus — 108
10. According to Aristoxenus, a tuning is musical if notes four steps away from each other (X → Y) complete a perfect fourth, or if notes five steps away from each other (X → Z) complete a perfect fifth — 112
11. A tuning is musical only if all the notes of two successive tetrachords are concordant — 113
12. The steps in Aristoxenus' argument that a fourth is equal to exactly two and a half tones — 115
13. Aristoxenus' experimental construction (on the left) beside a fragment of the tuning called the 'tonic chromatic' — 119
14. Aristoxenus' construction produces a series of small intervals which cannot be sung through in a 'musical' way as he defines 'musical movement' — 121
15. How the enharmonic tuning was made — 137

Preface

To ease access to the material I discuss here, I have transliterated Greek words and passages. The transliterations represent the Greek letter eta as ē and the Greek letter omega as ō. Iota 'subscripts' are transliterated as 'adscripts'. The transliteration does not distinguish between long and short when rendering upsilon, iota and alpha. Names, titles and Greek words in common use are not transliterated according to this system; they reflect accepted English (Latinized) usage. Authors and Titles are abbreviated according to the *Oxford Classical Dictionary*, 4th edition.

This book was substantially written on a research leave provided by the University of Missouri in 2015–2016, then completed during the first half of the academic year 2018–2019, when I was a member of the Institute for Advanced Study, thanks to funding provided by the Association of Members of the Institute for Advanced Study (AMIAS), which I gratefully acknowledge here. The figures contained in this book were brilliantly executed on the basis of my drawings by Gabriella Hoskin. I am also deeply grateful to the many friends and colleagues who have directly or indirectly contributed to my thinking, and also my well-being, while working on this book, including Nathan Martin, Pauline LeVen, John Franklin, Tosca Lynch, Eleonora Rocconi, Tim Power, Jonas Grethlein, Stephan Hagel, David Roselli, Nandini Pandey, Jim Porter, Verity Platt, Anatole Mori, David Schenker, Dennis Trout, Ray Marks, Barbara Wallach, Victoria Wohl, Paul Allen Miller, Erik Gunderson, Francesca Martelli, Scott McGill, Ellen Finckelpearl, Angelos Chaniotis, Heinrich von Staden, Sean Franzel, Carsten Strathausen, Sean Ireton and Roger Cook. Especial thanks to Sandeep Bhagwati, John Stewart, Sebastian Noelle, Lisa Rosenkrantz and to the marvellous members of the Columbia Jazz Orchestra for their raucous joy.

Introduction

I

In *The Audible Past* (2003), Jonathan Sterne argued that listening and hearing were 'developed and specialized practices, rather than inherent capacities',[1] acquired through training and amounting to 'a set of repeatable activities within a limited number of framed contexts'.[2] Focusing in particular on the professional training of sound telegraphers and doctors (who in the nineteenth century needed to master 'mediate auscultation', or listening to the inside of patients' bodies with an acoustic amplifier such as a stethoscope), Sterne documented the ways in which technical, pedagogical and cognitive apparatus were put to work to forge new forms of auditory attention, first among a restricted professional elite and then, by the middle of the twentieth century, in a widespread culture of listening oriented around radio and recorded sound. Sterne's thesis that listening is an acquired, cultural activity, which we can designate with the term 'auditory culture', elegantly threads the needle between imagining that things are what they are regardless of how they are perceived, and claiming that everything is dependent on some act of social or psychological construction. By 'thread the needle' I mean that it recognizes both of these propositions as partially true and perfectly compatible: if we accept that there is something like auditory culture, we also accept that one can only truly hear what there is to hear (for example the faintly audible signature of a heart in the early stages of cardiac failure) if one has submitted one's hearing to an intense training in which the data of the ear are enmeshed in a system of concepts and definitions that have nothing to do with the basic material of sound or the physiology of hearing. Such training seems like a turning away from sheer auditory experience, a socialization of the feral ear; and yet this is the only way one can become aware of what is actually there.

The paradox I am trying to articulate here may be present in every educational process. We begin in the world and of it; but that situation blinds us to much of what the world is, and it is only by turning away from this initial condition and enduring a long and difficult process of socialization and refinement that we become capable of discerning the enormous variety and detail which the world contains. From this perspective, which is, I think, the perspective opened to us by the idea of auditory culture, it is true both that the world's existence is independent of culture *and* that the world cannot be discerned except through culturally determined acts of intuition. Sound and hearer are both independent and interdependent: a finch's song has nothing to do with me, and yet without a certain amount of education in which I learn how finches sing, it will never be a finch's song, at least not for me. The idea is even further complicated when it becomes clear that in many cases the sounds I hear are as socially conditioned as my hearing happens to be. That finch's song is itself a function of at least two different cultural operations: the first is the set of historical and biological processes that led to the articulation of the finch's song, since finch music is itself learned and modified in social groups,[3] and the second is the complex of economic and ecological factors that led to my having a back deck close to a place where finches sing. Human and finch social systems are independent, but in listening their independence, paradoxically, becomes a kind of interdependence: both are needed for you to be able to hear the song.

'Auditory Culture' has a counter-intuitive aura. We do not normally think of our listening as learned behaviour, or as culturally conditioned: usually, it just seems like one of the ways we interface with the world. The reason for this, the concept of auditory culture proposes, is that listening is a learned behaviour that has become habitual; when we hear, *how* we hear is conditioned by cultural processes that have fallen beneath the threshold of awareness. As a result, hearing can be described as historical, as the embodiment of pre-existing, though barely acknowledged, practices. Glossing Sterne's approach in 2015, Brian Kane observed that scholars who study auditory culture

> seek to demonstrate the successions and relays between cognition and affect, or, speaking broadly, between the mind and the body. As listeners acquire new skills, much of the cognitive effort involved in the initial training is offloaded onto the body. At the same time, bodily capacities constitute both

the basis upon which training occurs and the ground for potential future cultivation [...] The capacities of the body are cultivated at the same time that cultures become embodied.[4]

This observation may be true, but it is no less difficult and paradoxical for that: it proposes that we are living a schism in which our immediate, personal and intimate sense of immersion in the world is influenced by histories of which we may be barely cognizant, experiences we hardly remember. This schism cannot be healed: the impression that my perceptions are simple and unfiltered cannot be reconciled with the fact that experience is learned and therefore cultural, as theorists of auditory culture claim. But if the two facts cannot be reconciled, they can still co-exist, though back to back, as it were, never quite able to look each other in the eye.

Both Kane and Sterne find a theoretical touchstone for the idea of auditory culture in the work of Marcel Mauss, who proposed an anthropological study of the techniques of the body. For Mauss, body techniques were acquired, effective and traditional forms of activity produced by formal or informal education; they revealed the body to be 'man's first and most natural technical object, and at the same time technical means'.[5] Mauss ascribed his own successful crystallization of the notion of bodily technique to his recollection that there exists in Plato a notion of 'technique in music and in particular ... in the dance'.[6] Mauss' invocation of Plato alerts us to the existence of classical precursors to the contemporary interest in auditory culture; but it also suggests that 'the body' needs to be taken in a broader sense than even Mauss himself lets on, since for Plato dance's training of the body was important primarily because of the effect it could have on a soul. Indeed, it may not be immediately clear why hearing (or any perceptual modality, for that matter) should be treated as a 'technique of the body' at all, as Sterne does. Though Mauss did acknowledge that even walking and swimming were 'physio-psycho-sociological assemblages',[7] he did not develop an explicit application of his framework for sensory practices, and one might observe that listening is considerably less tangible, less obviously bodily, than practices like walking or swimming – indeed, listening could be taken as quite explicitly psychological, a matter of mind. But a key, if undesignated, mediator between Mauss' approach to techniques of the body and Sterne's notion of audile technique is the work of Pierre Hadot, who emphasized that an important part of ancient philosophical practice was *askēsis* or 'discipline', which aimed to train and transform selves.[8] Hadot's perspective was particularly important for Jan Patočka, who though officially silenced by the Czechoslovakian authorities delivered an influential set of underground lectures on the topic of 'Plato and Europe' in which Plato's decisive contribution to what Patočka called 'the event of Europe' is 'the care of the soul'.[9] Michel Foucault acknowledged Patočka as an influence on his later work on the 'care of the self', most importantly instantiated in the first two volumes of *The History of Sexuality* and having its most significant outcome in the diagnosis of biopower, that function by which states extend authority over life-processes hitherto thought to be 'natural' and beyond the reach of culture.[10] Given this background it may come as no surprise that significant precursors to the contemporary notion of auditory culture can be found in antiquity. This book looks in particular at the work of Plato and Aristoxenus, both philosophers working in the fourth century BCE. In Plato's writing we see a process in which the conditioning of the senses through the dialogue form could lead to the acquisition of a cognitive comportment with a changed relation to sensuality in general, while Aristoxenus presumes that music is defined by rules embodied in musical perception, which he treats, paradoxically but not illogically, as both acculturated and autonomous.

Plato probably needs no introduction. A native of Athens and an important student of Socrates, he founded an influential school, taught Aristotle, and wrote a corpus of philosophical dialogues which are widely recognized as masterpieces of world literature. Aristoxenus is considerably less well known. He was born in Tarentum in southern Italy and studied at Athens with Aristotle before developing a remarkable and influential philosophy of music in the second half of the fourth century. They are very different figures.[11] To name just the most obvious point of divergence, Aristoxenus was deeply Aristotelian in orientation, and shows no sign of the idealist tendencies evinced throughout Plato's corpus. That said, there are moments of congruence. Andrew Barker has emphasized Aristoxenus' agreement with claims in Plato's *Laws* that serious music critics must have a deep and practised awareness of all the parts of music;[12] Barker also suggests that Aristoxenus' harmonic theory was designed to satisfy the *Philebus*' criteria for a science;[13] and in a crucial fragment Aristoxenus may in fact be defending Plato's musical knowledge.[14] But despite the apparent points of contact, there is another major obstacle to putting Plato and Aristoxenus together as I have done: the two corpora are incommensurable. Aristoxenus' writings challenge us in the first instance because they are extremely fragmentary. Crucial definitions of fundamental concepts are lost, we have no complete work, we do not know with certainty where what we do have comes from, and sizable amounts of material are reported at second hand. We are left with the delicate task of eliciting his teaching from an unstable and incomplete record – working with his texts is a bit like trying to learn what kind of animal is hidden behind a curtain by reaching your hand through a limited number of small openings. But at least we can be confident, in Aristoxenus' case, that there actually is an animal behind the curtain; whatever he said or meant, it added up to a theory of music. With Plato even that is open to doubt. This may seem surprising, since there is practically total consensus that Plato was a musical conservative,[15] that he thought music was mimetic and mistrusted it as such,[16] and that he was willing to countenance only a very limited range of musical expression within a well-ordered society.[17] Each of these claims is supported by passages from Plato's texts. But I am uneasy attributing opinions to Plato on the basis of his writing, which many have seen as constructed in order to prevent the extraction of teachings or authoritative opinions. Their dramatic form, their irrepressible playfulness, and their ever-changing answers to the same set of fundamental questions suggest that one must be profoundly careful in how one handles them. I find it safest to attend less to what the texts say, and more to what they seem to do. Music has proved crucial to helping me do that. Whatever they may or may not tell us about how Plato felt about musical developments in his day, his discussions of music can profitably be read as commentaries on the rhetorical aims of his own writings.

Any straightforward connection between Plato and Aristoxenus is therefore extremely difficult to make. We are dealing on the one hand with a philosopher attempting to delineate a positive theory of music, and on the other with a corpus of writing whose musical content is most safely taken as referring obliquely to itself. Different kinds of texts compel different methodologies: my essay on Aristoxenus (Part Two) is a more traditional example of an essay in the history of ideas, while my essay on Plato (Part One) reads his statements about music as self-reflexive guides to his textual strategies and his project of philosophical pedagogy. Although I do think that Aristoxenus responds to claims made in some of Plato's texts, I cannot say, and should not be taken as implying, that Aristoxenian music theory is in any kind of dialogue with *Plato's* views on music.[18]

What I can do is set Plato's textual strategies beside Aristoxenus' musical doctrine, collating the first's practice with the second's theory. Some illuminating points of comparison emerge when we do this. The most important concerns the status of perception. Reading Platonic textuality through the lens of its statements about music suggests that we could characterize his texts as control mechanisms intended to induce the soul to move in better, calmer ways which have both epistemological and metaphysical consequences, while in Aristoxenus music is a sensual comportment, brought about through generations of practice and resident as a set of axioms and rules in the ears of the musically acculturated. To put this slightly differently: I find in Plato's writing a dynamic system capable of reforming a reader's orientation to her perceptions, while Aristoxenus' theory describes music as the accomplishment of just such a reform. In this lies what I believe to be an important difference. Reading Plato's texts as I do suggests that calmer, more ordered perception is a *project*, something yet to come, while Aristoxenus asserts, to the contrary, that in music such ordered perception *already exists*. Platonic desires are transformed in Aristoxenus into established facts. But in this ill fit between a writing aimed at a futural perception and a theory describing the same perception as already established I discern a juxtaposition isologous to the inner contradiction implicit in the notion of auditory culture with which I began: we recognize that what induces us to perceive the world in a certain way is mediated by culture and education, and yet we also proceed as though our perceptions were immediate, un-fabricated or 'natural'. Sensual culture combines norm and fact in a manner which the collision of Platonic writing and Aristoxenian theory engineered here is meant to display.

The juxtaposition of Plato's writing and Aristoxenus' music theory I present here may do more than unfold some of what is implied by the concept of auditory culture; it may also contribute to a more vivid sense of what was at stake in an early and, I think, historically significant moment in the history of music theory. Aristoxenus' claims about what is and is not musical are supported by preliminary suppositions which would have a long history in theoretical accounts of music. Particularly notable are his explicit statement (for the first time that I am aware of) that music is made out of sequences of stable pitches, his argument that they must be sequenced in precisely quantized and interrelated temporal durations, and his innovative contention that musical meaning is derived from compositional choices. His most important contention, however, – and one that has had enduring influence on musical thought and practice – is that music is a highly organized form of auditory perception, the result of something like an aesthetic education. As we will see, this allows Aristoxenus to interpret music as at once norm and fact, that is, as ideal in a sense similar to my understanding of the tendencies implicit in Plato's writing project, and as accomplished in culture and therefore needing only to be described and preserved. To put this another way: at this early moment in the history of writing about music, the study of 'auditory culture' was encapsulated in the articulation of a 'music theory'.

II

Not all musics need a theory, nor do the theories they get always come from the women and men who play them. Indeed, theories do not always describe musics with perfect accuracy. 'All theories', according to Marc Perlman,

> are partial representations of music, since all theorists pass 'the raw material of practice through a filter of theoretical presuppositions' or confine them in the 'straightjacket of an intellectually respectable system'.[19] No theorist can resist 'the urge to idealize musical practice in ways congruent with one's world view'.[20] Music theory is never a direct insight into musical reality but is always culturally mediated: 'a music theory, like any kind of theory, is a construction, not an induction. It represents an interpretive grid superimposed upon musical material that determines the analytic questions to be posed, and the language and arguments deemed sufficient to answer them'.[21]

Perlman's own story tells of the emergence of indigenous Javanese gamelan music theory in partial response to exogenous theories produced by ethnomusicologists. The theories of music developed by Greek philosophers in the fourth century could also be described as exogenous relative to the musics they describe; they are related to and sometimes carefully derived from the observation of musical practice, but their ultimate concerns lie elsewhere. Reading Plato's references to music as instances in which his texts reflect on their own project and method, as I intend to do, emphasizes that their focus and frame of reference is philosophical writing. I hope it will emerge that Aristoxenus' work is ultimately as philosophical in orientation as Plato's.

Treating music in contexts whose concerns were different from those of musicians themselves was not a new thing in the fourth century. True, some early theorists were musicians. Lasus of Hermione, for example, had a hand in redesigning the music for the dithyrambic performances in the newly reformed festival of Dionysus,[22] and is also credited with the earliest known piece of writing *On Harmony*.[23] But most of the known names associated with early music theory were making their arguments in very different contexts. So the Athenian Damon: reputedly a figure closely affiliated with Pericles, and primarily a political adviser and operative,[24] he is linked to the idea that different soul-states or *ēthē* (*ēthos* in the singular) had affinities with different musical styles or modes (these may have been tunings, or rhythms, or combinations of the two; we simply do not have good enough evidence to know). Damon may be just as significant for the sociological event he marked as for the theory later attributed to him: here was a theorist who was not professionally engaged in making music, an intellectual and a political agent who described and made prescriptive statements about music for political reasons. Many of those who were important in music theory after Damon belong to a similar category. Using a combination of empirical research and mathematical construction, the south-Italian intellectuals Philolaus and Archytas saw music as a template for cosmic structures, and it was in their work that the old idea of cosmic harmony began to get a rigorous foundation.[25] It seems uncontroversial, likewise, to say that Plato's writings and Aristoxenus' theory were primarily aimed at the discursive and social circuits constituted by philosophical life and inquiry. I do not mean to indict or denigrate the philosophers' knowledge of music or their familiarity with musicians, but I do wish to emphasize that their discussions of musical thought were not primarily oriented to systems of knowledge or practice that were endogenous to musical performance and pedagogy. Some evidence from later centuries suggests that Aristoxenian theory had an impact on musical pedagogy,[26] but this could quite easily have been a development that post-dates Aristoxenus; his own language and approach suggest that his texts were written for intellectuals with an interest in music, not for musicians.

This is not to say that Plato and Aristoxenus were not part of the musical world in the broadest sense. Many modern scholars rightly insist that anyone connected to a musical performance in whatever capacity is involved in a common experience. Christopher Small called this common experience 'musicking'; Howard Becker captured it with the idea of 'art worlds'.[27] I am sympathetic with this point of view – I think we impoverish our understanding of what happens in a musical event if we focus only on the performer and ignore the bartender and the janitor, or if we overlook the fact that audiences themselves are highly composite and unpredictable collectivities. I also want to remain cognizant of the fact that within the collective totality of participants in any musical event there is also a multiplicity of different social systems at work, each one autonomous in its own way. It is true that the performer is playing to an audience, but the performer might be more interested in the pay cheque than the applause, and the bartender may actually be conducting research for a PhD thesis on Midwestern jazz audiences; those two audience members are courting, while the one over there is actually a critic and will publish a review the next day. And, finally, there are a few people close to the front who just like this kind of music. In addition to the various motivations that might bring different kinds of agents into the ambit of a musical event (economic, academic, emotional, vocational), different systems of *reaction* may also be at play. A musicologist with an interest in polyrhythm will react quite differently to a performance than someone who has just come to dance. The former may attempt to describe what he hears in terms of pulse, tempo and metre, eventually seeking to relate it to some pre-existing or not-quite-perfectly-elaborated set of categories or concepts; the latter will dance until the rhythm changes or his legs get too tired. It may be worth considering these reactions as different kinds of things – the musicologist could be working towards something called 'understanding', while the dancer might be looking for something more like 'immersion' or 'flow' or even 'ecstasy'.[28]

Plato and Aristoxenus should indeed be described as 'musicking' when they talk about music. But musicking itself, in turn, needs to be recognized as a system of systems, a hyper-organization in which many different kinds of activity jostle and contest, and in which from time to time new systems may emerge, old ones divide in two. Just this is what happened between music and philosophy in the fifth and fourth centuries BCE. In essence, what transpired was what some sociologists might call a process of functional differentiation: musicians and intellectuals began to form separate autonomous systems.[29] Thanks to the immense success of tragedy and comedy, musicians began to command large fees, and an economy of performance arose which allowed them to be first and only musicians.[30] The consequent professionalization made music into an independent sphere of practice, like all such social systems subject to internal protocols of operation and interfacing with other systems (like the state) only at certain points and in tightly constrained ways.[31] The same thing was happening with intellectuals at about the same time: aided by private wealth and based on a turn away from polis life, philosophy in the fourth century rapidly became an autonomous system of discussion which, while not closed to the outside world, increasingly sought to characterize that world in its own, internally generated, terms. In fact I will suggest that one of the greatest accomplishments of Aristoxenus' approach was to have created an image of music that philosophy could recognize. This becomes evident if we attend to two of his large-scale arguments: he rigidly delimits music to what is discerned by the musically acculturated, in effect closing it to anyone else; and he abstracts from this closed system a set of axioms which, he claims, cannot be violated, and on the basis of this, as I will try to show in the last part of this book, he interprets musical history as a comparatively stable system or set of systems. The validity of this claim as an evaluation of actual music seems to me impossible to assess, given the state of our evidence. What can be observed is that it makes music into a closed, auto-referential system just like Aristoxenian theory. Even as its independence had been articulated – indeed because its independence had been articulated – music had been claimed as a part of philosophy. The paradox here is important, for it sets music and philosophy up as a binary system involving two independent regions of practice whose very independence is maintained through each other.

One consequence of the philosophical system-reference characteristic of both my authors is that their works contribute to a vision in which music is subjected to *time binding*. This concept, first introduced by Alfred Korzybski in 1933, was elaborated into a major feature of social systems theory by Niklas Luhmann.[32] Time binding amounts to the capacity of physical, cognitive and social structures to reduce contingency and unpredictability. At the moment I am looking at a paper cup. The cup binds time in the sense that until it is recycled or breaks down naturally its materials are held in a particular configuration – the shape which holds coffee and makes it easy to drink. Perception of the cup also binds time, in the sense that I see, touch and use the cup as a cup, rapidly and unreflexively filtering out its ever-changing colours and sounds and weight as contingent 'noise' surrounding the object of my perception and use. Abstract models also bind time by offering forms which could describe a wide variety of possible variations, making complexity graspable through a single outline (I might have a 'theory of cups' that accounts for all kinds of different drinking vessels in all kinds of different states and forms; it could include a schematic drawing of the structural requirements for any such tool). Social organizations bind time, too: they feed events and people through mechanisms and procedures that maintain the organization's continuity, holding social components together just as my paper cup holds its materials together. In music, to use a few examples that will be relevant later, concepts like rhythm, which seek to lock temporal flow into recognizable and sharable forms, or 'tuning', which transforms a melodic sequence of pitches into a stable set, bind time by allowing shifting musical events to be seen as multiple instances of a finite set of forms. Auditory cultures bind time, too, by providing perceptual schemata that allow always-changing sounds to be perceived as stable entities – the sound of a siren is always the sound of a siren, and the sound of a flute is always that of a flute, though every instance is inevitably different.

When we compare Plato and Aristoxenus, we find that the two corpora have different but complementary orientations to time binding. Plato's texts tend to treat it as a desideratum: in the *Timaeus*, the title character expresses a preference for musical and psychic movements which are as regular as possible, maximally approximating the kind of movement exemplified by the world-soul, which in turn is said to imitate the timelessness which characterizes its eternal paradigm. Aristoxenus, by contrast, treats time binding as accomplished: music actually represents just the ordered movement dreamed of in the *Timaeus*. He finds in it not radical change and confusing instability but order and lawfulness; temporal contingency, and even time itself, is relegated to a remarkably small role.

That may seem extraordinary to many moderns. For several centuries music has been closely associated with change and movement, with time, as it were, unbound. Victor Zuckerkandl eloquently summed up this tendency, remarking 'with what uniformity, despite all differences between persons and periods, the idea of motion forced itself on thinkers and scholars when the question of designating the essential element of music arose'.[33] Zuckerkandl himself understood that the temporality of music was a profoundly non-Greek discovery: 'since the Greeks, no more far-reaching revolution in our symbol world has taken place. In music we have, on another plane, repeated the achievement of the Greeks; what they did for space, we have done for time. Greek art gave the world a new space image; our music has given it the first genuine time image'.[34] More recent scholars, most notably Carol Berger, have suggested that the propulsive linearity of musical temporality (whose significance he dates to no earlier than Mozart) is closely linked to the enlightenment belief in progress.[35] From this perspective it might come as no surprise that the ancient sources see time as a problem to be solved rather than a truth to be uncovered. Zuckerkandl does find reference to musical time in antiquity, particularly in Augustine; and of Augustine, after all a major theorist of time, he's surely right. Aristoxenian musicology, on the other hand, takes music as entailing change only in the least significant sense – and even there it is rigidly disciplined by reason. Music becomes a kind of immanent Platonic idea.

Perhaps our disorientation before engagements with music that emphasize not time but time binding is itself a consequence of the post-enlightenment sense of time to which most of us ascribe. After all, the sentience of major differences between historical periods is an inevitable result of modernity's temporal awareness, and the gulf between us and antiquity is an emblematic example. But post-enlightenment conceptions of historical time are internally fractured by a deep and perhaps inescapable contradiction. Modernity has long been felt as an experience of rapid and radical change, true, and nowhere more vividly than in music. But that sense of radical change has always been accompanied by a second impression: that we are bound by our epoch, that there is no escaping our mind-forged manacles, as Blake once put it. *This* intuition is not modern but ancient, and not historical but aesthetic; it is, I propose, closely related to the view of musical perception developed by Aristoxenus. In fact I hope it will become clear that Aristoxenian music theory doesn't just imply the reduction of contingency in the history and expression of music; it also forges a mechanism through which perception can frame an epoch.

That there are radical differences between historical periods is hardly an unfamiliar proposition. One thinks immediately of the epochs delineated by Vico, or of the historicism embraced by Herder, then elaborated into a world-historical system by Hegel. It survived in Hans-Georg Gadamer's philosophical hermeneutics, according to which every historical period is defined by a 'horizon' of meanings that is in principle closed to and different from the horizons of other periods: the practice of reading, for Gadamer, can be described as the pursuit of a 'fusion' of these horizons in which our context melds with the past context of a text, producing from the encounter a new and singular form of understanding.[36] Thomas Kuhn's theory of scientific revolutions also articulated a model in which periods were qualitatively distinct from each other, the transition from one to the next marked by a 'paradigm shift'.[37] In a slightly different mode, the early Foucault emphasized the difference between cultural moments, particularly in the history of science, as a difference between 'orders of discourse', systems of more-or-less rigorously policed standards of what can be said and understood within a constrained historical environment.[38] More recently, Jacques Rancière distinguished between 'symbolic regimes', which are shared assumptions about the nature of perception and art, as well as socially determining protocols for the recognition of certain subjects and classes as capable of being heard within decision-making systems.[39] In all these models (and in the many more like it) historical epochs are unified by their ability to forge perceptual communities through sensory techniques. Collective perceptions can define an epoch's limits as well, especially when alternative ways of hearing or seeing are excluded – though their exclusion may have its own role to play. Rancière's model may be the most explicit on this front, since he discerns a double process occurring both at the level of perception and at the level of politics. For Rancière access to political influence is brokered by a social construction of perception that makes certain forms of discourse and certain classes of humanity invisible and inaudible to power. We simply do not hear what is excluded, or we hear it only as noise. Such gestures, which appeal to a sensual process rather than to taste or cultural affiliation, lie at the heart of the way constituted modes of perception create historical closure. The emergence of music theory in fourth-century philosophy offers a blueprint for how such closure can occur. We will see that the consequences include an explicit naturalization of culture and the elimination of alternatives: music is a law-governed order of perception with a rigorously determined outside. But this is not just an example of what Rancière diagnosed: it is the condition for that diagnosis, because it articulates the closure of an aesthetic regime. Between aesthetic regimes, in this vision, there can only be relations of incommensurability: different epochs perceive in different ways. One consequence of this predicament is the paradoxical perception of continuity and change that seems so typical of historicism: our sense of music is fundamentally different from that of the Greeks, and yet, precisely because it performs an awareness of incommensurability designed by the Greek approach to musical perception, it is continuous with it. Perhaps, if it is true that the works of Plato and Aristoxenus contain views both radically different from and surprisingly similar to contemporary ideas about auditory culture, that is the unavoidable effect of the weird historicity to which we (and they) ascribe.

III

My discussions of Plato and Aristotle occasionally deal with details of ancient Greek music theory, so it seems worthwhile to provide a very basic background into the terminology and assumptions in this field.[40] In the centuries after Aristoxenus a more-or-less stable theoretical vernacular crystallized; we know this from 'handbooks', short texts written to introduce students to the subject,[41] and from the more original work of Aristides Quintilianus, Ptolemy and Boethius. Here I limit myself to what is directly relevant to my discussions and I leave out many of the elements of later systematizations. My aim is only to provide what a reader needs in order to follow some of the thornier discussions in Chapters 3, 4 and 5.

I will occasionally have recourse to illustrative diagrams. (I should say right away that Aristoxenus, for one, was highly critical of the use of diagrams for understanding musical sound. Even musical notation, which by his time had become a highly elaborate and sophisticated system, is criticized by Aristoxenus as having no explanatory power.[42] Indeed, we might need to recognize him as one of the few philosophical figures in antiquity who did not reinforce the hegemony of vision in his theoretical work. His was very much an *auditory* rationality. The needs of modern readers and the constraints of the printed

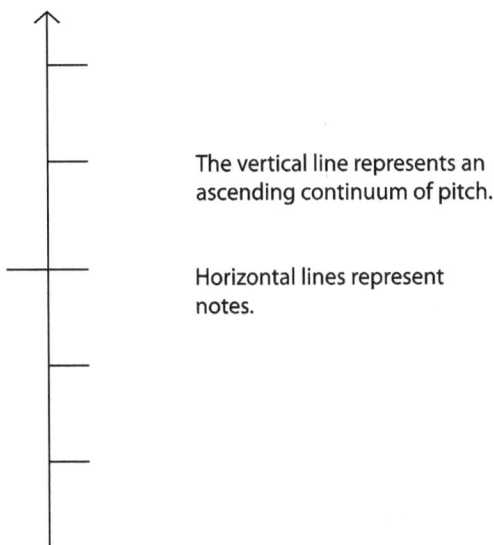

Figure 1 Basic format for the musical diagrams that follow.

book thus force me into acts of explanation that may well betray this particular author's insight.) In my diagrams pitches are represented as short lines set perpendicular to a longer, vertical line. The vertical line is to be read as representing a rising continuum of pitch: lower pitches are located towards the bottom of the line, and higher pitches are located towards the top (see Fig. 1).

The object of musical study was 'song' (*melos*); this was understood to be composed of 'harmony' (*harmonia*), 'rhythm' (*rhuthmos*) and 'diction' (*lexis* or *logos*).[43] It's a reasonable assumption that by 'diction' music writers meant the words of a song. 'Rhythm' referred to the specific sequence of durational expressions, either in the words or in an instrumental piece. 'Rhythmics' was an emerging topic in the fourth century which I discuss in Chapter 5, and I leave it aside until that point. 'Harmony' refers to what we could call the 'tuning' of a song, or, more basically, the choice of notes which were to be used. In most European-derived music, such choices are limited to twelve evenly spaced notes inside an octave, represented on the piano by the twelve white and black keys; the intervals separating these notes are conventionally called 'semitones' and are standardized by the factory settings on commercially released digital instruments (things are a little more complicated with voices and acoustic instruments). This musical system is called the 'twelve-tone equal temperament system'; it is a relatively recent development, dating to the nineteenth century. Although it was perfectly possible, if unlikely, for Greek songs to be tuned in a manner that approximated something we might play on a digital piano, there was nothing like the standardization that such an instrument represents (and enforces), and the tonal conceptions underlying how tunings were chosen and arrived at was fundamentally different.

The Greek ear acknowledged three concords or 'consonances': the octave, the fifth and the fourth. (In the Harold Arlen song 'Somewhere Over the Rainbow', the two notes on the word 'some-where' are an octave apart; in the children's song 'Twinkle Twinkle Little Star' the first 'twinkle' and the second 'twinkle' are a fifth apart; the first two notes of 'Amazing Grace' are a fourth apart).[44] Theorists thought these intervals sounded good and were easy to recognize. They were also easy to relate to each other: a voice singing up a fourth and then up a fifth would complete an octave (sing 'Ama-' of 'Amazing Grace', and then, starting on the same note as the second 'a', sing 'twinkle twinkle;' the first 'a' of 'Amazing Grace' and the second 'twinkle' should be the same distance apart as the first two notes in 'Somewhere Over the Rainbow'). Greek theorists also conceptualized the difference between the fourth and the fifth as a 'tone' (a tone is the difference between do and re if you sing 'do re me').

Since notes an octave apart are made by media vibrating at frequencies in a ratio of 2:1, the octave came to be known by that ratio – although in antiquity the ratios were never associated, as far as we can tell, with vibratory frequencies, but rather with the lengths of a vibrating string when it made each relative pitch. For the same reason, the fifth was designated with the ratio 3:2 and the fourth with 4:3. It turns out, too, that the difference between the fourth and the fifth, the tone, could be expressed as the ratio 9:8. So configured, the musical intervals are to be related mathematically in the same way that they are related in sound – just as a fifth plus a fourth produces an octave, so does 3:2 times 4:3 equal 2:1. This led to a major tradition of musical thinkers, including Plato but not Aristoxenus, who sought to work out harmonic relationships by relying on calculation rather than hearing.[45]

Of the three concords the smallest one, the fourth, was the most important for music theory. A fourth divided into four notes was called a 'tetrachord'.

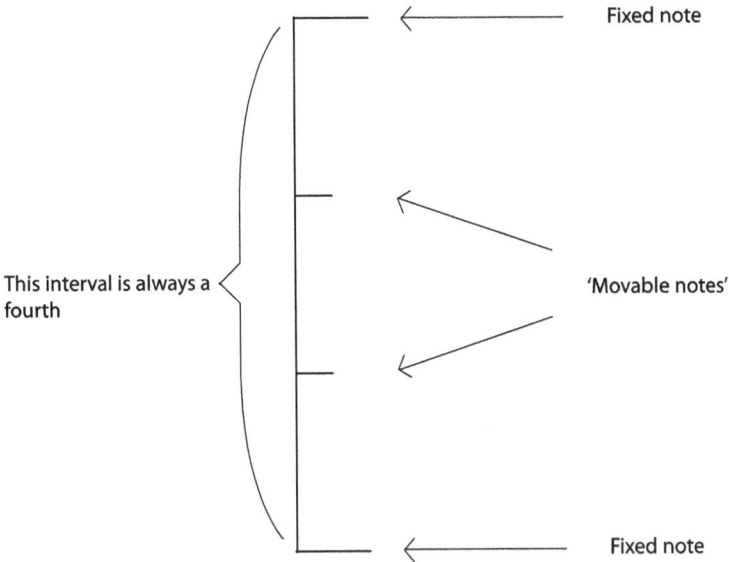

Figure 2 Basic form of the tetrachord.

While the outer notes of a tetrachord were always a fourth apart, the two inner notes could be located in any number of places; for this reason they were called 'movable notes', in contrast to the 'fixed notes' that bounded the tetrachord (see Fig. 2).

Tetrachords could be sequenced or spliced to produce larger combinations. There were two ways of splicing two tetrachords together. 'Conjunct' tetrachords shared a note; the top of the lower tetrachord was the same as the bottom of the upper tetrachord. 'Disjunct' tetrachords did not share a note, but they were related to each other in one and only one way: the bottom of the upper tetrachord was one tone higher than the top of the lower tetrachord, or one fifth higher than the bottom of the lower tetrachord. Most of the discussions of music in this book can be understood if we envisage a single octave composed of two disjunct tetrachords. After Aristoxenus, and perhaps before him as well, the names for the notes in this abstract schema were standardized as shown in Fig. 3.

The Greek meanings of the words appear to reflect the positions of strings on the lyre: the lowest-pitched note in this central octave is called 'highest' (*hupatē*) because its string was farthest from the ground (and closest to the player's chest) as a lyre was usually held. The note next 'up' from it is called

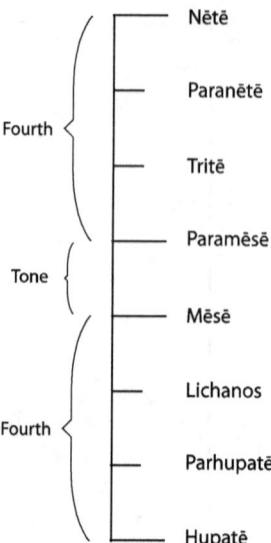

Figure 3 The central octave of the Greek tonal system, with note names. Note that the relative positions of Parhupatē, Lichanos, Tritē and Paranētē will have varied between different tunings.

'beside *hupatē*' (*parhupatē*); next comes the string played by the 'forefinger', *lichanos*, then the 'middle' note (*mesē*), followed by the note 'beside *mesē*' (*paramesē*); then the 'third' string (*trite*), the note 'beside *nētē* (*paranētē*), then, one octave higher than *hupatē*, was *nētē*. Aristoxenus himself tends to describe only the lower tetrachord, from *hupatē* to *mesē*. He does this because he presupposes that the notes of each tetrachord will 'agree' with each other – as *paramesē* is a fifth above *hupatē*, *tritē* will be a fifth above *parhupatē* and *paranētē* will be a fifth above *lichanos*.[46]

A fundamental way of distinguishing between tunings, as I've already intimated, was by means of the intervals separating the movable notes inside the tetrachord. They could be 'squished' down to the bottom of the tetrachord (when they were so squished they were called a 'compression' or a *puknon*). Depending on how squished they were, they could be treated as different 'kinds' or *genera* (see Fig. 4). The most compressed *puknon* produced the 'enharmonic' genus (which was sometimes just called 'the harmony'); a slightly less compressed *puknon* produced 'chromatic' tunings; and no compression at all produced what came to be called the 'diatonic' genus.

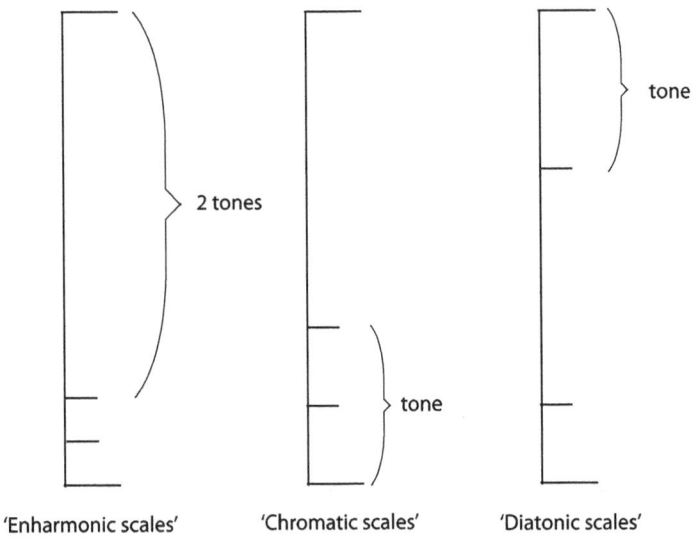

NB. these are <u>limits</u>: the movable notes may be found anywhere within this range.

Figure 4 Upper limits of movable notes in the three genera of tunings, according to Aristoxenus.

At some point before Aristoxenus, possibly during Plato's lifetime, tunings which had hitherto been treated as parts of separate traditions were interpreted as different 'species' of the basic tuning system we have been discussing. Imagine extending the octave scheme up a second octave; a musician might tune her lyre from *hupatē* to *netē*; or from *parhupatē* to *tritē*; or from *lichanos* to *paranētē*, etc. Each of these tunings could be called a 'scale species' – later European music theorists would systematize them as 'modes'. The most important of these for our purposes is the 'Dorian', which is the sequence from *hupatē* to *netē* I have illustrated in the diagrams so far. It is important to recall that each of these scale species could be actualized within any of the three genera of tunings (see earlier), so we are in no way speaking of something like 'scales' or 'modes' as modern musicians use these terms with reference to a piano keyboard. Rather we must imagine the availability of a wide range of intonational options. Both Aristoxenus and Plato devote energy to discussing which scale species are appropriate for what uses; Aristoxenus seems to have been interested as well, as we will see, in the correct relationship between scale species and genus in different compositions.[47]

Remarkably, there is little evidence of theoretical attention to the nature of individual tunes: even the area of theory called 'melic composition' or 'songwriting' (*melopoeia*) treated tunes in only the most perfunctory, schematic manner, and the sources are confused in a way that suggests the absence of any stable doctrine.[48] Of the theoretical topic called 'melody' (*melōidia*), practically nothing is preserved, but what there is suggests that it had to do with the performance of song or – better – the voicing of the structural choices made during composition, rather than with the nature, let alone the phenomenology, of tunes.[49] Rather, the best documented theorists mostly focused on the synthesis of music into a unified affect or *ēthos*. This synthetic aesthetic affect is consistently treated as a kind of emotional block or unit; in Aristoxenus (as I will argue) it is both the locus of musical meaning and the mitigation – in both theory and perception – of musical change.

IV

My theme throughout the book, then, is auditory culture's curious conglomeration of realism and social constructivism which describes hearing as simultaneously fact and norm: I seek to make this odd assemblage evident in the early development of music theory through the juxtaposition of Plato and Aristoxenus.

There are two parts. The first reads Plato's discussions of music as insights into the style and aims of his own writing. Chapter 1 addresses the nature of his texts and their unique hermeneutic difficulties. Like many recent readers, I am wary of attempts to attribute doctrines or beliefs in the texts to Plato himself, since so many of the formal characteristics of his writings seem to militate against doing so. I understand his dialogues to be aimed not at communicating content but at effecting change in the psychological behaviour of his readers, and I identify such an aim with music – an interpretive move that in turn suggests that the descriptions of music in the Platonic corpus could be read as rich descriptions of the rhetorical means of the texts themselves. Chapter 2 looks in more detail at musical passages in the *Republic*, the *Symposium* and the *Phaedrus*, and at the links between Socrates and the mythical figures of the Siren and the Satyr. Chapter 3 turns to the *Cratylus*, the *Timaeus* and more briefly to the *Laws*, where we find a physiology of hearing and music in which the soul is literally moved by what it hears; this provides a more-than-metaphorical basis for treating Platonic textuality as constructed to instill in the soul a motion conducive to philosophical life.

Part Two turns to Aristoxenus, who argued that there was an autonomous order in the rules of music, and gave voice to the idea that musical culture was a perceptual community. Chapter 4 is concerned with his work on harmonics. I emphasize Aristoxenus' contention that musical perception is autonomous and rule-governed and should be theorized only on its own terms. Chapter 5 turns to the issue of musical time. Although Aristoxenus acknowledges that music is temporal, he thinks neither theory nor the musically acculturated ear is much concerned with that temporality. Rather, music is both explained and experienced in terms that are meant to reduce contingency in musical expression. This is true both when individual pieces are listened to, and when musical culture occurs over generations: Aristoxenus' view of music history sees it as a relatively stable auditory and affective community in which change is minimized and major innovations are few and far between. This view of history is, I think, a necessary underpinning of his view of musical perception as autonomous and rule-governed: its autonomy and its basic regularity are predicated on the reinforcement of a sensory tradition across generations.[50]

If 'auditory culture' is a good tool for describing how listening happens, it is only one specific tool, and like all tools it has limitations as well as affordances. Of its limitations, above all the fact that auditory cultures may deafen us to sounds that do not fit their schemata, I will have little to say; I will have nothing to say of possible alternatives, and in a sense my critique ends with the observation with which I began: auditory culture requires that we live a schism between the impression of immediate perception and the knowledge that perception is always mediate. A corollary is that auditory culture, like Aristoxenian music theory, evinces a contradictory combination of the descriptive (this is how the world seems) and the prescriptive (this is how the world should be). If, by the final pages, I have set the stage for others to question how this configuration could be contested or even replaced, I will be satisfied.

Part One

Plato

Chapter 1

Plato started life in music. As a boy he composed hymns to Dionysus, then graduated to other genres, and eventually showed the skill and talent needed to compose entire tragedies. That's the story anyway,[1] and true or not it's a good one; it invites us to imagine his early life tending towards a position at the centre of Athenian public culture. Tragedy was a large-scale, high-budget mass entertainment; plays premiered, usually, in a spring festival attended not only by Athenians but also by many international visitors, accommodated by an enormous permanent theatre on the south-east slope of the acropolis.[2] It was a fully multi-media art form, a 'musical theatre' in the grandest sense of the expression. Highly paid actors spoke, chanted and sang to the accompaniment of a double-reed pipe known as an *aulos* (usually referred to in the plural as *auloi* because they were played in pairs), joined by a chorus of young citizens whose training had begun months in advance. Beautiful and expensive masks and costumes added to the sensual richness of the productions; even the art of backdrop design was invented for the form.[3] Shows began in the morning and lasted until well after noon; each day featured the work of a single playwright and a single company, who typically offered a 'tetralogy' consisting of three tragedies and a 'satyr play', a comic closer featuring a chorus of mostly drunk, easily aroused man-goat hybrids. There were three tetralogies by three playwrights performed over three days; they were judged in a competition, the winning producers often boasting of their victories by dedicating public monuments.[4] The art form to which Plato aspired was, in other words, a very big deal, a major sink of attention, expertise and cash. It was also an important driver of innovation, not just locally but also across the Greek diaspora: the style of music to which tragic words were sung was probably designed specifically for the genre in the later sixth century, and it developed rapidly in both expressive means and technical demands. By Plato's day it had reached a level of complexity and power few art forms ever attain.

Playwrights – they were called 'teachers', *didaskaloi* – were responsible for the music as well as the words; they also directed the production, coached the actors and assisted in the training of the chorus.[5] It's not known how an aspiring *didaskalos*, such as Plato was later said to be, broke into the profession.[6] There was a good-sized circuit of smaller stages in Attica and abroad,[7] and neophytes could have got a start there, but they still had to compete with major players from the central stage,[8] and I don't know of any evidence that this circuit was a breaking-in ground for younger dramatists. Aristophanes, a writer of comedies slightly younger than Euripides, seems to have begun by producing plays under the name of a better-known senior colleague.[9] Nepotism was another route to the stage: Euripides' nephew seems to have succeeded him as a playwright after his death.[10] There's no indication that Plato had family in the theatre, but he might have had a patron who could help him get a break. He probably knew Agathon, a tragic playwright associated with Euripides,[11] and he could have been assisted by either, if he was under the tutelage of anyone at all.

As it happened, things worked out differently – at least if the old story is true. He made the acquaintance, it is said, of a charismatic older Athenian who had an interest in intellectual innovations and a penchant for asking hard questions. Plato's encounter with Socrates, as he was called, was momentous. There are two tales about it. In one, Socrates dreamed that he held a swan in his lap, which suddenly sprouted plumage and a beautiful voice: he met Plato the next day. In the other, Plato burned his tragedies after the meeting, vowing never to compose again.[12] Either way, an epochal shift had occurred. Philosophy had taken music's place.[13]

But music didn't disappear completely from Plato's work.

An intellectual of Plato's age who wanted to speak of and to the city had the assembly and the law courts to disseminate his message, and there was an elaborate art form, that of rhetoric, to support him. Plato's writings deal repeatedly and extensively with matters of civic life: in the *Crito* he penned one of the most memorable and influential expressions of state ideology ever written (we owe our birth to the legal formation of the city, he says there, and so we owe it our death, if it should ask for it), and in the *Laws* he worked out an extraordinary and extensive legal system complete with philosophical rationale. The *Republic* explored the interactions between virtue and constitutional structure and made a compelling case for the centrality of education to civic stability. But even when they discuss politics his dialogues have nothing of the directness of rhetoric, not even when they mimic rhetorical forms (as in the *Apology*, the *Menexenus* and the *Phaedrus*). Rather they retain the obliqueness of tragedy. Tragedy was also a civic art form, to be sure: it was surrounded by major symbols of Athenian civic pride, and it was heavily invested in by men who played significant political roles. But a tragedy could only speak of politics obliquely, through the language of myth, through nuances of character and the ornaments of poetic speech – features that are easy to find in Plato's writing as well. Indeed, a sensitive reader might say that the skills of the tragedian are evident everywhere in his work. One of the great shortcomings of the way subjects are divided in the modern university, particularly when that is combined with the virtual disappearance of Greek from the educational experience of just about everyone, is that very few people are ever placed in a position to experience how good a writer he was. Every level of organization is virtuosic, from sound effects and word choice to sentence structure and overall design. Ancient readers were acutely aware of his abilities, and they tried to portray him as the continuator of the great tragedians. His dialogues were transmitted through the medieval period, and are still printed, in groups of four; these 'tetralogies' were created by editors to reinforce the idea that Plato wrote his philosophy in tragic style.[14] One biographer reports a viewpoint which analogized the history of tragedy to the history of the philosophical dialogue: just as in the earliest tragedies the chorus told the story alone until Thespis added a first actor, Aeschylus a second and Sophocles a third, so was philosophical discourse uniform (*monoeidēs*) and dedicated to natural questions until Socrates added ethics to the mix, and then Plato brought in dialectics and perfected philosophy.[15] It's not easy to tell who worked out this analogy. A similar version of tragedy's development is accepted by Aristotle,[16] so a fourth-century BCE date isn't impossible. But its exact origin is less important than the way it intimates a connection between Plato's writing and tragedy. The dialogue format itself may have encouraged the connection, and Plato's nearly obsessive return to settings involving Socrates close to the moment of his trial and execution certainly brings something like a tragic mood to much of his work. It may be, in fact, that the perceived similarities with tragedy could have given special importance to, or even led to the fabrication of, the story of Plato's early musical life with which I began.

The beauty and indirectness of his writing led to stories about his death, too. Here's one, told by the late antique commentator Olympiodorus:

> Just before his death Plato had a dream in which he had become a swan and was flying from branch to branch, and because of this gave a great deal of trouble to his hunters. The Socratic Simmias interpreted the dream as saying that he would be ungraspable by those who wanted to explain him: for exegetes were like hunters, seeking to hunt out the meanings of the ancients, and he couldn't be caught because his writings could be understood in a physical sense, an ethical sense, and a theological sense. To put it simply, they can be understood in many ways, just like the writings of Homer.[17]

This is undoubtedly a tale crafted relatively late in the history of Greek philosophy. Plato was not an 'ancient' when he died. But like the story about Plato's early aspirations to write tragedy, it has the merit of drawing our attention to the musicality of his writing. Reading Plato can be as overwhelming as a Brahms symphony or an Eric Dolphy recording; his work has power even before we begin to corral it into one of the higher orders of meaning articulated by Simmias.

Overwhelming – but also excruciatingly difficult to make sense of. While the dialogues beguile with the intricacy of their form, they also seduce us through an often frustrating inconclusiveness.[18] The issue isn't merely that Plato's works can be read in so many different ways, as Olympiodorus suggests; it's that they're almost impossible to read at all. A host of difficulties present themselves to anyone who aspires to derive philosophical doctrine, or even just positive opinions, from them; sometimes the corpus appears even to be designed to frustrate such a project. The features which give this impression are well known. Plato never presents himself as a character or writes in his own voice (outside a collection of letters, to which I will return). The unifying figure in the dialogues is Socrates, who appears in all of Plato's texts except the *Laws*, which Plato left unfinished at his death.[19] Plato is referred to by name only in the *Apology* and the *Phaedo*.[20] The dialogues can be catalogued, using a classification system developed in the *Republic*, into a set of 'mimetic' dialogues, in which every word is attributed to a speaking character (like a drama); and a set of 'diegetic' or narrative dialogues in which everything that is said is narrated by a single speaker, almost always Socrates or someone reporting a conversation told to them by Socrates,[21] but Plato never conjures with an extra-diegetic voice that could be associated with him (though of course we are constantly tempted to discern an authorial guiding hand), and so his writings present themselves as autonomous wholes, sealed off within their fictional worlds.[22] Their form at the very least proposes that we read them less as expositions of philosophical doctrine and more as dramas of ideas.[23]

To make matters even more complicated, nothing goes uncontested. Even Plato's notorious theory of ideas is less a solid entity than an evolving, fluctuating thing. The concepts articulated in the *Republic* are significantly expanded and elaborated in the *Philebus*, *Sophist* and *Statesman*, becoming a kind of logical atomism and theory of classification; they are supplemented with Pythagorean number-theory and a crossbreeding of materialism and geometry in the *Timaeus*; and they are *refuted* in the *Parmenides*. It's hard to know where to start with such a self-conflicting corpus.

Worse, there is at least one forceful reservation about the value of writing. The *Phaedrus* calls it a kind of game,[24] and compares texts to orphans, abandoned by their makers and subject to the outrages of unscrupulous readers.[25] Indeed, writers who do happen to put something true into writing, says Socrates there, will have to show that they did so by defending it in spoken dialogue, which would immediately make it clear that their writings are less important than their 'living speech', and that their claims to knowledge come not from writing but from the objects they have pursued in life.[26] These passages have been the object of high-level critical examination for a long time – indeed one could make the case that the modern humanities were seeded by them.[27] But it is still stunning to find such objections to writing in a text so brilliantly written and in a corpus replete with literary virtuosity. The comments in the *Phaedrus* come close to the end of a long and intricate work: how are we to react, after several hours of reading or listening, to the claim that what has so detained our attention and not a little amount of interpretive labour should be treated as no more than an entertainment, as at best an untrustworthy communicator of knowledge?

We find a similar sentiment expressed in the seventh of a body of letters supposedly written from Plato to friends and colleagues. Here a Sicilian politician is criticized for claiming to know 'Platonic philosophy' because he has read Plato's texts: but what Plato actually professed, the letter says, 'cannot be spoken like other kinds of learning; it takes a great deal of converse and long living together, and then suddenly a light flashes, as though leaping from a fire: and when it enters the soul it sustains itself'.[28] This doesn't just deny the written communicability of Plato's philosophical standpoint: it denies that it can be realized outside a community of practice. 'Converse and living together' seems to imply that one must debate, discuss and work with one's comrades before achieving the insight in question. You can't learn by proxy, by looking at or listening to the words of someone else; as far as wisdom is concerned, you have to do it yourself. The authenticity of this letter is frequently doubted,[29] and for good reason: if Plato had written it, the result would be to disauthenticate the whole corpus. Nothing Plato wrote could be taken as containing Platonic doctrine. Definitively ruling it out as Plato's work would leave us in a slightly better position, but there would still be the end of the *Phaedrus* to deal with, where we have at best a warning to consider carefully the status of the texts we read and at worst a disavowal of the text in which it is embodied.

These reflections do not mean that Plato's corpus should be set aside or ignored. While they do encourage caution about claims regarding 'Plato's teaching' on a subject, they also support even closer attention to the texture of his writings with a view to discerning how they are constructed and how they describe themselves. Plato's texts are nothing if not self-reflexive: arguments can develop in them that seem to be about themselves as much as about the purported philosophical subject. The judicious choice and juxtaposition of themes in Plato's work, in other words, gives us insight into what he is *doing*, if not what he is *saying*.

Case in point: a constancy in his work is a persistent epistemological anti-sensuality. We are told many times and in many different ways that the senses are unreliable, part of a world in constant change, and that knowledge is accessible only after the labour of the intellect, supported by communal conversation. One of the most concise expressions of this frequently articulated position comes in the *Cratylus*. Close to the end of that text Socrates links perception to Heraclitean flux, and then indicts both as incapable of either stability or fostering knowledge. If there were nothing but appearance, he says, things 'could not be known by anyone':

for as soon as you approach them in order to know about them they change, so you can't know what or how things are, since there can be no knowledge of what doesn't stand still [...] Nor is it likely that there is knowledge at all if everything changes and never stays the same; for if knowledge stayed itself and didn't change from its condition of being knowledge, then it would abide and indeed it would *be* knowledge. But if it always changes, then it would always not be knowledge, and for the same reason nothing could know or be known.[30]

Of all the statements in which something is conjured beyond the realm of sensation and change, this one is the shortest, the least complicated, and the most in need of further explanation. Without the apparent two-world idealism of the *Republic*, or the talk of being and becoming in the *Timaeus*, or the elaborate reformulations in the *Sophist* (to name the three most well-known texts), this passage would leave us with more questions than answers. As it is, we have more answers than we know what to do with. Any of those works could be taken as a gloss on what Socrates is talking about here. And yet their mutual divergence gives the impression that the desire we find expressed in the *Cratylus* was never fully realized; even the theory of ideas fluctuates, changes, comes into being and passes away. That leaves us with the *desire* for stability but little else: there must be something over and against the flux of phenomena which does not change and which can be known. But what?

The *Theaetetus* contains one of Plato's most detailed investigations into the epistemological status of perception. Responding to Theaetetus' assertion that 'knowledge is nothing other than perception', Socrates immediately links this definition with Protagoras' thesis that 'a person is the standard of measurement (*metron*) for all things, both of things that are, that they are, and of things that are not, that they are not',[31] which he explicates as meaning that things are for one as they appear to him and for another as they appear to her; if the wind seems warm to me and cool to you, it *is* warm and cool.[32] He then claims that this actually conceals a doctrine identical to that of Heraclitus, that 'there is no one in and of itself, and you couldn't correctly describe anything, but if you called it big, it would also seem small [...] but it is out of movement and change and combination (*krasis*) with one another that all things come into being, though we incorrectly say that they *are*'.[33] That things are in a state of constant change seems to be entailed by the claim that things are as they appear to me and you, since they would appear to change relative to each of us. That is to say: as percipients change, so do perceptibles.[34] Socrates finds this unacceptable: it seems to imply that one can both know and not know something at the same time;[35] it also seems to imply that insanity is a condition in which knowledge is possible, since even the insane perceive;[36] worse, it leads to the conclusion that perception both is and *is not* knowledge, since it may seem to be knowledge to me, but not to you, which leads to the extraordinary conclusion that 'a person is a measure of all things' – so long as it seems that way to the person in question.[37]

Socrates does not need to be taken as denying that there is a sense in which the Protagorean/Heraclitean model has value, since he doesn't deny that differences in perception occur. What he denies is that perception, and the state of change or flux with which it seems inevitably linked, is knowledge. If we know anything, he says, our knowledge must lie elsewhere. The nature of that stability upon which knowledge depends is itself variously formulated in the Platonic corpus, but again nearly always as a process of moving away from the immediate experiences provided by the senses. The *Republic* describes a philosophical ascent through a series of fields of inquiry that culminates in the form of the good using the image of a line divided into four sections. On the lower part of the line are experiences grounded in the senses; given the unreliability of these, thought is capable at best of opinion in these regions. On the upper part, one accedes to reflection on entities that have congress exclusively with the mind; knowledge is of these entities alone. Harmonics – defined in the *Republic*, significantly, as the study of movement[38] – is included among the higher, intellectual subjects. But it is not the study of anything audible: Socrates dismisses as ridiculous those theorists who 'lay their ears alongside [the vibrating string of a monochord], like neighbors hunting after voices; some say they hear a sound in between two others, and that this is the smallest interval by which a measurement can be made, while others dispute that and say that the two notes are the same – but all of them prefer their ears to their minds'.[39] The image is of theorists listening hard to the finest imaginable distinctions of pitch, getting their ears as close to a vibrating string to pick up as much information as possible, and then arguing about what is audible and what not – an 'empiricist' orientation far too dependent on sensuality for Socrates here. He likes another group better: they 'measure the numbers in harmony against each other', still proceeding inductively from music as heard but extracting certain mathematical ratios from the musical phenomena.[40] Ultimately, Socrates dismisses even these, as well as any theorists who 'prefer their ears to their minds': all such are doomed to fail because their method is sensual.

But the Platonic texts are themselves inevitably sensual, *in* and *of* the sphere of becoming, fated to communicate via eye and ear. This offers an explanation for why, even if the *Seventh Letter* turns out to not to be Platonic, it contains a valuable insight into the status of Plato's writing. Perhaps he never said so, but he could well have claimed never to have written his doctrine. And yet words were all he had, and one way or another he was constrained to make use of them in order to foster progress towards that spark of insight. How could he communicate a wisdom the medium cannot capture to minds that can only retrieve it by other means?

I think several interrelated approaches to this problem can be discerned in his work.

One was to offer images that could help someone grasp what they might fail to appreciate if it was uttered directly.[41] The *Republic*'s well-known story of the cave is an example of this kind. Socrates invited his interlocutors to imagine that there is a cave in which certain people are living, though bound in such a way that they cannot get up or look at anything other than the cave's back wall. On that wall are projected shadow-images, cast there by a crew of puppeteers who work with shadow puppets placed between the prisoners and a fire which provides light. Now Socrates envisages that one of the bound cave denizens should for some reason find his chains released: suddenly he can rise and turn towards the source of light behind him. This adventurer would realize that the images he had seen were just that – no more than images. And if he walked up the path leading out of the cave, he would soon realize that even that antral fire was poor and dim; in the clear air he would be beset by a bright light the likes of which he had never known, and he would see colours entirely unfamiliar to him as well. It would certainly take a while for his eyes to get used to this new spectacle, but in time he would be able to directly behold all there was to see, even to look almost directly at the sun. He would come to prefer the surface to the depths from which he had arisen, and he would choose, if he could, never to return there. But if he did go back, and if he tried to explain what he had seen to the other prisoners in the cave, they would laugh at him and treat him as though he were insane: if he tried to unchain them and lead them towards the light, they might even kill him to defend their bedarkened way of life.[42]

This image is not an expression of 'doctrine' in any direct or literal way. Rather, it is offered as an illustration or a likeness: Socrates invites his interlocutors to compare their situation with it, and then explains the analogy in detail.[43] As the philosopher ascends to the realm of ideas and beyond that to the form of the good, so does the figure in Socrates' image rise from the shadows and ascend slowly to the entrance of the cave, then into the light of day. Socrates adds a detail which goes some way to explaining the method of teaching through likenesses such as we see here. If such a man, Plato has Socrates say, were to try to explain what he had seen to the other prisoners chained down in the bottom of the cave, they would think he was crazy.[44] The unasked but crucial question here is how such a man could communicate his experience in a way that would both save him from ridicule and benefit his fellow prisoners, perhaps by instilling in them the desire to make the ascent out of the cave themselves. The allegory of the cave is already an answer to this question, since it itself speaks in images and likenesses, using the cultural means available to point beyond their own limitations.[45]

Plato is well known for the tales that somehow make concrete his most difficult proposals. (An off-the-cuff list of such tales would include the myth of Er at the end of the *Republic*, the allegory of the cave itself, the image of humankind as frogs gathered around a lake offered in the *Phaedo*; the judgement of the dead in the *Gorgias*.[46]) But it seems to me that the dialogues as a whole might be read as an extended application of this principle: they are engaging, often highly dramatic philosophical narratives which are aimed less at exposing a doctrine than at concretizing something which cannot be given directly in words.

Plato's texts teach in a second way as well: they use common modes of communication in a self-defeating or merely suggestive fashion, in effect teaching by refusing to teach, raising questions but remaining pointedly silent on the answers. A vast amount of Plato's work deploys this strategy: many of his dialogues end with all available answers to the central question (what is justice? what is friendship? what is knowledge?) refuted and no positive doctrine adopted. It would be a long list if we were to reckon up every dialogue which ended with one character remarking to another that the topic under consideration was still unresolved, and that they should certainly return to it on another occasion, casting readers unceremoniously into a silence which could be filled only by their own thoughts. Indeed, sometimes it is not just at the end that we are forced back on ourselves. 'In a number of Platonic dialogues,' writes Eva Brann,

> there are people present who say nothing or next to nothing out loud [...] The reader is, I think, invited to be present just as these people are, and with them to smile or snicker at witticisms and inside jokes, to nod approval at satisfying formulations, to recall contradicting passages of conversation, to appreciate the return of a theme, and, in sum, to check and fill out the recorded conversation with an unwritten inner accompaniment – to be always just on the brink of breaking in.[47]

To fail to answer its own questions, to almost compel us to speak back to it – this is a form of negative pedagogy, a kind of seduction whose greatest enticement lies in the withholding. It is also a deeply self-contradictory strategy, for it requires the texts to offer and withhold at the same time, to invite and refuse, to endorse study and yet refuse to yield what they promise.

There is a third mode of teaching or communicating in Plato's texts. We might think of them as engaging readers in a form of intellectual calisthenics, the goal of which was to accustom them to mental movements that would prove useful when the text falls silent. That reading is an ergonomic activity is a position that is now, I think, widely accepted. Psychologists observe that the eye jumps from one focal point to another in a line of text rather than gazing at every letter in sequence, and that a very small proportion of any text is actually in focus during any normal reading. Their model recognizes reading as a multilayered, recursive and self-correcting process involving the collaboration of eye and mind in gathering, theorizing about, and supplementing visual data about the text.[48] On the philosophical side, similar results have been acknowledged since Wolfgang Iser retrofitted Gadamer's notion of the hermeneutical fusion of horizons to describe individual acts of reading. Based on what I have read so far, I develop theories about what a text means, what will happen next, and so on. Progressively, my horizon of expectation shifts, as gaps in textual information are filled in and I become more confident that my view is consistent with the data I've gathered.[49] A favourite example for such models of reading is the detective novel, which is structured around a central gap or lack of information (whodunit?); I am kept reading by the constant revelation of new information which incessantly provokes me to modify what I think is going on. It seems clear that many Platonic dialogues are structured around a similar gap: we are drawn on by the question 'what is [love, friendship, knowledge, justice]?' That gap is accompanied by others, often of a dramatic or a meta-literary character: what is Gorgias really like? Who, or how, is Cephalus? What is the relationship between the elaborate cast of characters in the *Euthydemus* and the dialogue's central theme (what *is* the dialogue's central theme)? These are broad questions, but they initiate an engagement with the text which is dynamic and which depends on specific details; my contention is that such an engagement could be thought of as inducing a kind of movement in the soul that is in some ways more important than any individual question's actual answer. I will refer to this set of strategies as a 'gestural rhetoric'.

Jennifer Rapp's excellent book about the *Phaedrus* wrestles with the same interactions between the critique of writing, the oblique rhetoric of the dialogue form, and the project of pedagogy that I am trying to put my finger on here. In the following she is talking about how the dialogue form is an attempt to foster self-examination – a project which first entails the hardly trivial accomplishment of being able to discern the self:

> The replete and porous character of the self and the need to unmoor false conceptions of sovereignty in the self mean that direct, literal, and static modes of viewing will not be sufficient. Specifically, the ordinary oblivion of the self, which arises from its replete and porous nature, entail that angled vantage points and dynamic modes of viewing will be needed to see the obscure, fertile lacunae of the self.[50]

To catch a glimpse of your self, which is normally about as visible to you as the spot between your shoulder blades or as willing to stand still as your shadow, you have to move in a wily, oblique way, dipping and turning in thought, in an effort to catch its ever-receding outline. Rapp suggests that the dialogue form teaches you to move in just this way. Its very obliqueness, its refusal to stand still and its work with images involve us in a kind of whirling motion through which we begin to feel the hidden conditions of awareness.

Such a strategy is difficult to conceptualize because it starts from a refusal to communicate through concepts. There is a level of reading which accompanies the realization of propositional content but *is not itself* the realization of propositional content: it's the underside or the procedural unthought of interpretation. This level of reading could be taken as just as important, psychagogically speaking, as the actual comprehension of what is being said. After all, insight depends on a process of some kind, whether that be the process of dialogue, of slow and difficult collaborative investigation, or of entering a long period of concentration that finds fruition in a sudden flash of insight. What if in reading we were not extracting meaning but moving along with the text, synching up with it in the hope that it could somehow give us a kind of philosophical momentum?

Let us briefly reconsider the first two strategies listed above: on a second glance, both appear to be examples of this final one. I noted that many of Plato's dialogues can be taken as examples of negative pedagogy, of teaching by refusing to teach, since they pursue but do not attain solutions to their problems. But these works are not just teasers offering frustrating glimpses of answers that never come. They also contain something positive: a model of what you will have to do when you start to think for yourself. Plato once had Socrates define thought as 'a conversation with oneself in silence':[51] contemplation is a kind of inward self-interrogation much like the process of questioning typically evinced in his dialogues. Regardless of whether you read them silently or aloud to yourself, or even listen while others read or perform, your attention is entrained to the motion of an argument: and it is that motion, ultimately, that matters. The first strategy, to compose illustrative 'myths' or likenesses, can be taken in a similar way; to be sure, they are paradigms from which readers are invited to gain some insight into an often difficult argument. But, in addition to this, Plato's myths induce the soul to *move* in a fashion conducive to productive independent thought.[52] From the allegory of the cave, for example, we are asked to infer the nature of the process of intellectual awakening. Not only does the allegory give us an image which lets us understand how turning to thought works; *understanding the image by looking beyond it is itself an example of turning to thought*, so that, in effect, we have done what we are being taught when we understand the lesson.

If we consider Plato's writings as examples of this third strategy, the strategy of what I called 'gestural rhetoric', it becomes clear that following the course of an argument in order to realize a self-sustaining cognitive movement is just as important as the texts' propositional content. The point here isn't that Plato's writing is meaningless, or that meaning should be discarded when we approach it. Clearly such a claim would be nonsensical. Whatever we make of him, we do it because we have tried to understand him. But what matters beyond the conceptual or propositional content of his writings is a certain quality of cognitive activity. Thus – to take one particularly striking example from a corpus replete with similar instances – it is often noticed that the *Republic* has an unusual structure in which a preliminary question ('what is justice?') modulates into a broader discussion based on an analogy ('let us seek to understand justice in the soul by trying to understand justice in the state'), then seems to ground its initial question in the causal influence of the analogy ('a just soul is what is made by a just state'). This is an unsettlingly circular trajectory in which realities are derived from metaphors and vice versa. At the same time, exploring the nature of justice pushes Socrates and his interlocutors upwards through increasingly abstract levels of epistemological and ontological theory, at the highest limits of which there is no political consideration to be detected – and yet justice in both state and soul depends on the experience of this highly abstract contemplation. There is value in the very process of following the *Republic* through the circles of its argument: doing so prepares the mind to proceed in the direction the words seem to point. Thanks to its curious movement, at once self-devouring and self-transcending, the *Republic* stops looking like a work of mimetic art or even like a text with a political programme, and instead comes to resemble absolute writing, something more in the line of a novel by Alain Robbe-Grillet or Paul Auster.

Better: something more like a piece of music.[53] In the *Protagoras*, Plato attributed to Protagoras the idea that music represented a kind of first-line training in ethical behaviour,[54] and its ability to teach through gesture and habituation becomes a model both for Socratic and Platonic psychagogy, as we will see. As Brann put it with characteristic luminance, 'Socratic music is [...] *philosophical music*, the music of truth. Its special force will lie in this: that its *logoi* [words] are at the same time *erga* [deeds]'.[55] The *Republic* has Socrates embracing a theory of musical affect in which structural characteristics like tuning and rhythm have a powerful influence on the internal harmony of a hearer's soul, potentially leading it towards a state of harmony that is practically identical with prudence and justice;[56] this influence, as Barker has suggested, is slow and, crucially, subliminal.[57] Because of this, music offers an excellent analogy for the psychagogical force exerted by the gestural rhetoric of a Platonic text.[58] Nor do I foist the analogy onto the texts; it is contained within them. In the *Phaedo*, Socrates has turned in his final days to the composition of hymns. This is new, for he had elsewhere described philosophy as the best form of music;[59] in the *Republic*, it aims to produce a kind of harmony in the soul.[60] Plato comes close to equating his texts with music in the *Laws*, when the unnamed Athenian proposes that tragedy, which is again exiled from the ideal state,[61] could easily be replaced by the study of the *conversation the unnamed Athenian is having*.[62] Later he goes farther: 'we ourselves are the poets of the most beautiful and the best of tragedies – at least in so far as this is in our power – for our constitution is an imitation of the best and most beautiful life, and that is what we say is the truest tragedy'.[63] Substituting *itself* for musical culture, the *Laws* also appropriates a great deal of musical vocabulary to its own purposes. Ancestral monarchies were destroyed by the monarchs themselves, who 'did not harmonize (*sunephōnēsan*) with each other, but this dissonance (*diaphōnia*) was the greatest ignorance (so we say), though it looked like wisdom; and it destroyed everything because they were out of tune and bitterly unmusical'.[64] In another passage enjoining the use of preambles to explain the rationale of individual laws or policies, the unnamed Athenian comments that while all kinds of music have proems and introductions (*anakinēseis*), there are none for 'the things that are *really and truly nomoi*'.[65] *Nomos* was the name for a musical composition, a suite of constrained improvisations performed by aulos- and lyre-players in Greek festival competitions.[66] The *Laws* delegitimizes the musical meaning of the term, emphasizing that truly valid culture occurs only in laws – and, even more than this, in the text of the *Laws* itself. Of course that is not to say that philosophy *consists* in the reading of Plato, but, rather, that such reading would serve as a kind of overture, a tuning up of the soul in preparation for the contemplation that cannot be done other than in person.

In one of the most significant statements of philosophical method to be found in his corpus, Plato describes the aim of dialectics as 'showing which categories agree (*sumphōnei*) with each, and which do not go together'.[67] A bland or overly technical translation of this celebrated phrase would miss two things. First, the goal it describes coincides with the work a reader must have done when he approached the dialogue in which it is contained. Though modern editions identify the speakers by name, the original texts separated speakers only with a double point (:) and, perhaps, a small dash under the line of text to the right of the column (a *paragraphos*).[68] To identify who spoke meant categorizing each utterance and determining which went with which and who said what. One could learn what dialectics was, in other words, by performing it on the text one read. The second thing to remark about this description of dialectics is that it has strong musical overtones. In the process of sorting and sifting one discovers which things *sound together*: Plato's word is *sumphōneō*, a verb meaning to sing or speak together, to make a musical concord (*sumphōnia*). Here we have an ergonomic procedure – reading – linked to a philosophical procedure – dialectics – through the language of music. Actually, this is more than just linguistic mediation. The *Sophist*'s celebrated discussion of dialectics is led up to by a set of analogies, the last of which is music, 'the art of recognizing which sounds can be blended and which cannot'.[69] Recognizing what goes with what describes music, dialectics *and* the art of reading a dialogue.[70] I think music offers a way to imagine Plato's texts as a kinetic therapy aimed at calming and strengthening the senses and the soul, synchronizing them to a movement more germane to intellectual experience. At this level, his writings offer not a body of doctrine but a musical score of which the reader is both performer and instrument.

Following the lead provoked by these reflections, the next two chapters treat music as a symbolic realm in which Plato's texts talked about themselves. Chapter 2 attends to moments in which music is both disavowed *and* endorsed, in a contradictory gesture that is intimately related to Plato's stance vis-à-vis his own writing as an instance of negative pedagogy (or teaching by refusing to teach). The complex disavowal and endorsement of music emerges only when it is taken together with Plato's characterization of Socratic pedagogy, and his generalization from that to writing. In Chapter 3 I look at the association between music and the communication of movement. Here music is treated as useful because it affords a way to forge souls through psycho-kinetic communication and control. My emphasis is on the *Timaeus* and the *Laws*.

A number of warnings are appropriate. First, let me reassert what my project is: prompted by a few textual clues, I am using music in Plato to think about Plato's writing. What unfolds in the next two chapters is best understood as a creative, constructive attempt to get at the most challenging aspects of the dialogues through imagery associated with music. This is most plainly obvious in Chapter 3, where, although there are a few explicit connections to be found between music and textuality, there is no theory of textual kinesis that corresponds to the quite explicit theory of musical movement. But within the context of relevance provided by the analogy, the theory of musical movement poses what for me, anyway, is a useful question about reading Plato, though it is perhaps best answered not in print but during periods of introspection: do I move, cognitively speaking, when I read these texts, and is this movement good?

Second: while the analogy between music and Plato's texts helps us think about how we read, it is not exact. I do think the kinetic force of music helps us think about the ergonomic quality of his writing, but I do not think that music affects souls the same way that writing does. In fact there is a crucial difference between music and Plato's writing in that music, as it is imagined in the corpus, moves souls, while in reading a soul must move itself in response to structural features of the text. A related difference lies in the fact that in Plato's texts music is usually said to be effective because it manipulates perception, while writing would have psychic consequences because it compels a reader to work with meaning. What matters about the analogy of the cave isn't the sound of the words in which it is told (though Plato's a good enough writer to make that rewarding, too); the point is the way the analogy pushes us to understand something on the far side of what it presents. Nonetheless the differences themselves amount, it seems to me, to an important piece of information in their own right, provoking the reflection that Plato's texts, while in some way patterned on music, are also to be taken as a step beyond it. They are musical but not sensual; they demand (perhaps) a less embodied, more psychic kind of dance.

Chapter 2

In the tenth book of the *Republic* Socrates tells the story of Er, a man from Pamphylia who was killed on the battlefield, visited the afterlife, then returned to the living to report on what he had seen. At the end of his underworld tour, Er is given a sublime vision of the structure of the cosmos. The heaven is structured like a sequence of eight inset spinning whorls, on each one of which a Siren sits. Each Siren sings a single note, and together the eight notes make a perfect harmony.[1]

The *Republic* was not the first text in which music was affiliated with the structure and movement of the heavens. Anaximander seems to have claimed that the stars were fiery light shining through perforations in a dark screen; he likened these perforations to auloi or trumpets.[2] Other descriptions of the heavens did not evoke sound or musical instruments, but rather the ordered movement of dance.[3] The image appealed to Euripides, who returned to it repeatedly.[4] The important late-fifth-century Pythagorean theorist Philolaus mapped a universe circling a central fire in a movement he characterized as choric.[5] One scholar argues that Philolaus offered no theory of heavenly harmony at all.[6] But he did posit correspondences between musical and universal harmony; and he also argued that there were basic elements of the cosmos' constitution that could be explained using harmonic theory.[7] On this point, he has much in common with several authors in the Hippocratic corpus, who saw harmony operating in the body as it did in music.[8] In the *Republic* Plato himself has Socrates propose that the processes of decline and revolution that afflict every political organization were occasioned by astronomical movements connected to mathematical and harmonic speculations.[9]

But it is seldom suggested that you could *hear* the harmony of the heavens, as Socrates seems to imply in the myth of Er. Now, as it happens, Aristotle does report that some theorists thought the heavens made a musical sound.[10] Their argument went something like this: planetary bodies move; movement causes sound; different speeds cause different pitches; different planets move at different speeds. So each planet must make a different sound, and the sum total of these sounds is a harmony because the relative movements of the planets can be reconciled with the numerical relations of the concords.[11] Aristotle objects that if there really is an audible planetary music, it is curious that no one can actually hear it. An answer to this objection, attributed by Aristotle to certain 'Pythagoreans', is that since we are always exposed to the sound, we simply do not notice it, much as a coppersmith no longer hears the sounds of the smithy. Another attempt to address the fact that no one hears the heavenly sounds may be present in Archytas, who claimed that some sounds were too loud for the ears, likening them to rushing water that will not enter a narrow-necked vase.[12] But even here we have sound which, though in principle audible, is not heard in fact – it is not the actually audible heavenly music reported by Er.[13]

Outside the *Republic*, even Plato's works treat the music of the spheres as inaudible. In the *Timaeus* the world soul is constructed out of a material articulated according to the proportions of a musical scale (see later). But it is silent. Timaeus is quite specific on this matter: the movement of the world soul takes place 'without a note or a sound'.[14] This is quite in line with the *Timaeus'* hierarchy of values, since on the one hand sound is sensual and therefore less valuable than thought, and on the other, thinking, which is what the world soul does, is a silent dialogue.[15]

The *Republic's* image of heavenly harmony had a long career, and correspondences between music and planetary movement became a standard topic for music theory.[16] But normally audible music was either excluded or ignored. Cicero's *De re publica*, ending like Plato's with a sublime vision of the cosmos, had the dreaming Scipio seem to hear the music of the spheres,[17] while Macrobius, reading Cicero beside Plato, observed that the inaudibility of heavenly music was the result of our degraded, embodied condition: more refined minds would hear it better.[18] Ptolemy thought the mathematical structure of musical harmony corresponded closely with heavenly phenomena.[19] But nothing in Ptolemy suggests that he thought he was dealing with anything but a set of remarkable correspondences at a very high level of abstraction. Aristides Quintilianus outlined a long series of similarities between the structures of music and those of the heavens – but he, too, shied away from saying that the heavens made a sound you could hear. Rather, the numerical structures that prevail in the cosmos have gross and less accurate correspondences in the sensible realm: the senses are consistently presented as deaf to the harmonic truths resident only in numbers.[20]

Just as surprising is the fact that the *Republic*'s heavenly music is made by Sirens. In the *Odyssey*, after all, the Sirens are dread creatures. Anyone who hears them, we are told there, is drawn by an irresistible desire to listen and, forgetting their homeland, wastes away at their feet.[21] Hardly an auspicious precedent for the heavenly music heard by Er. To be sure, there are iconographical strains which could justify the Sirens' presence in this imagined underworld. In art, they are affiliated with the afterlife from quite early on,[22] and their eschatological undertones may well lie behind their appearance in the *Republic*. Walter Burkhert claimed that 'when we look beyond the facade of analysis and explication of the harmony of the spheres, what we find is neither empirical nor mathematical science, but eschatology'.[23] Still, there is something odd about the choice to use Sirens here, given the overwhelming cultural importance of the *Odyssey* and the generally menacing flavour of its musical monsters. Later readers of Plato were sensitive to this. One theory, repeated by Theon of Smyrna, explains the Sirens' presence by allegorizing them, via a quasi-Cratylean etymology, as planets; they twinkle (*seiriazein*). Theon adds that among the ancients the name 'Sirius' (which sounds a bit like 'Sirens') was used for any and all planets indiscriminately.[24] Others, including Plutarch and Macrobius, associated the Sirens with the Muses and understood Plato simply to be talking about the latter.[25] But the late-antique commentator Proclus would have none of this. Rather, he says with one ear on the *Timaeus*, Plato used Sirens to remind us that even heavenly music is embodied music. Proclus finds evidence for three different kinds of Sirens – those of the heavens, attested in the *Republic*, where he says they are associated with Zeus; those of the sea, attested in the *Odyssey*, and therefore associated with Poseidon, and those in the underworld, attested in the *Cratylus* and associated with Hades.[26] In distinction to these fleshy, time-bound Sirens, says Proclus, the Muses are responsible for 'noetic harmony'.[27] Proof for Proclus that the Sirens are subordinate to the Muses comes from the old tale that they challenged the Muses to a singing contest, lost, and were deprived of their feathers in punishment.[28] Ultimately, he concludes, the Sirens' music in the *Republic* has psychagogic value, allegorically speaking: it could lead us to the more rarified insights of the Muses.[29]

I am certain that one could profitably read Er's encounter with the Sirens as a statement reflecting fourth-century astronomy; a little deeper investigation would surely uncover some numerology and perhaps some mathematics at work here as well.[30] But I am moved by an implication in Proclus' reading of the Sirens as an allegory for philosophical pedagogy: perhaps there is an analogy between the Sirens and Plato's writing project. Both the *Republic* and the Sirens, at least as Proclus understands the latter, could be described as manipulations of the sensual realm intended to move others beyond sensuality. And like the Odyssean Sirens, these ones should not be dwelt with for too long. They make a sensual music that gets us started, as it were – but that should also be left behind at a certain point, as, indeed, it is: for the souls who hear this music depart the afterlife shortly thereafter. Note the complex, not to say contradictory, set of values which accrue to the Sirens if we understand them this way. On the one hand they are beautiful and beguiling; they may even evince a mathematical harmony still more ravishing than their sensual presence. On the other hand they should only be attended to for a while, since their aim is to lead us to the better music of the Muses. The Sirens are at once embraced and disavowed.

We can find other examples of the same combination of endorsement and disavowal associated with the most important musical figure in Plato's writing: Socrates himself.[31] Nobody is likely to be surprised, at this point in the development of Platonic scholarship, that Socrates cannot be summed up or defined by referring to his habit of refuting others through a series of questions. Asking questions and demanding comparatively short answers is not the only mode he works in: he can just as easily spin a tale, report a dialogue or improvise a sophistic demonstration of rhetoric. He's not best described as a rigorous logician, either: to be sure there are elements of what Aristotelians would call syllogistic in some of his arguments, but there is also a fair bit of bickering (as in the *Gorgias* and the *Protagoras*), teasing (especially with the young ones, as in the *Lysis* or the *Euthydemus*), long drawn-out stories about conversations he has had with others (*Republic, Symposium, Theaetetus*), puns (*Cratylus*), allegories (*Republic, Crito, Phaedo*) and myths (*Republic, Gorgias, Phaedrus*). What he does do consistently is exert a kind of fascination that lasts long after people have run into him and that influences far more than their ability to construct an argument. With Socrates it somehow becomes about more than how to think: he casts a kind of spell that forces you to feel that you must change your life (as Rilke put it long after). Consider Alcibiades' description of Socrates in the *Symposium*:

> I say he is most similar to those Silenoi that sit in sculpture dealers' shops; the craftsmen make them holding pan-pipes or auloi, and when you open them up they reveal images of the gods inside. I also say that he is like the satyr Marsyas [...] Aren't you [that is, Socrates] an aulete? You are, and much more amazing at it than [Marsyas] was. He entranced men with a musical instrument, through the power of his mouth, and even now people play his pieces – for I say the things Olympus played were from Marsyas, who taught them to him – so that whenever a good aulete plays them (or even a middling aulos-girl, really) they can possess you and through their divine powers reveal who is worthy of the gods and the mysteries. You are different from him only in the fact that you accomplish the same thing in bare words and without an instrument.[32]
>
> [...]
>
> When I hear him my heart pounds even more than that of the Corybants, and tears flow because of his words. And I see that everybody else suffers the same thing. I like listening to Pericles and the other good orators, but they never made me experience *that*. They didn't throw my soul into a tumult, or make me fault myself for being in the condition of a slave; but I have often been so broken down by this Marsyas here that I seem not to have a livable life. You won't say these things aren't true, Socrates: even now I know full well that if I were willing to lend my ears, I wouldn't be able to resist but would suffer the same things. He forces me to agree that I fall short, and yet I fail to take care of myself, even though I look after Athenian affairs. And so I forcefully withhold my ears, as though I were running from the Sirens, and I flee so as to escape growing old beside him.[33]

Readers coming to this passage from the *Republic* may be quite surprised to discover Socrates being compared to an aulos-player: *Republic* III had Socrates himself excluding the auloi from his thought-city on the grounds that it was 'many-voiced', capable of a wide variety of sounds that mimicked the multiformity of phenomena and degraded the pure and simple music validated there.[34] The *Republic* even excludes the 'instruments of Marsyas' as full of change and bad for the soul.[35] Perhaps part of what happens in Alcibiades' speech can be ascribed to the speaker's problematic status. Brilliant, energetic and morally dubious, Alcibiades might well have appeared as the great failure in Socratic pedagogy.[36] Indeed, the way he bursts in drunk at the end of the *Symposium*'s decidedly sober proceedings and goes on to reveal hitherto unaddressed aspects of Socrates' character has him reprising his role as a profaner of mysteries. The comparison to Marsyas has a pointed relationship to Alcibiades' own profile. A story is told that when it came time to teach him the auloi, he refused the instrument out of hand, proclaiming that nothing rejected by Athena was good for him, either.[37] The reference is to a myth that Athena created the auloi in order to imitate the lamentation of the Gorgons for their dead sister Medusa, but threw them away when she saw how she was forced to distort her face to make them speak. The auloi were then picked up, says the myth, by the satyr Marsyas, who became so proficient on them that he challenged Apollo to a contest. *That* didn't go well – he lost, and was flayed alive for his trouble. When Alcibiades compares Socrates to Marsyas, then, we have a complex set of associations at work: he professes overwhelming attraction to a figure he simultaneously rejects.

What Alcibiades experiences when he encounters Socrates is, it seems to me, an inversion of just the philosophical process Socrates says is the true content of erotic love. In the account Socrates reports having learned from Diotima, an early (and temporary) attraction to bodily beauty leads (at least for those who are attentive) to an even stronger attraction to the beauty of a soul, thence to the beauty of knowledge, and then, finally, to an eternal beauty that exists in and of itself.[38] Alcibiades gets this theory hilariously backwards. Diotima describes physical attraction leading to psychic attraction: Alcibiades begins with a psychic attraction to Socrates' words and proceeds from there to a desire for physical intimacy, climbing under the same cloak with him on a chilly night. Socrates never touches him – a behaviour Alcibiades perversely (and comedically) describes as an outrage.[39] When we read it against the background of Diotima's theory of philosophical love, Alcibiades' failure to initiate a physical encounter in this scene might be taken as a symbol not only of Socrates' virtue but also of Alcibiades' inadequacies. The latter fails, as it were, to capitalize on the opportunity given to him by his attraction to Socrates – not to seek caresses but to move beyond the semblance of corporeal Eros and to discern the beauty that lies in souls. Alcibiades tarries too long with the senses, and although he says he flees Socrates as one would flee a Siren, the reality is rather the opposite of this: he clings to Socrates like a sailor entranced by the Sirens' song. But while his actions are not ideal, his assessment of Socrates is basically right: the philosopher is a seductive, musical figure.

We find Socrates appearing as a musical figure in the *Phaedrus* as well. Almost from the beginning of this dialogue Socrates seems to assimilate himself to Corybantic inspiration. On the surface, this looks as though Socrates is saying that he and Phaedrus have both been initiated into the mystery religion to which Corybantic dancing belonged. But a second meaning is also suggested: Socrates and Phaedrus, who, after all, are both lovers of words, will together initiate themselves into the 'cult' of the sophist and rhetor Lysias through a collective contemplation of his written speech on love, which like the hierophantic objects of a mystery cult are concealed from the eyes of the uninitiated by the coils of a papyrus scroll. The initiation is compellingly musical, as we will see.

The *Phaedrus* is built as a sequence of speeches. The first is that written speech by Lysias, which argues that boys should give favours to men who do not love them: it is read out by Phaedrus from the scroll in which he keeps it. The next two are given by Socrates. In the first he makes the same argument as Lysias; and in the second he argues the opposite, that boys should choose to be with lovers. Socrates' first speech is repeatedly characterized as the result of inspiration, and hardly Socrates' *own* invention: his chest is filled like a vessel, he says, with a speech coming from somewhere else.[40] When he finishes it, he describes it to Phaedrus as '*your* speech, which *you* said through my medicated mouth'.[41] This speech seems to Socrates to take the form of a dithyramb and then to become epic in form.[42]

The references to inspiration surround Socrates' *first* speech. He renounces this speech, first by delivering it with his head covered in shame,[43] and then by offering a second speech, which he describes as a palinode akin to Stesichorus' revision of his song about Helen.[44] Perhaps the second speech comes from a more pronounced dedication to reason? In fact, no. The need for the second speech is suggested by Socrates' divine sign,[45] and the speech itself emphasizes the importance of Dionysiac enthusiasm. Socrates argues that love is a kind of madness, thanks to which we are led by the allure of sensual beauty towards the contemplation of greater truths. Our souls, he claims, are immortal: and when they are not tied to their mortal bodies they rise towards the heavens and the gods, who move through the sky in an everlasting circular procession. The memory of what the soul witnessed when it participated in this procession is a goad to the pursuit of moral excellence.

Socrates imagines the soul as a chariot pulled by two horses. One horse is sleek and white and well behaved, while the other is not; the task of the charioteer is to control this other horse and harmonize its movements with those of the good one. Socrates describes the bad horse as 'crooked, heavy, badly assembled',

> with a short neck and an apish face, black skin, and grey eyes, hot tempered, toxic and fraudulent, hairy around the ears and deaf, insensitive to whip and goad alike.[46]

Elizabeth Belfiore finds more than a slight resemblance to Satyrs in this description of the dark horse, which are (in her words) 'big, misshapen creatures with snub noses, high foreheads, shaggy hair, thick, short necks, large eyes, and large, erect phalluses. The black horse not only looks but acts like a satyr, beings characterized by *hubris* and a lack of restraint, especially in sex, and failing to achieve its sexual goals'.[47] Belfiore also points out that satyrs are sometimes portrayed on vase paintings as pulling chariots;[48] one notable instance contains an image of Zeus in a chariot on the inside, and an image of satyrs pulling a chariot on the outside.[49]

The stately procession of the gods in circular motion through the sky bears more than a passing resemblance to the circling Sirens in the myth of Er. But now things are orchestrated so that the divine procession from which the soul descends, to which it aspires to return, and in which it catches glimpses of sublime, eternal reality, recalls the Dionysian dance-song, the dithyramb, which is traditionally described as a 'circular chorus'.[50] Belfiore has collected the evidence plainly and convincingly:

> Each of the gods is a leader in the 'divine chorus' (*theiou chorou*, 247a7), moving through the heavens in an orderly choral arrangement (*kata taxin*, 247a3). Before it fell to earth, the soul-chariot of every human was a dancer (*choreutēs*, 252d1) in the chorus (*chorōi*, 250b6) led by one of the gods. The mortal lover attempts to rejoin this chorus in which he used to dance, imitating his own god and educating his beloved to follow the rhythm (*rhuthmizontes*) of the same god (253b5-6). Socrates' statement that Hestia

remains home (247a1-2) while the other gods move around in a circle (247d4-5) reflects the common idea that the stars are gods moving in a circular cosmic dance around a center.[51]

Belfiore concludes that Socrates has configured the philosophical process not only as a kind of madness related to erotic passion, but also as a dithyrambic dance.[52]

Belfiore also suggests that there is an analogy between the Satyrs associated with the dark horse and Socrates, that comic, snub-nosed hanger-about with whom Alcibiades compared Silenus and Marsyas in the *Symposium*. Satyrs are liminal beings associated with initiatory practice; they play a role in the transformation or improvement of adolescent souls – a role Socrates plays as well.[53] Note however that the Socrates–Satyr analogy, in the *Phaedrus* anyway, identifies the philosopher *not* with the whole cosmic dance, but with the *black horse*. This makes Socrates only *one element* of the process, not the dancer of the improving dance but rather more like what needs to be improved. Consider that in this dialogue of pairs, with Socrates' two speeches (which themselves correspond to 'good' and 'bad' horses), there are also two interlocutors: one looks like a Satyr and is comparable to the dark horse; and the other's name, *Phaedrus*, means 'bright' and 'shining', and thus invites comparison to the white horse.

In addition to the dithyrambic associations discerned by Belfiore, there may be tragic resonances as well. Jacqueline de Romilly observed close verbal parallels between the description of the soul-as-chariot in the *Phaedrus* and Hippolytus' disastrous chariot ride in Euripides' play.[54] The connection between the *Phaedrus* and Euripides is recommended by many other details as well – not least of which is the name of the dialogue's title character, which is merely the masculine form of Euripides' heroine, Phaedra. The *Hippolytus*, famously, was produced in two versions: it was by no means the only fifth-century drama to have been rewritten and reproduced,[55] but it was the most celebrated, and it might be taken as a natural point of contact for a text in which Socrates makes two speeches, each arguing the opposite point of view. In the first *Hippolytus*, Phaedra brazenly propositioned her stepson (and outraged the audience); Hippolytus reacted to Phaedra's advance by covering his head in shame. In the *Phaedrus*, Socrates' first speech is delivered with his head covered, in a gesture strongly reminiscent of the first Euripidean play. In the second *Hippolyus,* Phaedra committed suicide rather than be suspected of any unchaste action. In Socrates' second speech, love is shown to be a non-carnal, virtuous attraction. Do Socrates' two speeches mirror the two *Hippolytuses*?[56]

The musical thematics of the *Phaedrus* may also interface with the question of the value and force of Platonic textuality. It's worth recalling at this point that the *Phaedrus* begins with a scroll and ends with a lengthy assessment of writing and reading: 'literature' is a vibrant concern here. Granted, in the *Phaedrus* Plato gives voice to strong reservations about the value of writing. It destroys memory; it cannot be controlled but circulates far out of its author's reach, finding readers with whom it has no business, and it can't explain itself but just stands there in silence like a statue.[57] Familiar complaints, but also extremely paradoxical: this destroyer of memory is also a form of memory; and if Socrates thinks it wanders around too much, he *also* thinks it is uselessly immobile, like a statue. I've sometimes wondered if this wasn't so much a rejection of writing as a hesitant endorsement of it: you *can* use writing, as long as you use it right. That last comparison of writing to a statue evokes what by Plato's time had become a traditional contrast in which silent and dumb statues were unfavourably compared to song.[58] What if Plato were wryly suggesting that writing could be useful if it was more like music?

But things get tricky when it comes to a concrete application of this proposal. Socrates' next claim about writing is provocative, to say the least. The *true* writing, the really good philosophical writing, he says, is written in the soul of the interlocutor, and it grows there like a seed.[59] To plant that seed you don't just need to know the truth about your subject;[60] you must also know your audience profoundly enough to be able to tailor your speech to their soul – for each different kind of listener, a different kind of argument is needed.[61] This claim is thematically linked with erotic practice in the *Phaedrus* via a kind of typology: in Socrates' second speech, souls are said to dance in divine choruses led by different gods, and their sexual preferences are said to reflect these choruses – those souls who followed in the train of Zeus are naturally attracted to Zeus-like mortals, those who followed Hera prefer the Heraesque, and so on.[62] But there is also a cryptic musical allusion here; in the music theory Socrates articulates in the *Republic*, different kinds of soul are associated with different forms of music.[63] And there is something awry in the fact that the philosopher must know all the modes (of discourse): in this, in his multiformity, he bears a stunning resemblance to the composers criticized in the *Laws* for mixing modes and genera in order to satisfy the desires of their audience.[64] That this is how Socrates actually operates will be pretty obvious to many of Plato's readers: he persistently represents himself as merely giving voice to others' conceptions, drawing them towards pedagogically useful conclusions by matching his voice to theirs.

This makes the philosophical practice endorsed by Socrates remarkably similar to advanced Athenian art music, since both are mimetic and polyform, not only able to change based on the circumstances and the subject at hand, but practically defined by this idea. There is one major difference, however: Athenian art music is not endorsed. In fact it is consistently and quite aggressively criticized. The *Republic* is notoriously clear on this subject; among the musical features which a well-run polity should prohibit, Socrates argues there, are just the polyformity and mimesis we have seen embraced, at least implicitly, at the end of the *Phaedrus*.[65] In addition to excluding all but the 'Dorian' and the 'Phrygian' modes from his city in words, and accepting an equally restricted set of rhythms, Socrates proposes to prevent 'imitators' from performing. 'Imitators' do not tell a story in their own voice: rather, they speak in the voices of their characters. Such men are so shameful that they will happily imitate anything – 'thunder and the sounds of the wind, hail and axles and pulleys, and the voices of trumpets and *auloi* and *syrinxes* and of all the musical instruments, and even the sounds of dogs and sheep and birds'.[66] While this is presented as a discussion of storytellers, it has a musical application as well: 'many-stringed' instruments constructed so as to support modulation between three different tunings, and the 'many-voiced' *aulos*, which is capable, says Socrates, of the greatest variety of sounds imaginable, are also to be left out of the city.[67]

Socrates also says in the *Republic* that no one should consider themselves an expert in music

> until we know the forms of prudence and courage and liberality and magnanimity and whatever is akin to these, and also the opposites that one can find everywhere, and until we perceive the contents in which they occur, both them and their images, and not overlook them in small or large issues but believe them to be the substance of art and discipline.[68]

This looks similar to the claim in the *Phaedrus* that one must know all the different kinds of soul in order to declare oneself a competent rhetor. On a closer look, however, we see a rather significant difference in the application of the idea that one must have a variegated understanding of the spectrum of ethical states. In the *Republic* the purpose is to allow one to act as judge, regulator or censor: understanding the elements of morality allows one to recognize and eliminate the corresponding structures in music. In the *Phaedrus*, by contrast, the perspective is practical: broad knowledge of character is needed in order to be able to persuade others. One must know the multiform in order to *be* multiform, responsible to the immediate rhetorical situation, as it were. Given that Socrates' tendency in the *Phaedrus* is clearly to describe and endorse a 'rhetoric' that is actually a philosophical pedagogy or dialectics, I do not see how to avoid identifying a conflict between this and the critical method of the *Republic*. The challenge posed by the contradiction is mitigated, however, if we recall that in the *Republic* Socrates is tailoring his argument to the points of view of his interlocutors, who at this moment happen to be Glaucon, a figure described as having a more-than-passing interest in musical matters, and the one who had thrown Socrates' utopian society into disarray by insisting that its cuisine have more flavour and interest – an introduction of luxury that required an elaborate rebalancing of politics, culture and education.[69] That is, the 'juridical' method of musical criticism, which entails a rejection of profligate mimeticism and polyformity, is an application of the same polyformity endorsed in the *Phaedrus* as a central method of philosophical pedagogy. The surprising co-ordination between musical multiformity and Socratic practice is therefore explainable, I would suggest, via the idea that it is a necessary strategy within the world: nothing else would work, pedagogically speaking.

And what holds for Socrates holds, too, for the writings in which he appears. The Socratic *logos*, a genre Aristotle called nameless, could also be said to lack a concept.[70] Even its integrity as 'a' genre is difficult to establish. As I remarked in Chapter 1, some of Plato's works are 'diegetic', narrated by a consistent voice, while others are 'mimetic', shifting voices with no narrative mediator; some have elaborate frames in which 'the story of the story' is told, along with its genealogy in an oral or written tradition, while some have no frame at all; many maintain a disciplined series of questions and answers, while others (such as the *Symposium* and the *Phaedrus*) are sequences of speeches – one (the

Menexenus) is a speech framed by a dialogue, and one (the *Apology*) is a speech with no frame at all (but it contains a mini-dialogue). Nor is Socrates himself a constant or stable character: sometimes he professes ignorance, sometimes he leads the conversation in a strong dogmatic fashion; in several he is a minor player. Every topic is available for discussion, including physics, despite the legendary 'Socratic turn' from astronomy to human ethics. Other texts, and sometimes entire genres, seem to drift just below the surface.[71] I find the analogy between his writing and the 'bad' music that is so notoriously criticized in his political writings to be striking and noteworthy. This contradictory gesture, in which a certain kind of music is disavowed as a performative practice but also apparently embodied both in Socrates and Platonic textuality, seems similar to the way writing is handled in Plato's corpus: the *Phaedrus* (and the seventh letter) disavows it, and yet here is a voluminous and virtuosic corpus.

Thus far I have followed a set of images which seem to describe both musical performance and Socratic pedagogy. But we encounter the same unsettling identification when Plato's writing turns from metaphor and myth towards a more analytical mode. Socrates commonly associates art with a process of mimetic descent. In a memorable passage of the *Ion* he claims that rhapsodes who perform and interpret Homer do not have an art, but rather a divine power,

> which moves you like the power in that stone Euripides calls Magnetic but most call Heracleian. That stone doesn't just move rings [*daktulioi*] of iron; it also puts its power in the rings, so that they can do the same thing – I mean attract other rings. Sometimes a very great chain of iron rings hanging from each other is attached to the stone, and the power is put in many such rings by the original one. Similarly, the Muse herself makes people inspired, and through those a chain is assembled of other, equally inspired people. For all good epic poets are good not because of art, but because they are inspired, and when they are possessed they utter beautiful poems. Good musicians [*melopoiai*], too: just as the Corybants dance when they are not in their right minds, so do musicians make beautiful songs when they are not in *their* right minds. When they enter into the matter of harmony and rhythm they are like Bacchants and possessed.[72]

Socrates' reference to iron rings (*daktulioi*) plays some extremely complex games of association, linking magnetic stones to the Corybants, who were closely associated with the Idaean Dactyls[73] – mythical figures associated closely both with magic and with inspired dances in armour and the protection of the infant Zeus from his father. 'Dactyl' was also the name for the characteristic metrical foot of epic;[74] so we could very well be looking at a pun linking the effect of magnets on *daktulioi* of iron to the *daktuloi* of epic metre.[75] In a further complication, we learn from the scholia on Aristophanes' *Clouds* that the dactyl was the rhythm played by the aulete who accompanied (or perhaps introduced: the word is *krouma*) the dancers in a song to the Kouretes (another variant of Corybants, also associated with the Cretan Ida, the dance in armour, and ecstatic dances around the cult of the infant Zeus); in this performance there actually was a chain of metrical *dactuloi* accompanying inspired music.

A mimetic chain similar to the one in the *Ion* plays an important role in the *Republic*'s argument that art is ontologically degraded: since (Socrates proposes) a painting of a table is an imitation of a table, and a table is an imitation of the idea of a table, the painting is, in effect, a copy of a copy.[76] This objection is then applied to music and tragedy, though Socrates is vague about the exact details; his point is that they too are 'twice removed from the truth'.[77] Poets who make imitations like the painting of the table deal in falsehoods and copies, and Socrates insists in the *Republic* that their works do not appeal to the better part of the soul, but rather to sensual pleasure, making it harder for reason to intervene and calm the soul's lesser components;[78] what you experience in the theatre has a habit of gradually taking over your whole life, and you risk becoming habitually passionate instead of rational.[79] A mimetic poet can therefore be compared to someone who kills good rulers and replaces them with bad ones; effectively, such works of art 'place a bad *politeia* in the private soul of each person'.[80] The *Republic* offers a detailed account of the formal characteristics of this bad music under the heading of what should be avoided in designing musical institutions for an ideal state, some details of which we have already encountered earlier. In book three Socrates introduces a distinction between those narrative forms in which the singer or storyteller speaks in his or her own voice, and those in which the performer imitates the characters in the tale. The Homeric epics mix these two styles together: tragedy, in which there is no narrator, is wholly of the latter style. Starting from the twin principles that one should aim to be good at one thing rather than mediocre at many[81] and that one tends to become what one imitates repeatedly,[82] Socrates reaches the conclusion that in the education of the guardians of his imaginary city only storytelling in which the narrator speaks in his own voice should be adopted.[83] Of professional imitators by contrast, we have just seen that Socrates has little good to say.[84] It's not just that such artists are shamefully willing to be seen in public imitating all kinds of people and things; worse, they have become ontologically unstable, adhering in diction, music and words to no simple standard but instead forever changing into something else.

But here again I detect a description of Socratic conversation, or Platonic dialogue, or both. When considering the various critiques of mimesis and mimetic descent, we should note that Socrates himself sometimes presents his positions as merely passed on from someone else (Diotima in the *Symposium* and Aspasia in the *Menexenus*); sometimes, too, the dialogues are reported versions of conversations witnessed by others;[85] and Plato's adherence to Socrates makes him part of a mimetic tradition.[86] I would connect these observations with the second of the three means of philosophical teaching I adumbrated in Chapter 1: that 'negative pedagogy' in which Plato teaches by failing to teach. We might ask why such self-disavowals don't ultimately characterize his work as little more than a game of hide and seek: if Plato's writings not only cannot communicate whatever he is supposedly about, why not simply stop reading and head straight for the truth? The answer here could be that we can't head for the truth itself. In the allegory of the cave we are chained to our seats and would need some kind of help to get unbound; there must be something about the texts that helps us make progress, though that progress will eventually make us put them down. That 'something' could well be the way they involve us, through narrative structure and ergonomic design, in certain intellectual movements that condition us for insight. This would be the third mode of psychagogy I referred to earlier, the gestural rhetoric that, I claimed, made his writings most like music. I turn to this in Chapter 3.

Chapter 3

I

Let me start with a text that has little to do, on the surface, at least, with music. Plato's *Cratylus* is commonly held to be a dialogue about language.[1] It opens, after all, with a debate about words. Do they have some essential relationship with what they mean, or do we understand them just because we agree on their use? But the dialogue's real target is perception; language is no more than a field in which to explore the instability that Plato thinks characterizes all sensual experience. The *Cratylus* is of interest to me above all because it establishes a clear association between sensibility and instability, and then *performs* this association, involving both the characters and the reader in a kaleidoscopic and disorienting series of transformations.

The dialogue pursues its argument through an extraordinary series of etymologies, covering words drawn from every corner of experience from the human to the divine, which take up a large portion of the text.[2] Those etymologies, in turn, seem calibrated to dramatize and expose the dialogue's broader argumentative aim to address the epistemic value of perception. Etymology, after all, establishes the filiation and reference of words by exploiting their sounds, deriving knowledge about their meaning and even their 'truth' from their sensual appearances. Through the sensual method of etymology, the history of language itself is presented as a matter of sense and sensuality: once coined (more on that in a moment), words are gradually deformed because the speakers of the language have a tendency to prefer sensual pleasure over denominative correctness.[3] In effect, sensuality produces linguistic history by obscuring whatever insight was supposedly contained in the original expressions. Two factors coincide in this model. First: language has a history, that is, it is subject to change; and this change is momentous enough to make its interpretation a significant challenge (as is evidenced by the extensive effort expended on etymology in the dialogue). Second: the major driver of this change is sensuality, a delight in the pleasures of the mouth.

The connection between sensuality and change doesn't just drive the history of language: it is also the truth disclosed by language's origin. A core idea in the dialogue is that Greek as Socrates and his interlocutors speak it is descended from a language invented by certain name-givers. These name-givers meant the language to have an essential relationship to things, but they proceeded on dubious principles:[4] they trusted their senses, and consequently took the world to be in constant and bewildering motion.

> Those very ancient men who established words were most of all like many of today's wise men, who get dizzy from spinning around as they search for an answer to the way things are, and then it seems to them that *things* are spinning and always moving. They think the cause of this opinion is not their own inner experience, but that things themselves are such as to never rest or be stable but to flow and move and always to be full of motion and becoming.[5]

For example, the gods are named *theoi*, Socrates says, because they appeared to be always running (*theontes*) – the original gods being, apparently, the sun, moon, stars and heavens.[6] The sun seems to be in constant motion; the air seems to flow, and the aether seems to go around the air.[7] Hestia is either essence (*essia*) or flux (*ōthoun*, connected to *ōsia*);[8] Kronos and Rhea are names of streams, as is Oceanus, while Tethys is what is strained or filtered (*diattōmenon, ēthoumenon*).[9] Persephone's real name is Perepapha or Perephatta, because she touches what is in motion (*tou pheromenou ephaptomenē*).[10] Often Socrates includes a reference to the Heraclitean idea of change, as though the name-givers were themselves Heraclitean in orientation.[11]

The inventors of language, viewing what they thought was a world in motion, imitated it with motions of the mouth. For example, *r* represents motion because the tongue moves when it is made;[12] *d* and *t*, closing the mouth and stopping the breath, imitate stoppage.[13] At this most basic level, where primary words imitate phenomena, the mimesis is kinetic: movement, imitation and sensuality coalesce in an original vocal choreography, as the mouth moves in imitation of the world. The very strategy of developing a world-description out of the movement of the mouth reproduces, at the fundamental level of basic poetic principles, the same principle perceived in phenomena: both the apparent world and language are basically kinetic, flux of word responding to an apparent flux of world.

These theses are enacted in the form of the dialogue. The argument spins and whirls, as though the investigation had catapulted Socrates and his interlocutors into a vortex of shifting perspectives. Close to the beginning Socrates refutes Hermogenes' proposition that words have meaning only 'by convention', or on the basis of intersubjective agreement, and arrives at the conclusion that language exists thanks to some attempt to get at the nature of things – a position close, if not identical, to the contention of the other interlocutor in the dialogue, Cratylus, who holds that words have an essential relationship to things.[14] But in his conversation with Cratylus, Socrates leads the group towards the realization that convention must play a role in the shared meaning of words.[15] Thus over the course of the dialogue both Hermogenes and Cratylus are brought to agree with positions more or less opposite to where they started. This is excellent dramaturgy: it shows the parties to a philosophical investigation veering around unpredictably just like the world as it was supposedly experienced by language's creators. No surprise, really: Socrates and his friends have been following their ears, relying on perception in much the same way the inventors of language are imagined to have done.

And we, who have been following Socrates and his friends on this roundabout tour of theories about language, may also have begun to spin and whirl – especially if we are trying to figure out what, if anything, is being said here. But it seems that the bewilderment we are in by the text's end served a purpose, for just before closing the proceedings, Socrates makes one final suggestion: there can be no knowledge in a Heraclitean world of constant change, and there must be some stable, noetic, non-sensual way of knowing.[16] One could draw conclusions about language from this observation (as Socrates himself does):[17] language will be useless if its components do not refer to things that are stable and knowable – not sensible objects but mental entities, which we might as well go ahead and call ideas. Which need not mean that words *do* refer to such things, but so long as they *don't*, that is so long as speakers cannot claim to know whereof they speak, language will be of little value as an epistemic tool. But one should not miss the broader point, that is, that one cannot rely on epistemologies grounded in perception such as the one Socrates finds encoded in Greek.

What matters to me here is that the *Cratylus* has induced in us the same movement it critiques: we have been taken on a wild ride, undergone a circular argument, experienced self-contradictions produced by a reliance on our ears. How could we learn from within such a textual vortex? Perhaps the trick would be to hear the distant intimations of ideality even in the most worldly music; in one's encounter with a Platonic dialogue one must enter the dance in such a way that one's orientation was away from the threshold in becoming where one began. No, not 'enter the dance' – we are already moving. Rather, we must learn to move with the motion of the world, in such a way that our soul begins to turn as one with the original and best motions of the universe.

II

Plato imagines such a process in the *Timaeus*. This text presents many of the same interpretive problems posed by Plato's corpus as a whole. The speech that makes up most of the dialogue, and to which an enormous amount of commentarial activity in both antiquity and modernity has been directed,[18] is attributed to the text's title character, Timaeus; he opens by articulating a perspective that immediately puts his own story into some doubt. He starts with a distinction between being, which is eternal (*to on aei, genesin de ouk echon*) and becoming, which has no share in being (*to gignomenon men aei, on de oudepote*).[19] The former, he said, can be grasped by thought via reason, and the latter by opinion via perception.[20] The cosmos or the heaven was created, that is, it *became*, because it is perceptible (28b); but being created it must have been brought about by some cause (28c). Already at this point two difficulties have been introduced. The first concerns what exactly is being described in this discourse concerning the heavens. Being created and perceptible, the heaven is, by very virtue of that fact, only graspable by opinion and perception. Whatever Timaeus may say of it can only be a provisional fiction built in and for the senses. For the same reason a second difficulty immediately arises: 'it would be a tough job to discover the maker and cause of the cosmos, and impossible to name him for all' (28c).

Timaeus asserts that anything created on the model of being must be beautiful (28a–b); since the cosmos does happen to be beautiful, Timaeus concludes that its creator must have made it as a copy of eternal being (29a).

But Timaeus also claims that whatever is copied from a copy cannot be beautiful (28b). This raises the possibility of a distinction between kinds of accounts, which Timaeus shortly develops: stories which are concerned with the never-changing paradigm, i.e. with being, will themselves be never-changing and secure, while stories concerning the ever-changing copy will be ever-changing like the copy (29b–c).

> And so, Socrates, if we are unable to provide precise accounts which agree with each other completely on all matters concerning the gods and the genesis of the all, do not be amazed. But if what we say is no less likely than others' accounts, that should please you, remembering that I who speak and you who judge have a human nature, so that it is appropriate to provide a likely story about these things and to seek no farther than this. (29c–d)

To provide accounts that 'agree with each other' is a constant desideratum of Plato's Socrates. Knowing his audience, perhaps, Timaeus here begs that his tale not be taken as likely to survive a vigorous Socratic cross-examination. Remarkably, he grounds this plea in a theory concerning the nature of being. His story will not fully agree in its parts not because he is remiss in his intellectual responsibilities, but rather because he is describing a sensible and created thing – whatever his individual failings there is a greater structural obstacle to perfect truth here. It is thus more than just prophylaxis against Socratic questioning when he warns us to 'seek no farther' than a likely story: it amounts to a kind of ethical imperative. No human account of the created cosmos could be more than likely, and to demand total coherence would be, in effect, hubristic. Timaeus' 'seek no farther' echoes traditional musical themes. Coming from the voice, say, of a Pindar, it would mean that since we are human we should seek no more than human excellence.[21]

But his apotropaic gesture also raises the question why we should abide with Timaeus' extended discourse at all. Wouldn't it be more profitable to attempt to generate our own cosmology, or, better, to go straight to the paradigm, accounts of which he says can be trusted and stable? Either Timaeus means what he says here, or he doesn't: if he does, we can enjoy his account as a pleasant entertainment but will inevitably disagree, though we do not have licence to criticize his account as absolutely wrong (it is only a likely story; 'right' and 'wrong', in their absolute senses, should not apply here). If he doesn't mean what he says, or if there is something in his account which points beyond likelihood towards an experience close to thought and reason, we are justified in asking why he doesn't focus on that.

As I have presented it, the dilemma leaves out at least one other possibility: we might stay with Timaeus' story, even knowing from the outset that it cannot coincide perfectly with the way things appear to us, because the very act of following along is beneficial somehow, perhaps as a form of cognitive kinetics that, beneath or beside or at the edges of the propositional content, itself orients us in a beneficial way. Timaeus' cosmology does contain, I believe, a model of just such a non-propositional communication, which I propose to take as a description of the work's psychagogic poetics. The model is musical, and it relies on a willingness to think of music as a platform for teaching without meaning through the structuring of motion.

That movement is a key theme of the *Timaeus* is clear from the dialogue's opening. It takes place on the day after Socrates had delivered an extensive account of a conversation whose main heading was the nature of the best constitution and the kinds of men who live in it (17c–19a). The summary is suspiciously similar to the main points of the political parts of the *Republic*; this has suggested to many that the *Timaeus* describes the aftermath of the telling of the *Republic* (17c–19a).[22] At the end of his summary of this conversation, Socrates remarks:

> Listen to what I have suffered regarding the republic which we have gone over. My experience was like that of someone who, after beholding a beautiful animal either worked out in a painting or actually living but resting quietly, is overcome by a desire to see it moving and entering into a contest over something which is appropriate to their bodies. Just this is what I experienced regarding the city we described. (19b–c)

That conversation was like a fixed and immovable picture, so beautiful and beguiling that Socrates is overcome by passion to see its parts moving; now he would hear a tale of the ideal city acting in history. The immediate consequence of Socrates' wish is Critias' tale of just such an ideal republic: he reports a story (which he says he heard from his grandfather, who heard it from Solon, who heard it from an Egyptian priest) in which ancient Athens fought a war with Atlantis (21e–26e). But Socrates' desire also articulates the theme of Timaeus' much longer cosmogonic speech: that of the relationship between a stable image and the movement that relates to it.

Timaeus' cosmology is described, metaphorically, as a musical performance. After he has laid out the distinction between being and becoming we have discussed, raised the possibility that the sphere of becoming was created by some kind of god, and warned us that his account can only be a 'likely story', Socrates bids him continue:

> We have received this *prooimion* from with you awe: now complete your *nomos* for us straightway. (29d)

In a gesture Plato would make much more of in the *Laws*, Timaeus' account is reconfigured as a musical composition or *nomos*: his initial definitions (which we have just discussed) are the *prooimion*, the introductory song during which a singer invokes his tutelary deity.[23] Imagining the cosmology as a song may help to underscore some of its more striking structural details, most crucially the introduction of a second cosmogonic account just over halfway through;[24] traditional nomes were typically built in multiple parts, often with a modulation in mode or performative method.[25] For now what matters is that in Timaeus' tale music has a kind of sensual force, potentially affecting a reorientation of the soul through non-propositional channels.

The created world is alive, endowed with a soul and a mind (30b). This is because the demiurge, being good, wants everything to be like him, since goodness entails generosity (29f). But everything visible (I take 'visible' to be metonymic for 'perceptible') was moving in a disordered and chaotic fashion, and so he gave it order (30a). Since what has a mind is better than what is mindless, and since nothing without a soul can have a mind, he created the all as a living being with a soul. That this is only a likely story is indicated by the fact that the demiurge learned that mind was better than no mind because he saw this to be the case in created creatures (30b); but nothing has been created yet. Timaeus' incoherence can be explained by the fact that his tale is based on his observations of the world, which are prior to the account of creation, though *in* the account they must be posterior. Timaeus claims, in fact, that the demiurge created the universe in the image not of any creature that was part of the universe, but rather in the image of the creature that contains them all (30c–d). But where did the demiurge see this creature? In fact he could not have seen it, since nothing has yet come into being. The demiurge must therefore have imagined, or perhaps simply thought to himself, that the universe must be one thing containing everything else. In effect, in other words, the cosmos is the outward expression of the demiurge's theory of being. Just as Timaeus' tale is a likely story, so, in a sense, is the created world – it is a likeness of likelihood, if I can put it this way.

The material of the created cosmos was determined, again, on the basis of certain theoretical considerations that seem to have originated with the demiurge. Working, at first, with fire and earth, the demiurge needed a bond to link them together. Air and water are used for this purpose (32a–b). The demiurge uses *all* fire, air, water and earth; any remainder would raise the possibility of a second universe being created (32a). The resulting cosmos was not only one and complete; it was also round, because the sphere contains all other shapes (33b). Because there was nothing outside it, there was nothing to perceive, ingest or manipulate, and there was nowhere to go, and so it had no senses, organs, or hands and feet (33d). That's not to say the cosmos doesn't move, just that its movement is of the best kind, which Timaeus says is circular; it revolves around a single point (34a).

Within this spherical, rotating body is set and extended the soul of the world (34b). The soul is made of a mixture of the 'self-same' and of the 'other', which Timaeus also calls a mixture of being and becoming (35a). These are 'fitted together by force' (*sunarmottōn biai*, 35a–b); it is as though the soul of the world is an unwilling combination of the transcendent and the immanent. This mixture is then divided in a series of proportions that have what appears to be musical significance. In what follows I reproduce Barker's admirable translation into modern numerical relationships: Plato's terminology is considerably less easy to understand for those (like me) who only have an amateur knowledge of mathematics.[26] Taking portions from this assembled material, he creates sections of matter whose sizes correspond to two numerical series: one of double intervals (1, 2, 4, 8), and another of triple intervals (1, 3, 9, 27). In both of these series, the intermediate value between any two is a *geometrical mean* – that is, it is the square root of their product (2 is the square root of the product of 1 and 4; 9 is the square root of the product of 3 and 27). Converting the double and triple series into multiples of six, we get the following sequence of relative proportions:

6 12 24 48
6 18 54 162

The demiurge now creates smaller portions, such that between any two values in each series there appears both the arithmetic mean (a value y halfway between x and z, such that $y - x = z - y$) and the harmonic mean (a value b between x and z such that $x{:}b = b{:}z$). Inserting the arithmetic and harmonic means gives the following series:

6 8 9 12 16 18 24 32 36 48
6 9 12 18 27 36 54 81 108 162

Collapsing these series produces a single sequence with relative sizes of

6 8 9 12 16 18 24 27 32 36 48 54 81 108 162

Now the numbers of this series are related in proportions that correspond to the intervals of fourths (4:3), fifths (3:2) and tones (9:8) (see Fig. 5).

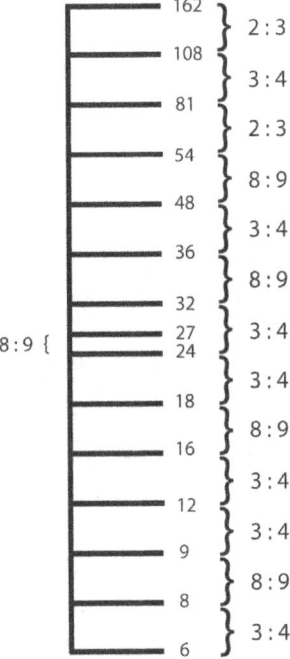

Figure 5 The ratios corresponding to the musical intervals produced during the demiurge's construction of the world soul in Plato's *Timaeus*.

The demiurge's next step is to fill up all the intervals of 4:3 with intervals of 9:8 and one *leimma* (a *leimma* is the difference between 4:3 and $(9:8)^2$, that is 256:243): the result is a series of intervals, two sequences of which (the lowest and third octaves) match the diatonic scale traditionally attributed to Philolaus (see Fig. 6).[27]

This series of proportions, partly corresponding to what appears to be a hypothetical diatonic scale, is the world soul. It is constructed exclusively on the basis of numerical relationships, and the intervals within it are mathematically definable.

Understanding the construction as Timaeus describes it is – to put it mildly – challenging. Major questions go unanswered. What operation, exactly, is the demiurge executing on this plastic material mixed from sameness, difference and being? Timaeus says that he 'distributes' (*dieneimen*), 'divides' (*diairein*) or takes portions away (*apheilen*, 35b) from the created material; his language suggests that each of the portions is a chunk or strip of some basic material. At the end of the first step he would appear to have seven strips or pieces. At the next step, however, new portions are cut out – but it isn't at all

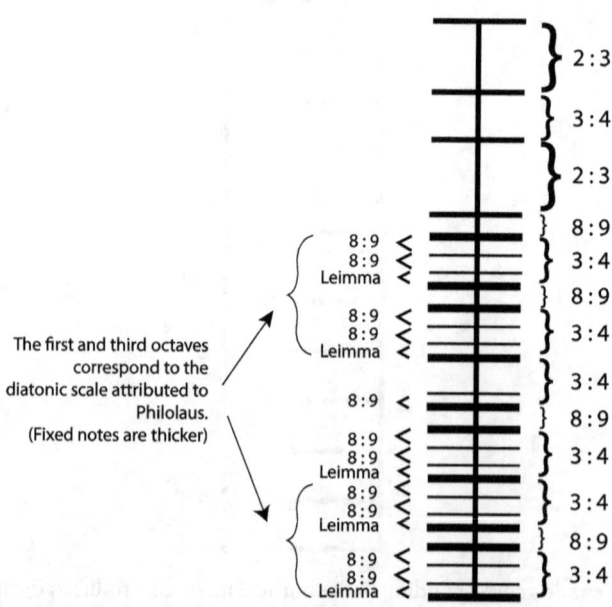

Figure 6 The completed world soul in Plato's *Timaeus*.

clear from where. Timaeus says 'from there' (*ekeithen*), which could refer to the original mass or the already taken portions (36a). Then they are placed 'between' the already taken parts. Where is this 'between'? Shortly after this these new pieces, which are called 'bonds', have their intervals filled with new portions, corresponding to 9:8 and the *leimma*. There is little difficulty if we imagine that the demiurge is working with abstract numbers, but he is *not* working with abstract numbers; he is working with *stuff*, and we are bound to ask where the stuff is placed and how it is arranged. The easiest way to picture the procedure would be to imagine strips laid out next to each other (see Fig. 7).

And in fact visualizing things in this way is perfectly adequate for the apparent goal of the exercise, namely the discernment in the world soul of something resembling the proportions detailed earlier. But Timaeus almost immediately makes such a visualization impossible: after he has created these proportions, says Timaeus, the demiurge cuts the whole system in two, *kata mēkos*, which seems to mean 'along its length', and then joins the ends of each of the two strips to each other, creating two circles which he sets rotating the one within the other (36b–c). That suggests that the whole exercise has been aimed at marking sections on a strip of material (see Fig. 8). This could even be the description of the base of a monochord,

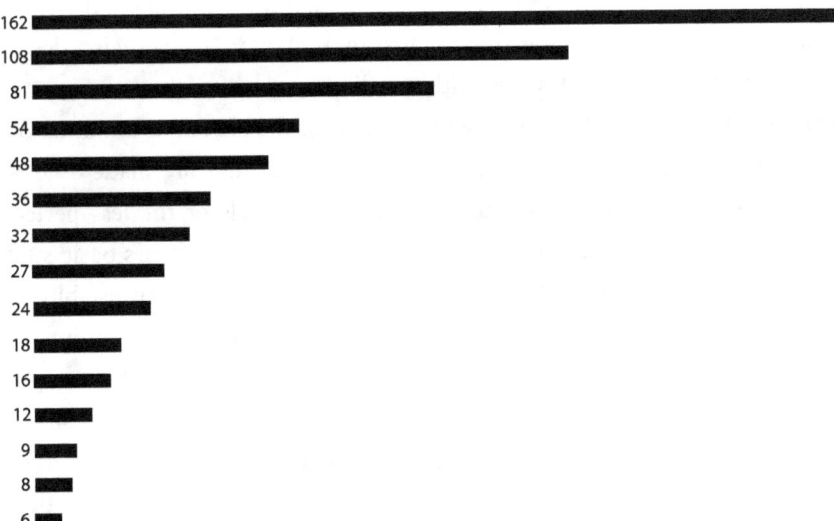

Figure 7 The first set of proportions, imagined as strips of material.

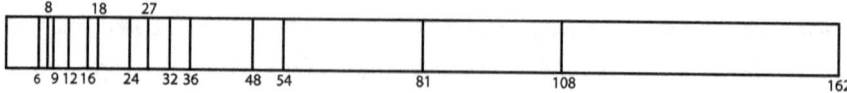

Figure 8 The first set of proportions imagined as marks on a single strip of material.

that one-stringed experimental tool favoured by practitioners of mathematical musicology.[28]

We could attribute these difficulties to the fact that Timaeus is trying to describe processes that took place before there was anything like the perceptible world; indeed, it all took place, we are told, before there was time (time is created at 37d–e). Even though the numerical part of the procedure is a quasi-mythic etiology which reverse-engineers mathematico-musical proportions, it is also clearly *not* meant to be an abstracted representation of sound; perhaps music inspired the model, but the model is not of any sensual music, nor is it produced with any explicit reference to music. My diagrams fail to explain what the demiurge did, perhaps, for the same reason Timaeus' story is hard to follow: both are sensual representations of abstract processes, copies of copies.

At this point the demiurge seems to have completed his initial task – to create a cosmos that was a living being endowed with soul, one and perfect. What follows is a kind of excess – a hypertrophy of creation that, while it leads to a world that resembles ours, also causes a significant falling off from the more perfect cosmos elaborated in the first movement.[29] The cause is a desire for a world stuffed, as it were, with a full panoply of creatures. Time is introduced and associated with the movements of the planets as an imitation of the eternity of the paradigm (37e–38c); then creatures are made – gods, birds, fishes and terrestrial beings (39e–40a). The souls of the less perfect creatures are made by mixing diluted versions of the world soul's basic stuff 'just about the same way' (41d) as he mixed the world soul. This establishes that each soul has a built-in affinity for the cosmic harmony; that affinity will be crucial to explaining the psychagogic value of music below. He then assigns each soul to a star; as they travel through the heavens, the demiurge shows them the nature of the cosmos (41e). When they are placed in bodies they will be part of the generalized flux, with matter entering and exiting them; they will necessarily have perception, erotic pleasure and pain, fear and rage, and the whole panoply of emotions (42a). Timaeus explains a little farther on how perception and passion occur to embodied humans. While the world soul moves in an orderly if complex manner, the motion of mortal beings is tumultuous and noisy (*thorubōdē*) and overpowered by constant disturbance (42c-d).[30] They are enmeshed in the great river of becoming, carried along and moved in such a way that every part of them is set in motion, and this motion is disordered and irrational (43a-b). Timaeus likens the movement of the material river from which mortal beings cannot be separated to a massive wave whose ebb and flow causes tumult (*thorubos*) within the creatures it flows over and through (43b). The energy and confusion caused by the constant collision of material bodies in the vicinity of mortal souls produces sensation:

> These souls, which were deeply immersed in the river [of becoming], neither governed nor were governed but bore and were borne by force. The result was that the whole living being was moved in a disordered fashion willy nilly and without reason, since it was possessed by all six types of directional motion (that is, forward, backward, left, right, and up and down). While the waxing and waning wave that provided nourishment was great, the affections which were caused by the external collisions caused an even greater uproar in each of them: when the body of someone struck against some fire which remolded it from without, or was caught by the gale of winds born by the air, the motions of all these things were carried through the body and fell upon the soul. They have since been called *aisthēseis* ['perceptions'] because of this, and they are still so called. (43a–c)

Aisthēsis, 'perception', sounds a bit like *aissō*, 'to dart about'.[31] This recalls the *Cratylus*, where the possibility of etymology is linked to the confusion experienced by the inventors of language when they perceived the universe (see earlier). Timaeus links that disruption to the condition of being created: sensation is the kinetic consequence of embodiment.

But the creation of mortal beings doesn't just disturb them: it disturbs everything. The agitations upset the regular course of the world soul, introducing backflows and turbulences (43d.1–2). Perception detunes the cosmos, throwing the original proportions governing the concords out of whack, perturbed by all kinds of 'turnings' (*strophas*) and 'refractions' (*klaseis*) and deteriorations (*diaphoras*) in the circles that had earlier characterized its ordered movement. The result is like when a man rests his head on the earth and throws his feet up in the air; 'the things on the right will seem on the left and those on the left will seem to be on the right' (43d–44a).

The condition of turbulence, of taking-in and letting-out, of hearing and speaking, eating and shitting, to which we are submitted as embodied creatures represents a significant danger, for it gives rise to the passions and perceptions, which, in turn, can have real consequences for the condition of our lives:

> If someone governed these [passions] he would live justly, but if they governed him, he would live unjustly. If someone lived his appointed time well, then he would return to live with his allotted star, and enjoy the happy life that he was made for. But failing in these things he would take the nature of a woman in his second birth [Timaeus apparently thinks this is a bad thing]; and if he didn't stop from evil even then, he would change into the nature of some beast who was similar in its manner of being to the ways in which he was evil. (42b–d)

Motion begets motion: a soul that yields to the tumult of the created flux is set on a path of death and rebirth. Here Timaeus interfaces with the myth of the 'heavenly chorus' articulated in the *Phaedrus* and also, in a different way, with the *Republic*'s myth of Er. Vice, that is, addiction to embodiment, leads to further embodiment, while a commitment to the opposite stands to return the soul to its happier origin.

Elsewhere Timaeus puts this differently: when the flux abates, he says, the movement of the soul reverts to its own nature, with the result that it becomes capable of accurately naming things and thinking reasonably about them. He equates this process with education, which is imagined as a kind of kinetic calming or restraint (44b–c). It's notable that he seems to conflate what might seem to us to be two different orders of causality. The social or the cultural, in the form of education, is said to be able to restore dominance to the circle of the same in the mortal soul. But a physiological process can accomplish the same thing: the abatement, if that is the right word, of the in- and efflux of data (sights, sound, food) simply ceases to overwhelm the soul, much as receding weather might calm a sea, revealing more constant currents beneath the temporary choppiness of the waves.

Almost immediately, we are given a gloss on this process in the form of a description of vision. There is, we are told, a pure fire within us which gives light without burning: this flows through the eyes into the outer world. The stream of inner light, meeting with outer light, coalesces with that 'as like to like', and a single body is formed from inner and outer which then communicates the motions of that body back to the soul, presumably via the sensitive medium of the eye-beams (45b–d). The result appears to be a becoming-like of soul and world, at least on the plane of motion: the same motion occurs in both the world and the soul, and that is experienced as vision. Timaeus doesn't say so here, but this theory of vision helps to explain – again by purely physiological means – the psychagogic value of astronomy. Sight is given us, we are told,

> so that beholding the circles of the mind in the heaven we may make use of them in the movements of our own minds, which are related [*sungeneis*] to them, as ordered is related to disordered, and so that learning and partaking in the correctness of reasonings according to nature, we might imitate the altogether unerring movements of God, and make steady the wandering movements within us. (47b–c)

Beholding and reasoning about the motions of the superior mind, we are supposed to imitate the unwandering movements of the world soul by stabilizing the errors of our own. Plato's language seems to elide the difference between psychic and physiological: we reason about the starry motions, but in doing so we *partake* of and thus imitate them.

Music has a value similar to that of the heavens:

> Harmony, which has motions akin to the circular progressions in our souls, does not seem to the devotee of the Muses who has any sense to be useful for some irrational pleasure, as is now generally thought, but was given by the Muse as an ally in ordering and making concordant the inharmonic movement which has arisen in our soul. (47c–e)[32]

This harmony is an 'ally' of the *katakosmēsis* of the soul. Timaeus does not immediately provide an explanation of how harmony could help us order the movements of our soul, as he had done for vision. Instead he appears to interrupt himself and to introduce a new topic: an account of things that come into being not by mind but by necessity. Mind, we are told, started the creation of the cosmos but then persuaded necessity to finish the work (48a). Here we must remember that in creating the cosmos the demiurge made use of four basic materials (earth, air, fire and water); the account of necessity will be grounded in an assessment of their nature. Despite the fact that he calls it 'necessity', a term which would appear to imply some fated or incontrovertible causality, Timaeus also calls it the 'wandering cause' (48a). It is wandering, I think, because it consists in the flux of variable matter that defines existence as corporeal presence.[33]

Timaeus asserts three times that his discourse about necessity constitutes a new beginning (48b, twice at 48e). But in fact this is not a radical interruption. Rather, it is the natural continuation of what Timaeus has already said. Once the demiurge had created stuff, a theory of stuff was inevitable. Further, the appearance of this new approach at exactly the place where it occurs – after a physiology of vision and mid-phrase, as it were, as a physiology of hearing is being introduced, seems well motivated. Vision is consistently, if not notoriously, favoured in Plato's writing as a figure for the philosophical project. In the *Republic* the form of the good is equated with the sun in that all is illuminated by it, while thinking is likened to an inner vision.[34] The same appears to be true in the *Timaeus*; both heavenly bodies and the soul's capacity for seeing are made from fire (45c–46d), and that fiery element is the key to the contemplation of the heavens and the consequent calming of psychic motion. Just as the level of turbulence increases as Timaeus progresses 'down' through the orders of creation into embodied beings, so does his account abandon mind at just the point when light ceases to be in want of explanation. At the same time, the new theory becomes increasingly mechanical and separated from the benevolent intentionality of the creator god. Thus is it is that the order of explanations is suddenly reversed: so long as the cause in question was the demiurge, the order of operation was from the intellectual down to the corporeal. But in the new account, which deals with the sphere of matter, Timaeus proceeds up, from the basic conditions of matter and movement towards the psychological operation of the senses; he deals with touch first, then taste and smell, before finally returning to sound.[35]

'Let us posit (*thōmen*) sound (*phōnē*) to be a blow which comes through the ears,' he says,

> and is given by the air in the head and the blood to the soul; and let us posit that the movement which is caused by it, beginning in the head and ending in the area around the liver, is hearing (*akoē*). If it is fast movement, then it is high-pitched, and if it is slower it is lower.[36] If the movement is consistent

(*homoia*), then it is equal and smooth, and if it is the opposite of this, it's harsh. If it's great, then it's loud, and quiet if the opposite. (67b)[37]

Note that Timaeus never strays from the methodological postulate that this is a 'likely story': he does not say what sound *is*, but proposes a certain definition (*thōmen*). It is as though the theory is independent of the experience – as though Timaeus wanted to recognize that we would hear things regardless of how we theorized hearing. Much of the account he offers is clear: a blow enters the ear and is transmitted through the blood to the liver where it is communicated to the soul. We have every reason to assume that the movement from ear to liver is isologous to the movement outside the body. There is also a coordination between the nature of movement and its phenomenology: speed produces pitch, amplitude loudness, proportionality smoothness. Where Timaeus is much less clear is over the nature of the movement caused by the blow and the means by which it is transmitted to the liver.[38]

The historical context provides limited clarity. Early discussions of the voice credited some kind of impact as its source. Anaxagoras thought it was the result of breath striking air; the blow was then 'conveyed' to the hearing.[39] This is reported by the doxographer Aetius: Diogenes Laertius attributes the earliest use of the theory to Archelaos, 'the first to bring physical theory from Ionia to Athens' and reputedly a teacher of Socrates.[40] Both were unmistakably trying to explain the nature of voices – the role of breath makes that hard to deny. But Archelaos' account suggests that the principle could be applied more broadly, such that, though the breath plays a role primarily in voices, the blow (*plēxis*) was thought to be the source of all sound. Indeed, it is plausible that his theory of the voice was derived from a general account of sound: one cannot see or experience a blow when one speaks, but one can clearly observe that clapping one's hands together produces an audible sound. That observation could then be collated with the tangible vibration in the throat when one speaks.

Our incomplete records give no hint as to how any theorist earlier than Democritus thought the sound of a voice might have been transmitted to the ear. Aetius reports Democritus' claim that the air was broken up into similar shapes when it was struck by the voice.[41] Theophrastus, closer to Democritus' time, attributes to him a slightly different view, claiming that voice (*phōnē*) is made out of 'a compression of the air which forcefully enters the ear'.[42] The event described here occurs at the other end of the transmission from what is reported by Aetius, who focuses on the voice at its moment of emergence from the mouth; Theophrastus, who is actually writing about hearing, is interested in how it arrives at the soul. The context of Theophrastus' account suggests that the 'compression' is caused by the 'bottleneck' of the ear canal; once it had cleared this space, he reports, Democritus thought the voice scattered swiftly throughout the hearer's body. Both after the mouth *and* after the ear, in other words, the air is broken up into commensurate shapes by a violent impact, almost as though the ear were a second mouth; metaphorically, at least, sounds are 'spoken' by the ear to the inward parts of a body. Similar doctrines can be found in Archytas, writing in the first half of the fourth century.[43] 'It is not possible for a sound to exist,' he writes, 'unless some blow takes place between things.'[44] Sounds which reach our ears quickly and strongly appear high in pitch ('sharp': *oxea*), while what comes slowly and weakly seems low ('dull' or 'flat': *barus*). Thus, he says, if you move a staff slowly and weakly through the air (perhaps by spinning it), you will produce a low-pitched sound, while if you move it swiftly and vigorously, you will produce a high-pitched sound. No mention of the voice, yet, in his discussion. The subsequent argument, however, makes it clear that, while 'sound' is being treated as a general class, its paradigm was that subset of sounds produced by the human vocal tract.

> Whenever we need to utter something loud and high, either singing or speaking, we do so with a great deal of breath. It is like with missiles; if we throw them hard, they go far, and if we throw them softly, they don't. [...] So it is with the voice: what is carried by a strong breath is great and sharp, and what is carried by a soft breath is low and small.[45]

This brief overview makes it clear that Timaeus follows a major tributary of Pre-Socratic theory about audition. In other ways, however, what he has to say is quite singular. The most distinctive element may arise as a consequence of his denial of the existence of void within the created universe (79b). This is a significant divergence from theorists working closer to the main stream of atomic theory, where void played a constitutive role. Timaeus' denial of void means that a kind of 'law of conservation of density' prevails in his cosmos: the movement of one element entails a reshuffling of others. Breathing, medical cupping, drinking and ballistics are all explained as a function of this endless and compulsory circulation of matter (79a–80a). In this context, Timaeus describes the cause of musical concords:

> The fast and slow sounds seem high and low, and they are sometimes ill-attuned because of the inequality of the movements caused in us by them, and sometimes concordant because of the equality. For the slower movements catch up to the earlier and faster ones which have stopped and already arrived at equality [to the slower sound]: and the later ones add themselves to the earlier ones and move them; but when they catch up they do not disturb them by adding a different motion, but they add the beginning of a slower movement which is in accord with that of the faster, and they create a single experience out of high and low. This causes pleasure to the foolish, but happiness to those with some intelligence because it is an imitation of the divine harmony, though it arises in mortal motions. (80a–c)[46]

This passage is difficult to explicate. Once again the basics are relatively clear: when the movements of two notes are equal, they appear as concords: they sound ill-attuned when they are unequal. After that, things get hazy. Higher pitches being faster, they arrive earlier to the ear, while lower pitches, being slower, arrive later. When these (s)lower pitches catch up with the faster sounds, the latter are in the process of slowing down, so that the velocities of the two sounds approximate each other. The slower sound adds its own movement to the faster sound, producing a single, compound experience out of high and low. This is an obscurely explained process, at best. What set of conditions allows the faster sound and the slower sound to meet just when the faster sound is equal to the slower one? How does the slower sound help the faster one in such a way that a single experience is produced? If the faster sound is slowing down so as to approximate the slower one, why is the result not just one sound?[47] How are we to explain this in terms of the dominant dynamic process being described throughout this section of the text, namely the circulation of matter in a cosmos devoid of void?

Given these unclarities, we might be well advised to recall Timaeus' own warning that his account is no more than a likely story. A kind of coherence is achieved nonetheless: in giving equality such a central role in his account, Timaeus has recalled his initial set of acoustic claims, in which equal or proportionate movements produced smooth sounds. Perhaps we may conclude, at least, that concords are experienced as smooth. That would be consistent with Timaeus' basic perspective, since – as Lyon has brilliantly observed – the liver, that point at which the soul receives sound from the body, is itself smooth;[48] the liver would naturally experience a certain pleasure at encountering sounds that help it to return to its natural state, and returning to one's natural state is, according to Timaeus, what causes pleasure (64d).[49]

But Timaeus also says that pleasure at concords is only experienced by the imprudent, while the wise experience something more like cognitive delight (*euphrosunē*). Such auditors experience concords as 'an imitation of the divine harmony, though it arises in mortal motions'. Why there should be two different kinds of responses here is, again, unclear; it may be that all Timaeus wants to emphasize is that however they come about, and whatever the exact process involved, concords signify cosmic harmony to thinking people. Elsewhere, Timaeus imagines a process of maturation in which we are gradually able to dissociate the rational part of our souls from the turbulence of appetite and sensation (44b–c); perhaps the audition of concords, by communicating a better motion to such persons' already improved souls, helps this process along. After all, 'there is one therapy for all things':

> to give the nurture and the motions that are appropriate to each. And the motions in us which are most akin to the god are the thoughts and revolutions of the all. Each must follow these, and by learning the harmonies and revolutions of the all, must correct the destructive circles in our heads which we get from coming-into-being; and he should make the thinker equal to the thought in accordance with his original nature, and so having made himself equal he should have as his goal that best life which was established in advance for men by the gods, now and evermore. (90c–d)

We note again the importance of harmonious or proportional movement: listening to concords can set off in us a better kind of movement.

Although the second part of the *Timaeus*, the 'account of necessity', offers what can be described as a mechanical description of the corporeal sphere, it remains a likely story. But with its persistent suggestion that mechanical causes can encourage the soul's entrainment to the better motions of the world soul, the account of necessity also suggests that a likely story may in fact be good enough, since even the lesser harmonies of the audible sphere can begin to synch us to the better harmonies of the intellectual. The *Timaeus*, in other words, offers an account of hearing that seems to suggest that there is a way, even for us who are completely imbricated within a created world of flux and change, to begin to approximate those better motions of the heavens. This bears comparison with the use of what I called a 'gestural rhetoric' in Plato's writing, where the text requires of readers certain operations that are themselves already philosophical. That characteristic, which I have described as ergonomic, is embodied in formal elements of the dialogues: the drama of the unfolding of an argument, just following which might habituate a reader to the movement of ascent described in the allegory of the cave; or the fundamental work of recognizing who is speaking, done for us by modern editors but left to the reader by the ancient conventions of dialogue.[50] Timaeus' model of musical affect could provide one paradigm for the gestural rhetoric of a pedagogy that works without words.

III

The *Laws* contain Plato's most explicit statements on kinetic persuasion or gestural rhetoric, thanks to a systematic and coherent vision that encompasses the workings of the cosmos, social coherence, and the human organism within a single purview. Here as in the *Timaeus* the phenomenal universe is a dynamic realm defined by the interaction of movements: in the context of an attempt to legislate a city into existence, this model transforms itself into a political kinesiology.[51] The *Laws* finds causality in the contagion of movement within and between spheres of activity – between performance and the body, the body and the soul, the individual and the state, the cosmos and the senses. The importance of kinetic contagion in the *Laws* is best exemplified by a passage late in the work where the unnamed Athenian speaker offers a proof of the immortality of the soul. The form of movement by which a thing moves itself must be treated as first and best, he says, since a self-moved mover will not only move itself but can also be identified as the origin of other forms of movement. Anything which moves itself may be described as living: the soul is the principle of life, and thus the capacity of self-movement that causes other kinds of movement.[52] The universe, which also moves, must be inhabited by souls much as bodies are.[53] Good and ordered movement is circular motion around a still centre.[54] The planets are moved by a good and wise soul.[55] (In the course of this argument there is a shift from what appears to be the soul contained in each individual, to soul as a principle of cosmic movement. This is an ambiguity that runs through Plato's later philosophical work, and it is crucial to my understanding of how philosophy could become a method of bringing the individual soul into harmony with the world soul.)

A similar 'downward' communication of ordered movement seems to function as a paradigm for the political management of music, which the *Laws* imagines as an attempt to impose good, ordered motions in the relatively unstable material of culture and individuals. As in the *Republic*, music is treated under the heading of education (*paideia*), which is defined as 'a drawing (*holkē*) and leading (*agōgē*) towards the reason (*logos*) called correct (*orthos*) by the law (*hupo tou nomou*)'.[56] The law, in turn, is the externalization of reasoned judgement in the fabric of the city.[57] The *Laws*' narrative, in as much as it has a narrative, is one in which the unnamed Athenian works out the best way to live, then creates a civic structure that embodies that through a legislated educational framework: because education may be said to forge or direct behaviour, it is in effect a kind of kinetic conditioning. As a consequence the emphasis is not on the imparting of information, or even on the explicit teaching of certain forms of thought or argumentation, but rather on what can be called the cybernetic control of bodies and minds: the soul is dragged or led towards right reasoning not so much by content or example as by a set of practices. Music is recognized as one of the most important, if not *the* most important, of these practices, and the unnamed Athenian shows a corresponding level of concern over its management.

We are born as frenzied bundles of chaotic movement. 'No young creature,' Plato has the unnamed Athenian assert, 'can keep the peace, as it were, with its body or its voice. They are always trying to move and speak, zigzagging all over the place as though they were getting pleasure out of dancing and goofing around and uttering all kinds of sounds.'[58] This primitive state of turbulent disruption is treated as problematic: the infant's movements are frenetic, disordered, unproductive and hard to control. Babies, we could say, are possessed by their coming into being, that turbulent process theorized as the source of perception in the *Timaeus*. Noting that exercise strengthens the body and calms the soul, and that being carried around seems to have a similar effect on roosters,[59] the unnamed Athenian opines that infants should be held in constant motion – they should even, were it possible, spend their whole early life on ships. Indeed, the value of such a practice is suggested by the tendency of mothers to put children to sleep not by making them still but by rocking them, and to assuage fear by singing and dancing. The principle at work here is the transmission of movement: 'An applied external movement governs the inner movement, which is frenzied and fearful, and when it has taken control it causes a peaceful calm to appear in the soul in the place of the troubling throbbing around the heart that was there before – this is something utterly pleasing'.[60] This is the paradigm which governs Plato's view of musical pedagogy: musical culture amounts to a set of movements that can calm a soul.

The unnamed Athenian displays a surprising degree of unwillingness to directly legislate in this area. He remarks that the practices and lifestyles within family units are very diverse; this diversity naturally leads to conflicting inclinations and behaviour patterns which are presented as harmful to the polis. And yet, although these divergences pose a real danger to public order, taken individually they are too trivial, and taken collectively too widespread, to make them the target of formal legislation; the law would seem both petty and overly oppressive if such divagations were explicitly forbidden.[61] Instead, the unnamed Athenian would have his advice uttered, but as 'teaching and advice', not as laws,[62] and they are to convince people that there are real benefits in the voluntary observance of sound musical practices. The laws, then, will not directly legislate household practice, but can affect it by crafting supplementary discourses: these stand to calm the household much as music and dance order and calm the soul.[63]

The general principle that not all practices are best managed by direct legislation had been set forth by the unnamed Athenian in *Laws* IV, where he observed that while most lawmakers limit themselves to the articulation of rules which favour the *force* of law, a second option is still available, and that is to accompany the law proper with a persuasive discourse 'so that the one to whom the lawmaker speaks will accept the directive (*epitaxis*), that is, the law, benevolently, and therefore also be more inclined to learn it'.[64] To illustrate the form he has in mind – a law prefaced by a persuasive discourse – the unnamed Athenian turns to the example of music.

> There are *prooimia* and introductions (*anakinēseis*), as it were, for all discourses and whatever a voice begins to utter, which offer a kind of technical preparation useful for whatever is going to be performed. Indeed,

there are marvelously wrought *prooimia* for the citharodic songs called *nomoi* ('laws'), and for every kind of music. But for the things that are *really* laws, which we call political, no composer has ever said or brought a *prooimia* into the light, as though it had no natural existence.[65]

This crucial passage connects the *Laws* to the musical *nomos* and provides a formal explanation for much of what the text actually contains: not just laws but also persuasive introductions, as it were, aimed at making legitimate behaviour voluntary. The non-legislation around kinetic and musical education we have been discussing is a superb example of the application of this principle. Indeed, the reason for having at least principles, if not laws, around movement and music, is, remarkably, also an application of the reason for having persuasive discourses to supplement laws: both concern, at least metaphorically, a kinetic communication. Not accidentally, I think, does the unnamed Athenian call the persuasive *prooimion* a 'starting up of motion' (*anakinēsis*).

After discussing child-rearing, he addresses the kinetic regulation of the body in dancing and wrestling,[66] then the regulation of games,[67] then finally turns to music.[68] The unnamed Athenian celebrates the Egyptians for their extreme cultural conservatism: they consecrated musical forms by law and thoroughly resisted innovation.[69] Musical forms are to be tightly tied to religious festivals as specified in the official calendar, and all deviations from the dictates of the law are to be prohibited; this provides the city with a way of regulating cultural practice. Music should contain appropriate prayers to the gods and never say anything that is contrary to the laws.[70] In order to enforce these requirements, a board of elders is to be appointed to make a selection from the old songs; musical experts will be consulted only as technicians, and at no time will their preferences be given hegemonic status.[71] The judges are to curate a musical culture using criteria laid down by the city's lawgiver, rather than on the basis of aesthetic pleasure or desire.[72] Ultimately their main question should be whether a species of music can make someone better or not.[73]

> Every disordered study of music which acquires some order is much better, even if it doesn't set aside the sweet Muse for the better kind. For sweetness is common to all: if a man who has lived from youth until the settled and wise age in a prudent and ordered music hears the opposite he will hate it and accuse it of illiberality. But if he's been raised in the common and sweet

music, he will say that the opposite kind is frigid and bitter. Thus, as was just now said, neither kind has more sweetness or bitterness, except that the one makes men better if they are raised on it, and the other makes men worse.[74]

That music is a kind of culture, rather than simply a material realized in performance, is particularly clear here: you like the music you have been raised listening to. But the criterion the unnamed Athenian really cares about is whether a given musical culture will improve you. In a deliberately curated culture such as the one he envisages, the criteria of pleasure and betterment will presumably coincide.

Tragedy will not be included in the unnamed Athenian's playlist. He complains that it is ritually inappropriate, full of sub-genres and vocal sounds that do not fit a sacrificial context.[75] Earlier in the dialogue he had also criticized its tendency to target the pleasure of its audience: in the course of a discussion of the relative value of different state structures, with a major secondary interest in the historical progression between them, the unnamed Athenian describes certain musical-cultural events and their consequences for the development of democracy. In the good old times, musical expression was divided strictly into genres: each form of song was kept distinct, and it was forbidden to mix them with each other. The rules governing such generic distinctions were enforced by certain men who listened in silence and compelled the broader audience to do so as well. More recently the authority of the august judges has been usurped by poets who were inspired by a kind of Bacchic frenzy (*bakcheuontes*) to mix (*keranuntes*) the different genres. The assumption of these musicians was that the only standard of correctness was the pleasure of whoever delighted in the music. Thus pleasured, audiences began to cry out their approval of certain performances, and the old aristocratic and carefully regulated music was replaced by a wild and libidinal theatrocracy.[76] Although this passage is often thought to be a direct criticism of the music of the later fifth century,[77] little that is said here could not be said of the genre as a whole. Tragedy had been polygeneric practically from its introduction at Athens. The form, in which a chorus interacted with one or more actors in telling a story, involved a fundamental mixing of Ionian and Dorian musical styles, while the (Doricizing) choral songs themselves, because they occur within the imaginary space of a story, could take on the character of many different genres depending on the tale being told.[78] Ultimately, though, the specific musical style being attacked matters less than its features: this is music that mixes genres, that is, that contains within it a discernible impurity of expression and a high degree of change. It appeals to audiences that are interested only in the pleasure it gives them; and the pursuit of that pleasure is a major driver of musical and then political decline.

Just as rocking can have an effect on a child's soul, so does the communication of movement underlie music's capacity to affect citizens and states. This is clearest in the unnamed Athenian's discussion of dance. In a discussion of the kinds of dance to be promulgated in the unnamed Athenian's projected state, he provides an etiology of dance, which can be described as a cultural institutionalization of the typical movements of different kinds of people. Courageous and temperate people typically move their bodies and voices in a more constrained way; those who lack courage and temperance engage in greater and more modulating movements. The forms of movement imitative of these characters have similar features. Such relations are to be studied and promulgated within the state so that the best movements can be imparted to bodies and thence to souls.[79] The unnamed Athenian is not explicit on how dance affects souls; he presents it as a form of bodily exemplarity, such that we can learn how to act and how not to act just by studying it. But his discussion of early childhood education suggests that dance might condition souls kinesthetically as it were, communicating inward what begins as a visible, bodily motion.

The *Laws*' musical culture is managed from within. The unnamed Athenian emphasizes the importance of having judges who can choose what music to include or exclude; but these judges are part of the system, not separate from it. The qualifications for musical judgement were established early on in the *Laws*, in Book II, and they are worth paying attention to at this point. A critic must know what the music is imitating, whether the imitation is correct, and then whether it is beautiful.[80] The implication seems to be that critics must first and foremost be experts in what art imitates, that is, in the nature of good and bad actions and character. But the critic must also know the mechanics of musical expression. Judging the correctness of a musical imitation requires knowledge of rhythm, harmony and words, because one must be able to assess whether these have been combined effectively in an imitation.[81] Further, the judges learn about musical culture by *engaging in it*. The unnamed Athenian is very clear: after some training in music theory they must learn how to dance and sing in the most appropriate ways.[82] Such judges are quite different from the silent and authoritarian judges who governed musical culture in the days before tragedy (see earlier): they do curate music for the city, and they certainly judge it, but they have dance in their background (and also presumably in their present), and they are far from using corporal punishment to enforce order: their deep involvement in the musical culture of the city allows them to create order by managing culture.

Just before he says this, the unnamed Athenian makes a curious series of statements in which he compares current composers with the Muses. The Muses, he says, always associate tonal material with rhythms and dance moves that are appropriate to each other and to the meanings of the words of their songs.[83] They would not combine the words of men with the dances of women, or the songs of free men with the rhythms of slaves; nor would they 'put together the voices of beasts and men and instruments and all kinds of sounds as though they were imitating something'.[84] This is the sort of nonsense only human poets get involved in. More crucially and damningly, human poets also use rhythms without harmony, expressing themselves, in other words, in words without melody; they even engage in instrumental performances with no singing, a practice which makes it extremely difficult to tell what they're imitating.[85] These criticisms are directed at tragedy – words without melody are a feature of tragedy from the moment the first actor is introduced (in the second half of the sixth century). But they also aim at the older festival music associated with Delphi, where music without words, in the form of solo aulos and kithara performances, was a feature from the early sixth century; in that context Sacadas had introduced sound effects imitating animals.[86] Everything is excluded, in other words, except choral music. Why? Maybe it is through dance that good character is communicated to the souls of citizens. The very process of dancing and singing compels them to learn to move and think in the best possible way – so long, that is, as the music and its movements are imitations of the best sorts of characters. Or it could be that non-choral musics emphasize a division into performer and audience, while choral music is participatory, and it is through choral acculturation that musical judges are trained; the culture, as I noted earlier, is perpetuated from within. Thus when tragic poets are banned from the new city the unnamed Athenian's reason is that the city itself is a tragedy, an 'imitation of the most beautiful and best life – and that is what we hold to be the best tragedy'.[87] This pushes the unnamed Athenian's emphasis on immanent participation to an extreme: the city itself is a kind of choral performance, participating in which leads one towards the best kind of life.

It is also possible to read about the city in which one lives: in fact, it is required. While discussing what written literature should be taught in the new state, the unnamed Athenian suggests the following:

> At this moment, as I look at the arguments which we have been running through since dawn – not without some inspiration from the gods, it seems to me – they seem to me to have been spoken in a manner very like that of a kind of poem. At the same time an experience has come over me which isn't surprising at all: I am utterly delighted as I look at these collected and comely discourses. Of all the texts which I have read or listened to either in poems or prose these seem to me the most measured (*metriōtatoi*) and especially appropriate for young people to listen to.[88]

He goes on to propose that their conversation should be studied and approved by every teacher and every student.[89] This prescription is no less grounded in a vision of immanence than the remark on tragedy we have just discussed: for here the conversational prelude to a constitution is studied by the citizens of a state forged by that constitution. At the same time, the dialogue itself will function as a kind of *prooimion* not unlike the persuasive discourse used to encourage mothers and nurses to calm their children's souls with healthful motions (see earlier). There's a sort of pun at work when the unnamed Athenian proposes that his discourse on the laws is 'the most measured' of texts, both prose and poetry. The *Laws* does not scan the way a poem does; it does not have 'feet' or 'metra' in the poetological sense. But it does contain content the contemplation of which is supposed to be capable of improving souls; it is in this sense that it is 'most measured'.

At this point it may be worth turning briefly to the *Philebus*, in which Socrates offers an extended discussion of measure (*metron*) and why it matters. He proposes that things can be approached in terms of two poles and the intermediate points between them. At one pole there is 'the one': at the other, 'the unlimited', and in between there is the space of 'number'. The voice, for example, is a single thing capable of infinite kinds of sounds. In attempting to get a grasp on the voice, you can start at one pole or the other, but you should not progress from the 'one' to the 'infinite' until you have dealt exhaustively and systematically with what lies in between. This is what the inventor of the alphabet (here, as in the *Phaedrus*, the Egyptian god Thoth) did: he perceived the infinity of the voice and attempted to specify the distinct sounds that come out of it – vowels and consonants and possible combinations of these. His analysis of the sounds, which he called the art of letters (*technē grammatikē*), was based on a finite enumeration of sounds extracted from the voice by analysis.[90] It helps to appreciate this theory if we remind ourselves that 'infinite' and 'finite' are not primarily numerical concepts, but instead refer to the clarity of borders (*perata*) – the voice is 'infinite' (*apeiros*) in as much as the many sounds it makes glide into each other. Socrates imagines the infinite as defined by gradations of comparative binaries – 'more' and 'less', 'tall' and 'short', terms of which there may always be more or less without limit. 'In the case of high pitch and low pitch,' we are told, 'and also fast and slow speeds, which are indefinite (*apeiroi*), these things (limit and number) are introduced, and that establishes limits and sets up a completed music.'[91] Similarly, the alphabet makes these continua definite by imposing clear distinctions.

In the *Philebus* the mixture of limit and unlimited produces the determinate though changing world, which is a 'coming into being resulting from standards of measurement which are worked out with the help of the limit'.[92] The world, then, is a determinate set of measured components imposed on an indeterminate material. There is an optimal configuration for such impositions. In medicine, says Socrates, this optimal state is called 'health': in music, it is 'harmony'.[93] Pleasure comes when we approach that optimal state; pain, when we leave it.[94] Intellect is the *cause* of the mixture: it chooses the measures and imposes them on the material. That, not at all incidentally, makes intellect more important than pleasure and leads to its being preferred. Socrates concludes:

> every compound (*sunkrasis*) which does not happen to have a share, one way or another, of measure and commensurability, necessarily destroys its components (*ta kerannumena*) and also itself above all. For truly what results is not a mixture but rather an unmixed jumble. [...] But now the power of the good has fled into the nature of the beautiful. For measuredness and commensurability turn out to be beautiful and good in every case.[95]

Connected to these reflections are a number of observations concerning the nature of art (*technē*). Take away number and limit, says Socrates, and you are left with guesswork, buttressed perhaps by practice but with no inherent reliability (Socrates is speaking to Protarchus: I have reproduced the dialogue as I imagine it might have been found in a fourth-century book-scroll):

> If someone were to remove counting and measuring and weighing from all the arts, what would be left of each would be trivial. : Trivial indeed. : What would be left after that would be estimation and the nurture of the senses with experience and practice, making use of those capacities for guessing which many call arts after they have built up their strength through work and practice.[96]

This particular idea is frequent in Plato's works. The *Gorgias* had Socrates object that any so-called *technē* that did not have a coherent theory of its object was no art at all but merely an acquired skill, the result of practice (*tribē*).[97] The *Philebus* maintains the distinction, but now *technē* does not require a theory. Rather, it needs measure and a rational method based on that measure. In the *Philebus*, Socrates claims that music lacked this measure. In 'music', he says, 'which fits together concords not by measurement but by practised guess, most of all [in] the art of aulos playing, since it hunts after the measure of each note by guesswork, much that is unclear and nothing that is certain is mixed in'.[98] The *Timaeus* takes a more moderate point of view, suggesting that even audible concords can help a soul not only to appreciate the better motions of the world soul, but also to approximate them. They are, in a sense, the healthful alternative to the unmeasured sensual music criticized in the *Philebus*. The *Laws* proposes another alternative, not in what can be heard but in the inaudible meaning communicated by speech: just as good music tempers and calms a soul, so do certain texts. If, as Michael Frede and Jill Gordon (among others) have suggested, the tendency in Plato is to demand that we examine the life we live, that should mean that we must ask what motions reading him has required of us.[99] Could it be that just making sense of the *Laws* compels us to achieve a calmer, more law-abiding state of soul? If that is a natural inference then it may be that the musical experience that matters, at some level, is the one embodied in the writings themselves.

We thus find in the *Laws* a single model of efficacious movement applied at several different levels of analysis: just as the nurse calms the frenetic movements of a baby by imparting to it a gentle rocking motion, so does the lawmaker calm and regulate the terrific variety of household practices by a persuasive discourse that leads to conformity without applying coercive authority. This kinetic control is lexically associated with music: as we have seen, the persuasive prefaces intended to encourage without legislation are characterized as *prooimia*, that early part of a musical performance when the singer invokes the gods; the laws themselves are *nomoi*, a word which designates both legal framework and musical composition. These associations between the subject of the dialogue and music are perhaps best summed up in the claim we have just been discussing, that the *Laws* is the best kind of tragedy. What the *Laws* do not contain is anything like an explicit attempt to associate the psychosomatic kinesiology that is so central to the management of musical culture with reading as a cognitive process. On the topic of textual pedagogy that leaves us less with a conclusion than with a question, a hypothesis for further research: when I read, does my mind (or soul) move in a fashion that could be conducive to a philosophical outlook? This research, as I suggested close to the end of Chapter 1, may not have results that can be set forth in print; they may need to be pursued privately, in the secret, as Petrarch might say, of one's study.

In both the ontology of perception developed in the *Timaeus* and the model of education through music made explicit in the *Laws* we find what I think are enticing similarities to the notion of auditory culture developed more recently by figures like Jonathan Sterne. (This is no surprise since, as I suggested in the Introduction, 'audile technique' is inspired by Mauss' notion of bodily technique, and that, in turn, seems to have been catalysed by a reading of the *Laws*.) Here we find music being used as both a tool and a cultural 'surround': as a tool, because the right music can communicate dispositions and ethical orientations that are considered proper to the great city; as a 'surround' because the choral and participatory nature of this culture establishes a coherence thanks to which there is no outside, but rather a shared worlding produced by the fact that selves have been subjected to a common fabrication. Crucially, however, the *Laws* presents these possibilities as a project: we read a philosophical fantasy which proposes political change through musical and thereby sensual reform. But what is articulated here as desired finds an afterlife, surprisingly recharacterized as accomplished, in the work of Aristoxenus. I turn to him in Part Two.

Part Two

Aristoxenus

Chapter 4

A student of Aristotle active in the later portion of the fourth century BCE, Aristoxenus came from a family of musicians in the western Greek town of Tarentum, a place Plato may have visited in the early part of the century. His Italian roots and musical connections could both have been factors in his decision to study with a Pythagorean by the name of Xenophilus,[1] but eventually he drifted into Aristotle's circle.[2] Like many who had been exposed to the peripatetic's systematic approach to research, he was enormously prolific.[3] Music, or subjects proximal to music, played a large role in his writings: there were numerous texts on Pythagoras and Pythagorean doctrine,[4] biographies of Archytas,[5] Socrates[6] and Plato,[7] works on harmonic theory, on rhythm, on composition (*melopoeia*), on musical instruments,[8] on choral dancing[9] and on tragedy.[10]

Of this massive output only three reasonably large texts are available to modern readers, all gathered together under the title *Elements of Harmonics*.[11] There are also good sized but lamentably disconnected and ill contextualized fragments and summaries of a parallel text called *Elements of Rhythm*.[12] Significant but ultimately uncertain amounts of Aristoxenus' work seem to lie behind the large theoretical synthesis by Aristides Quintilianus (*On Music*) and the unpolished but very valuable *On Music* falsely attributed to Plutarch;[13] a number of brief 'introductions to music', particularly those of Cleonides and Gaudentius, seem to include some Aristoxenian material as well.[14]

The *Elements of Harmonics* presents a unique set of problems. The three 'books' which the surviving collection contains certainly do not all come from the same original work. Book One and Book Two have what appear to be different doctrinal contents. They divide the subject of 'harmonics' up into different sub-headings;[15] they each offer a catalogue of basic assumptions, but there are five in Book One and two in Book Two;[16] and a crucial concept, that of harmonic 'potential', occurs only in Book Two.[17] Book Two is also unmistakably the start of something – it begins with an overview of its subject. But it also contains several passages which suggest that it may have been developed, in part, in response to objections to an earlier work on the same subject.[18] These considerations suggest that the first two books come from different works. Book One offers itself as an articulation of principles combined with a critique of the approach of certain *harmonikoi*, whom Aristoxenus says he had also attacked in earlier (but now lost) work.[19] Book Two could be taken as more constructive and less destructive, or as a reconsidered and more tightly organized articulation of whatever was contained in the text originally containing Book One. Book Three, on the other hand, has a completely different form. It contains a series of demonstrations relying on a few axiomatic principles – usually the same two assumptions that are articulated in Book Two (I will discuss these later), but with a methodology that is less inductive and more deductive than anything that happened there.[20]

Despite the divergences, the three books of the *Elements of Harmonics* share a fundamental question: 'what is the nature of music?' (*hoian echei phusin to kata mousikēn;*[21] *ti pote estin hē phusis autou*).[22] A surprising question, coming from a student of Aristotle, especially one who clings as closely to the teacher's doctrine as Aristoxenus sometimes does.[23] As Barker pointed out, Aristotle distinguished sharply between things that come into being by nature, and things that come into being with the agency of art.[24] Music, we might expect, would be an example of something that comes into being thanks to art; but Aristoxenus clearly and consistently treats it as something with a nature; and, worse, he seems to understand *physis* in a strictly Aristotelian sense. The distinguishing feature of things that come about by nature, says Aristotle, is that they have a principle of movement and rest within themselves.[25] Things that come about by means of art have no *inner* or *ownmost* principle of change: that comes, instead, from without. We might think that music, being made by musicians, would have its principle of change in the musician or in his/her soul, and that therefore it could not be said to have a nature.[26] But in the *harmonics* Aristoxenus assumes the opposite: it is not just a manner of speaking when he asks 'what is the nature of music?' Music's principles, for Aristoxenus, are musically immanent.[27]

Not a small amount of energy is spent in the *Harmonics* excluding certain subjects as external causes and therefore irrelevant to music. Musical instruments, for example, have little or nothing to contribute to our understanding the nature of harmonics, he says, because they are ultimately guided and governed by the musician's ear.[28] Likewise the material conditions of sound: if one were to start from the idea that sound is motion of the air, that would be to engage with ideas unrelated to the subject.[29] This last exclusion is particularly crucial for Aristoxenus, since one of his primary propositions is that in music voices move in what he calls a 'discontinuous manner', appearing to stop on certain pitches and then to jump to other pitches.[30] Such a claim would have contradicted a common theoretical postulate that sound was constituted by movement;[31] Aristoxenus finds, however, that such theories are irrelevant in the study of music. Whatever may be the case in the material world, in music, he asserts, the language of rest is neither metaphorical nor inaccurate: here, the voice *just and literally rests* on stable pitches. His licence to make this claim is that he is describing not physical facts but appearances; his focus is on music as a strictly perceptual sphere. 'All of these things must be understood according to the way things appear in perception (*kata tēn tēs aisthēseōs phantasian*), he says.[32] This is a fundamental methodological postulate, on which much depends: any attempt to describe the nature of song must be an account of what appears, what occurs within perception. This excludes not just material causes, but also mathematical speculations such as those we have seen playing such an important role in Plato's *Timaeus*:

> We will try to give demonstrations that agree with appearances, not like those who came before us who talked about outside subjects and turned aside perception as inaccurate, making up noetic causes and saying that there were certain ratios of intervals and a disposition towards each other in which high and low arose, uttering totally irrelevant things that completely opposed appearance.[33]

With this Aristoxenus distinguishes his approach to music from a long and important tradition reaching back through Plato to Archytas and Philolaus, and claiming its origins in the Pythagorean discovery that the concordant intervals of octave, fifth and fourth could be expressed as the ratios of 2:1, 3:2 and 4:3.[34] Aristoxenus' origins in Tarentum, a major Pythagorean centre and the base of operations for both Philolaus and Archytas, might have exposed him to this tradition, and his early contacts in Athens were Pythagoreans,[35] which suggests that he was initially at least friendly with such approaches. Nonetheless, by the time he was writing about harmonics it is clear that he had rejected its more anti-sensualist tendencies.[36]

Aristoxenus insists, as we have seen, that music is to be explained in a manner that 'agrees with appearances'. This methodological assertion is central and definitive, since the nature of music, its immanent cause, will turn out to be a set of rules governing the behaviour of what appears in perception. I will turn to these rules later: what matters first is Aristoxenus' assertion that music is defined as an entity which occurs *exclusively* in and as perception; because it only occurs here, it can be described as having a nature on the Aristotelian account.[37] Because music has a nature – i.e. because it is treated as not caused by anything outside perception – it can also be described as *autonomous*; because its nature consists in certain rules, it is *law abiding* or *regular*; and because it is both autonomous and law-abiding, music proves to have an order which is unparalleled among perceptible things.

> There is a wondrous order (*taxis*) to the system of song, although despite this it has been accused of great disorder by some, thanks to those who have worked on the subject up to now. In truth, though, no other sensible thing has such orderliness, nor so much.[38]

There is an added, crucial stipulation: harmonics doesn't just describe music as perceptible, but only as what appears to 'those with experience in music (*tois empeirois mousikēs*)'.[39] 'Experienced' here translates the adjective *empeiros*: *empeiria*, in Aristotle's schema, is the experience that comes through repeated exposure to the same phenomena.[40] Music, we must understand, is only available to be studied in those acculturated to it: its 'nature' resides, in fact, in an already-acquired form of auditory culture. I will argue in Chapter 5 that Aristoxenus' theorization of music as a region of quasi-ideal stability within perception relies, at a crucial moment, on a vision of history: the 'nature' of music, in the end, turns out to be a culture in which change is minimized. Perception is defensible, in the end, primarily because music is nothing more or less than a *common set of auditory practices*. At which point someone might observe that music has, in fact, been caused by something outside itself: cultural self-reinforcement is the ultimate source of the rules that determine music as a highly ordered class of perceptibles.

This chapter details how Aristoxenus constructs music as a kind of ideality within hearing. The next chapter turns to his theory of musical temporality: while he recognizes that music takes place in time, he also intends that theory should bind time, making musical expression as predictable as possible. That leads me to a discussion of his vision of musical history.

I

Although Aristoxenus insists that the study of harmonics must attend exclusively to perception and disregard the physical basis of sound (as I have just pointed out), it would be a mistake to call this a rejection of acoustic ontology or a radical turn away from natural philosophy. To the contrary, Aristoxenus' analysis of music as a form of auditory culture depends on an ontology of sound in which there is a radical distinction between sound's materiality and its perception. This was relatively new, but not unprecedented.

While in the *Timaeus* sensation was part of a unified process joining body and world on a single plane,[41] many of Plato's younger contemporaries and successors introduced a cut at the interface of sense and world, often arguing or implying that perception was different from the material stimulation that provoked it. In the auditory realm this meant distinguishing between hearing and sound, where 'sound' designates external processes and events and 'hearing' is the psychological process they provoke.[42] One of the most salient differences between sound and hearing was that sound was commonly associated with motion – or even defined in terms of it – while hearing was taken to be the mitigation, transformation, or even elimination of movement.

A particularly vivid articulation can be discerned in Xenocrates, who was the third head of Plato's Academy and slightly younger than Aristotle.[43] For Xenocrates – at least as his views are reported by the late antique commentator Porphyry – sound was constituted by a series of discrete impacts separated by silence, while hearing perceived instead a single, continuous sound.

> Often if a cone is spinning and there is a white or black point on the cone, it happens that a circle appears that is the same color as the point. Likewise if there is a single white or black line on the moving cone, the whole cone seems to acquire the same color as the line. In these circumstances you can't even make out the point as a part of the circle, or the line as a part of the apparent color; the eye just can't discern such details.[44]

Xenocrates endorsed the common hypothesis that the material basis of sound was an impact or blow, but he realized that if impacts are indeed the basis for sound, sound had to be fundamentally different from what we experience when we hear: for a blow is a discrete, single event, while what we hear is continuous. Xenocrates' model is remarkably similar to the modern account of pitch-perception, which treats sound as a series of pressure-waves communicated through a medium like air to the ear where, thanks to a sophisticated combination of mechanical and electrical processes, the frequency with which those pressure waves strike the ear-drum is converted into the neurologic basis for the experience of pitch, a continuous and qualitative perception quite different from the discontinuous, essentially quantitative stimulus. Again, like the modern account, Xenocrates' implies that while perception is caused by sound, sound is not perfectly translated into a *perceptum*. Something is lost when hearing takes place: the movement itself. Like the spinning dot or line, a series of impacts on the ear is converted by hearing into the perception of a single note. The moving dot associates sound with kinetics, while the perceived circular line associates perception with a kind of stability.

Aristoxenus' own advanced training took place under Aristotle, and it is likely from him, rather than from Plato's successors, that he learned to treat perception as distinct from its causes. Indeed, the peripatos in general appears to have made the distinction almost habitually. Let us start with the founder. For Aristotle sound is propagated through a medium (*to metaxu*, 'the between'): the sounding object moves the medium, and the moving medium moves the organ of hearing. Usually the medium is air; water can also serve this function, though less efficiently.[45] Following the main stream of acoustic theorists before him, Aristotle identifies the origin of sound as a sudden, violent striking of one thing against another. Not just any thing will produce a sound when struck: the medium must move as a continuous mass, and this comes about when it is trapped by a hollow object or in contact with a smooth surface. Smooth things, like bronze, and hollow things, like *auloi*, are optimal sound-producers because they prevent the medium from escaping during the striking action.[46] Just as sharp things stab the flesh and blunt things press against it, so, thinks Aristotle, do high-pitched sounds move the ear very intensely for a short period of time while low-pitched sounds move it less intensely for a longer period of time.[47]

High-pitched sounds, in other words, come into being more quickly (they are more like a quick jab from a sharp knife), while low sounds emerge slowly (as though one were gently pushed by a broad, flat object). Aristotle offers more detail and an illuminating explanation of what he means in *On the Generation of Animals*. There, he rejects the thesis that pitch is related to the magnitude of the thing moved; on such a thesis, a greater mass of air would be moved more slowly than a smaller mass of air, and pitch would be a function of the amount of air that is moved when the medium is in contact with the striking motion. Aristotle thinks this would mean that high notes were necessarily produced by small voices, but he observes that there are animals with large, high-pitched voices as well as animals with small, low-pitched voices. Instead, he proposes that pitch arises from the relationship between the strength of a voice and the size of the medium that it moves. Large quantities of air are harder to move than small ones, and thus require more strength; a strong voice may move a very large mass of air slowly (and create a lower pitch) or quickly (to create a higher pitch), while a weak voice will produce low pitches when it tries to move a mass of air that is too big for its strength, and can produce high pitches only when it deals with a mass of air that is proportional to its strength.[48] Aristotle's explanation is exactly analogous to the case of a person trying to move a stone: a strong person will be able to move a large stone quickly or slowly, but a weaker person will be able to move a large stone only slowly. I think we must infer that what determines pitch is the speed with which the air is *set in motion*, not frequency or the speed with which it traverses space.[49]

Hearing is a perceptual capacity of the soul, and is therefore treated in *On the Soul*. For Aristotle perception is a capacity that receives the shape or form of what is perceived but not its matter. He compares perception to the imprint made in wax by a signet ring: the imprint contains a trance of the ring's shape, but in no way becomes the ring's material.[50] A sense, in sensing, is a form in the making; so long as it is being moved, it is not quite or not yet actually the form, that is, it is not quite or not yet actually the same as the stimulus;[51] it will be formally the same as the stimulating object when the moving (that is the perceiving) is over.[52] Aristotle seems to be making a distinction between achieved sensation, when the form has been actualized in the faculty of sense, and incipient sensation, when it is still coming into being. In incipient sensation the object is not yet perceived; it is only being assembled, so to speak.

Perceptions can be compiled into higher-order cognitive entities like mental images, thoughts and art. Close to the end of the *Posterior Analytics*, he acknowledges the need for a non-demonstrable kind of knowledge which could provide a basis for argumentation. This knowledge needs to be 'true, first, immediate [meaning not arrived at through the mediation of other principles or data], more knowable, prior to and the cause of' any conclusions that are drawn from it.[53] We cannot get such premises (which can be definitions, theses, hypotheses or axioms)[54] from any kind of demonstration or argument. Instead, we get them from a capacity that is common to all animals: it is a 'faculty of discrimination' called 'aesthesis'.[55] Perceptions lead to memory; if we have more than one memory of the same thing then we have experience (*empeiria*) of that thing. A single form in the soul, produced by and having to do with many perceptual events, experience is the starting point both of art (*technē*) and knowledge (*ēpistemē*).[56] Aristotle likens the genesis of experience to what happens in a retreating army when one soldier stops and makes a stand, then another one does, and so on, and eventually the army reconstitutes itself. The idea seems to be that a multitude of individual perceptual events can be compiled into a categorical impression. Just as we have a perception when the process of becoming stops (see earlier), so do we begin to have concepts when multiple perceptions stop or come to rest in the soul.

Sound and hearing are, in this account, materially different – only the form of the sounding object is produced in the hearing – and that may be sufficient to show that there is a difference between sound and hearing in Aristotle's approach. But since both sound and hearing are described in terms of form and formal genesis, one might be prompted to observe that we have here a theory that posits a basic similarity between sound and perception, not discontinuity. But recall our observation that for Aristotle the perceived sound is an achieved form, while what gives it its characteristic quality is the nature of the process by which it came into being. A finished perception, in other words, is a stopping, a stasis or stability, while the factors that determine its qualities are movements, comings-into-being of form. There is a difference between the impression left by a signet ring in wax and the manner in which the signet ring is pressed down into it; the latter certainly has an effect on the characteristics of the former, but it cannot be identified with it. Similarly in sound: the specific way a sound is made conditions the quality of the sound when it is perceived, but the formative activity cannot be identified with the perceived sound.

An entirely different model of sound propagation and perception appears in a fragment of text also contained in Porphyry's commentary on Ptolemy's *Harmonics*; this fragment is now known as the *de audibilibus*.[57] But it, too, makes a distinction between sound and hearing. Here we are given an extensive physiology of voices, the characteristics of which derive from the condition of the bodies that propel the breath forward. Sounds propagate, it is said here, because the air is moved or pushed by the breath; that movement continues through space.[58] The spaces through which the air moves affect its appearance, and the *De audibilibus* goes into great length discussing the physical conditions that influence the pitch and timbre of sounds. For example, a long and narrow windpipe imposes greater effort on a speaker; such voices are strong but cannot be sustained and do not go far, while short windpipes force speakers to breathe out more swiftly, producing a stronger impact and a higher pitch. Flexibility – the ability to produce a range of motion – also influences vocal characteristics: the text singles out the mouth in particular as a cause of great variation: some people can use their mouths to imitate the voices of many species of animals. A large, elastic lung can produce a great variety of vocal sounds, whereas a small, hard lung is limited to making a few weak sounds.[59]

The fact that physical causes of sonic qualities can be identified does not mean that what we hear *is* those physical causes. The author of the *De audibilibus* asserts that the sounds that reach our ears are analogous to the original blows which produced the sound.[60] But there is also a crucial and definitive difference between the material processes of sound propagation and production and the perception of these processes: while a string strikes the air many times, the ear itself hears only one sound. Perhaps referring to the same phenomenon remarked by Xenocrates (see earlier), our author offers an analogy in the fact that discrete coloured patches seem to be connected if they are in rapid motion: similarly, we do not hear the individual blows of a string because they are too close together.[61] Perception, that is, represents unities where the stimuli are in fact multiple, stability when the stimuli are in motion. By this very fact the physical stimulus is distinguished from the perceptual experience. The *De audibilibus* offers concords as another example of the same fact: we hear one sound when the stimulus is actually two.[62] That this should happen in the case of concords seems especially important: this account implies a distinction between matter and perception right at the core of musical experience, and implies that music essentially belies its material basis. We are not far here (though nothing in the actual text says as much) from asserting the autonomy of perception, particularly in the region of music – just the step Aristoxenus takes in his work on harmonics.

It may be that the peripatetic whose discussion of perception and music comes closest to those of Aristoxenus is Theophrastus, who wrote extensively on psychology and perception, and at least one important work on music.[63] What we know of his writings on perception suggest that he operated primarily as an interpreter of Aristotle, seeking above all to explain and to refine the teacher's doctrines.[64] But it is clear that Theophrastus' exegeses of Aristotle also included refinements. According to Priscian, he tried to resolve Aristotle's apparent endorsement of the Empedoclean idea that perception was somehow a ratio (*logos*) by claiming (alas, in a passage that has not survived) that the ratio was between the perception and its object.[65] Likewise he responded to Aristotle's insistence that all perception required a medium to connect (or separate) sense and sense-object, which raised the inevitable question of how exactly such media actually worked: what was it about air and water, for example, that allowed them to operate as the media for sound? Theophrastus appears to have claimed that it was not air or water *per se* that received and transmitted the forms we experience as sounds, but rather their *transonance* (*to diēches*); similarly, it was air's *transparence* that made it amenable to the communication of seen things, and its *trans-odiference* (*to diosmos*) that made it capable of carrying the forms of odours (etc).[66] In an attempt to explain why the air that Aristotle and Theophrastus mistakenly believed existed inside the ear did not make its own sounds, Theophrastus insisted that sound required a blow to be produced, and that nothing struck anything else in the inner ear; he went on to speculate that the movement of the ear air was the kind of movement associated with life, and then he argued that life-movement was not sonorous.[67]

As Aristotle distinguished between sound and hearing, so did Theophrastus. He endorsed Aristotle's claim that perception acquired the form, but not the material, of its objects,[68] and he distinguished between theories of perception in which sense and sense-object are different and those which posit an identity between acts of sensing and sensible stimuli. Theophrastus called these theories 'perception-by-same' theories; he thought Heraclitus and Plato were the leading exponents, and he criticized them in depth, a fact which implies his own espousal of a position in which sound and hearing were to be distinguished.[69] That the distinction between sound and hearing was a basic assumption in his thinking about music is also, I think, an unavoidable conclusion from the lengthy fragment of his essay *On Music*, preserved by Porphyry.[70] Porphyry cites Theophrastus as an authority against the assertion that number is the basis of pitch. According to Porphyry, Theophrastus argued in this passage that it is not 'quantity' (*posotēs*) but 'quality' (*poiotēs*) that determines pitch.[71] The first half of the cited fragment has Theophrastus asserting that number cannot be the basis of music: if it were, then everything that had number would be melodic. Neither numerical relations, nor any physical process, determine whether a note will be high or low.[72] This might appear to go even farther than Aristoxenus. Aristoxenus rules out noetic and material causes as irrelevant to harmonics: in the passage I have been discussing, Theophrastus appears to deny that noetic or material factors in any way cause differences between pitch. Instead, we might be prompted to conclude – as Porphyry clearly wants us to – that Theophrastus thought that it was the quality of a sound that determined its pitch.

But there are a number of problems with this reading, as Massimo Raffa has recently pointed out quite decisively.[73] The first is that, as an acoustic doctrine, that is, as an attempt to explain why certain sounds have the pitches they have, it leaves us with very little at all. Theophrastus doesn't actually say that pitch is caused by a sound's quality. Rather, his statements are limited to asserting that the ear receives high pitches more quickly than lower ones because of their characteristic qualities: it's not the pitch *per se* that is influenced by the sound's characteristics, but the specific manner and timing of its perception. I struggle to see that Theophrastus is making any kind of positive claim about the causes of pitch here, other than that it cannot be reduced to numbers. Theophrastus has not answered the question of why a sound sounds the way it does, though he has not ruled out the possibility that a sound is somehow formal in nature, and this is exactly the answer we would expect him to give if we pressed him on this point, since it is the Aristotelian answer (as we have seen). But – and this is the second problem – even Aristotle had admitted that speed played a factor in the determination of a pitch, which on Ptolemy's reading Theophrastus denies.

We could also observe that the text itself doesn't seem to be about the acoustic conditions of sound – that's Porphyry's theme, not Theophrastus'. Theophrastus' subject is announced in the first few sentences:

> The song-singing movement which arises in the soul is extremely accurate whenever the soul wants to express it with the voice, and it turns the voice however it wants, insofar as it is possible to turn an irrational entity. Some ascribed its accuracy to numbers, saying that its precision in producing intervals is a result of the ratios that are in them.[74]

The theory of number is raised here as an explanation, not for specific pitches, but for the soul's accuracy in moving the voice in a musical way. That, someone might observe, is an extremely fine distinction, but it's also a distinction that matters, because it articulates the difference between a physics of sound and a psychology of music. Whoever these numerical musicologists are, they are saying that the numbers start in the soul, and are then passed on, somehow, to the music. One implication of such a theory might be that our souls partake of a divine harmony, which was itself somehow a matter of numerical relationships, and it was this that was communicated – with enormous precision, apparently – to the voice. Theophrastus turns to the physics of sound only in order to attack the theory that *musical sounds* are caused by numbers: there are no numbers in sound, so numbers in the soul cannot be their cause.

After he has argued against number as the cause of the soul's accuracy in turning the voice to make music, Theophrastus addresses a second and apparently unrelated theory. There are those who claim that it is 'interval' that makes music musical.

> Nor are the intervals the causes of the differences [sc. between notes], as some say, and therefore the causes [of the soul's ability to turn the voice with such accuracy], since if you removed them the differences would continue. For when things are left out, these are not the causes of existence; they didn't make it but just don't prevent it any more. Being unmusical is not a cause of being musical just because what is musical would not arise unless what is not musical is removed. Nor does anything else associated with knowledge come into being unless the opposite of knowledge, that is ignorance, is banished; ignorance is not the cause of knowledge inasmuch as it exists, but rather inasmuch as it is set aside and does not prevent it [i.e. knowledge]. Thus the intervals are not the causes of song in that they

create it, but rather in that they don't prevent it. For if someone were to utter the notes in succession and also all the intermediate pitches, would this not produce an unmusical sound? Therefore, although when these things are not sent away the result is not-music, it doesn't mean that leaving them out is the cause of music, just because they prevent it if they are not removed.[75]

His language is unusually contorted here, as though he were having trouble finding an intuitive way to articulate what is, in fact, a relatively straightforward point: intervals do not cause music because intervals are just the spaces left when unmusical sounds are removed, and one does not define something as the absence of what prevents it.[76] (Aristoxenus shows an analogous unwillingness to think about the 'space between notes', at least in certain contexts, as we will see.) Porphyry's claim that Theophrastus' argument concerns the role of number in determining pitch leaves this new topic completely unmotivated: why, after what we have been led to believe is a polemic about acoustics, are we now dealing not with theories that seek to explain what makes a pitch a pitch, but rather with theories attempting to explain what makes an interval musical? The transition is motivated, though, if we realize that Theophrastus' text is an attempt to explain the source of the soul's ability to control the voice so precisely in making music. In this passage, he is claiming simply that it is not its ability to avoid inharmonic notes that makes the soul musical.

Perhaps if we asked Theophrastus what it was that underpinned the creation, propagation and perception of pitched tones he would reply more or less as Aristotle had: it was the relative speed of the coming into being of forms produced when air comes into collision with something hard.[77] But here his concern is not the causes of pitch, but the cause of music, and so once his negative arguments are complete he returns to the theme with which the passage began: music and its relationship to the soul. 'Music has one nature: it is a motion of the soul which arises in accordance with the resolution of the ills which come from emotion. And if it weren't this, it wouldn't be the nature of music,' he says – and then Porphyry ends his citation.[78] We learn from Plutarch and Aelius Festus Aphthonius that the emotions that played a particularly important role in the provocation of music according to Theophrastus were pleasure, anger, and enthusiasm.[79] We know from the beginning of the passage that to get rid of these, the soul will 'turn' the voice – presumably by imparting form to it, much as the soul creates voice in Aristotle – however it wants to, depending on the needs of its particular healing process. Theophrastus also claimed that the emotions were the price souls paid for their attachment to a body,[80] so we might imagine that music is the soul straining towards a solution to its incarnation. (If this reading is right, Theophrastus could be described as engaged in a sophisticated dialogue with the *Timaeus*, or ideas like the ones expressed there: on the one hand, the numerology is rejected, but the existential postulate that creation or embodiment is a condition from which music can help us recover, is retained).

There is much more to say on Theophrastus' remarkable text, but I will stop here and return to the main point which, I hope, is reasonably clear: Theophrastus should be expected to follow Aristotle on the distinction between sound and hearing, in that hearing is a formal but not material process of becoming similar to the sound that stimulates it. His denial that *music* resides in the physical causes he mentions links this particular area of auditory experience to Aristoxenus' own insistence on the autonomy of musical perception.

The positions I have run through share a common assumption that there is a difference between the material events that I have called 'sound' and the psychological process that I have called 'hearing'. Aristoxenus' insistence that music is to be explained only with reference to appearance relies on the same assumption. Whatever music is, it is not 'sound': it concerns 'hearing' alone, in as much as it occupies an autonomous space occurring within the realm of perception. This treats music not only negatively as *not* number or material movement, but also positively as an inherently structured, autonomous system of perceptual behaviours. As Barker put it,

> No rules are imposed on *melos* externally, from the repertoires of mathematics or physics; correspondingly, it imposes its nature on nothing else. Its behaviour, and the principles underlying it, have no implications of a metaphysical or cosmological sort; there can, for instance, be no authentically Aristoxenian theory of the 'harmony of the heavens'. Since the subject whose behaviour harmonics investigates inhabits only the perceptible realm, and since its nature is autonomous, the evidence on which the science can legitimately draw is in the strictest sense empirical.[81]

It is to this musical autonomy that I now turn.

II

Aristoxenus' conceptual lexicon consistently assumes that musical perception is autonomous. Consider the central concept of 'potentiality' (*dunamis*). Close to the beginning of Book Two Aristoxenus remarks that he intends to address the question of whether notes are 'pitches, as most people suppose, or potentialities (*dunameis*)'; he also plans to say 'just what a potentiality is'.[82] No definition is forthcoming in any of his extant works, but his use of the concept adequately illuminates what he means. Within any given harmonious scale there are many intervals of a fourth and a fifth, but all of these intervals are dynamically or potentially different.[83] We can think of Aristoxenian *dunamis* as referring to what some moderns might call 'degrees'. In the modern piano key of C major (i.e. using all the white keys on the piano but none of the black keys), the first degree (C) is different from the second (D) because of the kinds of movements that are possible from it: you can go up a major third from the first degree (C) but not from the second (D). Similarly, to move stepwise from C to F involves the sequence of intervals tone-tone-semitone, but to go from D to G (the same distance in absolute tonal space) involves the sequence tone-semitone-tone. In the Aristoxenian system, a singer performing in an enharmonic tuning could cover a perfect fourth by rising from *nētē* to *mesē* or from *lichanos* to the conjunct *tritē*. But passing stepwise through the tuning to cover the same space the singer would sing two quartertones and a ditone in the first case and a ditone then two quartertones in the second. *Dunamis* interprets a note as the set of notes which could follow from it (see Fig. 9).[84]

Aristoxenus must have been influenced, here, by Aristotelian concepts. A potentiality, says Aristotle, is an origin of change (*archē metabolēs*), either in something else or in itself.[85] In the broadest terms, the change of which potentiality is the origin can be described as a movement (*kinēsis*) or as an actualization. But not everything is potentially everything else: a piece of bronze, for example, is potentially a statue, but not potentially a ship. Actualization, then, is a constrained form of movement, in which the outcomes are defined by the specifics of a substance. Similarly, in Aristoxenus a note is potentially some set of other notes and only that set; vocal 'movement' is a process of actualizing some note from this constrained group of possibilities. As Barker put it, a note 'is not just a fixed point, a pitch, but something with its

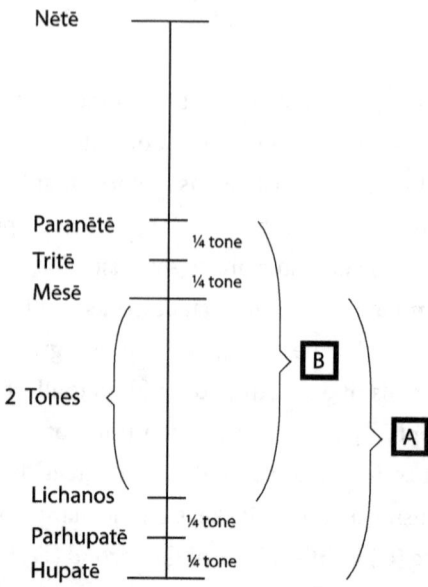

Figure 9 Two conjunct tetrachords in the enharmonic genus. Both intervals A and B are Fourths, but to sing through A one must sing ¼ Tone – ¼ Tone – 2 Tone, and to sing through B one must sing 2 Tone – ¼ Tone – ¼ Tone. Similarly, the potential notes one may sing from mesē are different from the potential notes one may sing from lichanos.

own dynamic properties, which (for example) impel the voice to move next, in its melodious trajectory, through no distance upwards less than that which separates *lichanos* from the highest note of its tetrachord, *mesē*.[86] The third book of the *Harmonics* contains a series of propositions whose goal is to specify the potential routes (Aristoxenus calls them *hodoi*, 'roads') from any given note in a musical system.[87] These specifications are quite limited, as we will see.

What Aristoxenus says of notes is true only in *musical* singing and perception. Outside of that enclosure he recognizes that a wider variety of pitches and movement is possible. Speech, for example, is contrasted with singing in that a speaking voice 'glides' or slides, while a singing voice 'jumps' from one note to another;[88] and Aristoxenus describes the process by which one readies a string or a voice for the production of a new pitch as 'tightening' or 'loosening': in musical singing, these tightenings or loosenings are inaudible, and only the stable incidence of pitch is heard.[89] The doctrine of potentialities depends on a state of appearances, then, that prevails only in musical perception; a completely different auditory topology prevails elsewhere.

The idea that notes were potentialities led Aristoxenus to assert that they could always have the same names regardless of their absolute pitch. That is, the note one step down from *mesē* would always be called *lichanos* regardless of the specific size of the step that brought the voice there. This seems to have boggled some of his hearers' minds, for he cites a lengthy objection to it.

> Some people have wondered how there can only be one *lichanos* if the interval between *lichanos* and *mesē* changes. For there is one interval separating *mesē* and *paramesē* and again separating *mesē* from *hupatē*, and all of the other fixed notes, but many intervals must be posited between *mesē* and *lichanos*. It would be better to change the names of the notes and not to call the others *lichanos*, and just to call one of them *lichanos* – say the ditone *lichanos*, or whatever. For notes that bound different intervals must be different notes: and the opposite must be the same too: notes bounding equal intervals must be the same notes.[90]

The objection seems straightforward. In different tunings, the note one step down from *mesē* may have different pitches. Doesn't it make sense to give these different pitches different names? But this objection is based on an incorrect assumption, says Aristoxenus: that there is a relationship between the names of notes and the size of the intervals that separate them. In fact, it often occurs that the same interval separates notes with different names.

> We see that *nētē* and *mesē* differ from *nētē* and *lichanos* in their potential (*kata tēn dunamin*), and likewise *paranētē* and *lichanos* from *paramesē* and *hupatē* – and that is why they each have a separate name. But a single interval separates all these pairs: the fifth. It is clear, therefore, that a difference in the size of intervals does not follow on a difference in the names of notes.[91]

Notes are not named on the basis of the size of the intervals separating them. Rather, they are named on the basis of their *dunameis*: even though the pairs of notes identified here are all separated by an identical 'distance', they have different potentials within the tuning, and therefore different names.

Aristoxenus has a second objection to the idea that each pitch should have a different name, and therefore that the interpretation of notes as potentialities should be abandoned: there is an infinite number of tunings, he says, and so there would need to be an infinite number of note names.[92] When he claims that there is an infinite number of tunings, he means that within a tetrachord bounded by fixed notes any given tuning may set the other two notes anywhere on a limited continuum: *lichanos* may be anywhere between two and one tones lower than *mesē*, for example (see Fig. 4). This is, on the one hand, a plausible response to what must have been a quite diverse musical environment: in the absence of any standard, and in the context of a culture that was largely oral and inevitably local, both instrument construction and individual musicians' preferences must have varied greatly. Given this great variation, Aristoxenus seems to have concluded that basing one's claims on any actual interval size would inevitably rule out microtonal nuances that should not be ruled out. 'Each of the subjects in music,' he says, 'must be ordered and disposed within the sciences [i.e. treated within a systematic framework] to the degree that it is determinate, and left alone if it is indeterminate (*apeiros*). In the matter of song, issues regarding the sizes of intervals and pitches seem to be indeterminate, but they are defined and ordered regarding potentiality, form, and composition.'[93] That is: we cannot predict exactly where *lichanos* will be pitched in a given composition. But we *can* predict that it will be two steps up from *hupatē* and one step below *mesē*. Given the open nature of musical culture as Aristoxenus understood it, such an approach seems eminently practical. But it also reflects a strong epistemological conviction: one can only *know* what is clear and defined and, above all, stable.

Aristoxenus has one more defence of the concept that notes are potentials. An approach that measured intervals and grounded its claims, for example, in saying that *lichanos* must be two tones below *mesē* to make an enharmonic tuning would fundamentally falsify perception, he says, not in the sense that it would be wrong, but in the sense that this is not how perception works. For the ear does not measure intervals: it simply recognizes that certain tunings are alike in being 'chromatic', while others are diatonic or enharmonic.[94] *How* it does this is particularly complex, and I will return to this question in Chapter 5. For the moment what matters is that in Aristoxenus' object area, that is, in the perceptions of those with experience in music, these recognitions simply happen. Although potentiality is itself a theoretical entity, reasoned about by the mind,[95] its value is that it can explain what happens in perception, conceived as an autonomous region of musical experience.[96]

Once notes are understood as potentialities, a second concept comes suddenly into focus, again via a recollected Aristotelian definition. The concept is that of 'continuity' (*sunecheia, hē sunechēs, to hexēs*).[97] For Aristotle, continuity is defined as a relationship between two things such that they share a limit: the line segments AB and BC are continuous because the one stops and the other begins at the same point, B.[98] Notes in Aristoxenus' vision of music are continuous because there is nothing separating one from another. Aristoxenus remarks that continuity can best be understood by analogy with the construction of words out of letters. 'When we speak,' he says, 'the voice by nature places the first, second, third, fourth, and the rest of the letters in order in each syllable, and not any letter after any letter, but there is a certain natural way of growing an utterance by combining letters' (I have paraphrased slightly).[99] This seems to be a reference to the fact that languages have rules about the combinations of phonemes: in certain languages certain sounds never occur in word-final or word-initial position, or in combination with other sounds. There is, as it were, a law of combination governing the elements of language. This is an insight reaching back to Plato's *Cratylus*, and it may well be grounded in the materialist combinatorics of Democritean materialism. The fact that letters are 'elements' (*stoicheiai*) suggests that the 'elements' of Aristoxenus' apparent title may refer not only to Euclidean geometry but also to the quest for a set of basic units and rules of combination within the space of musical perception. In any case, Aristoxenus goes on to claim that music is just like language, in that only certain combinations of notes and intervals are made by the musical voice.[100]

The letters in a word are to be understood as continuous because there is no gradual transition from the one to the next; one pronounces /c/, then /u/, then /p/. Modern linguists might object that speaking does not produce sounds that are as discrete as this argument suggests. In fact, the exact pronunciation of phonemes (like the exact intonations of pitches) is influenced by the surrounding sounds: /a/ after /m/ is different from /a/ after /d/, and the identity of the letters depends on the cognitive segmentation of an ever-changing stream of sounds.[101] This isn't a very strong objection, though, since Aristoxenus asserts that such acoustic details are not part of what harmonics aims to study: the *musical* ear just hears pitches. Here, too, the continuity of notes is a function of autonomous musical perception – a cognitive rather than acoustic process.

The succession of notes in continuity is governed, Aristoxenus suggests, by a finite set of rules.[102] Some combinations of notes are musical, and some are not: discerning the principles that distinguish between them is a major goal of harmonics as Aristoxenus conceives it. In Book Two he articulates two of these principles. He calls the first one 'the most necessary of all the things pervading a musical combination of intervals',[103] adding that while it alone does not define musical tunings, it is a condition satisfied by all of them.

> In any genus, moving in continuous motion from any note to a higher or a lower one, let the concord of a fourth be taken on the fourth step, or a concord of a fifth on the fifth step. A note where neither of these happens will not be musical relative to all those notes with which it does not produce a concord ascending in the degrees I have indicated.[104]

See Fig. 10, and imagine a singer singing a rising series of notes from some initial note X – say what we know today as middle C. On Aristoxenus' account, the second note in the series can be a variety of distances away from the first. The third note can also be a variety of distances away from the second. But the fourth note must be a fourth away from the first note: that is, no matter what the second and third notes are, the fourth – Y in the diagram – should be what we today

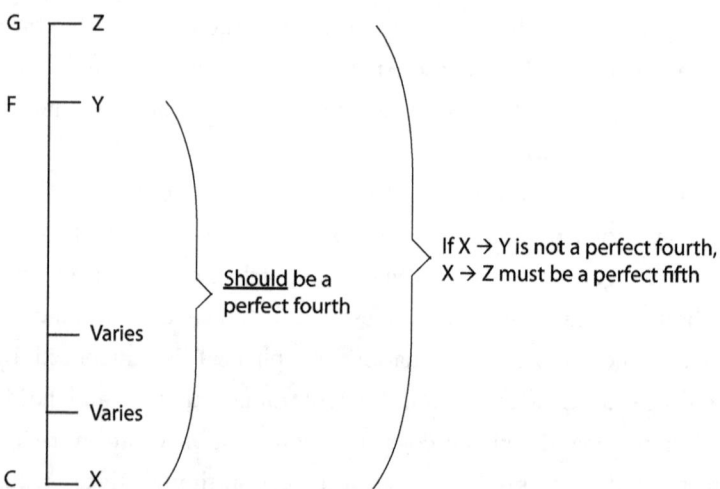

Figure 10 According to Aristoxenus, a tuning is musical if notes four steps away from each other (X → Y) complete a perfect fourth, or if notes five steps away from each other (X → Z) complete a perfect fifth.

call F; and if it is not, the fifth note – Z in the diagram – must be a fifth away from the starting point. That is, it must be what we call G.

A second, equally binding condition concerns the relations between tetrachords.

> It is necessary for tetrachords that belong to the same system either to be concordant with each other so that each note is concordant with its counterpart, or to be concordant with the same tetrachord, each being continuous with it but not in the same direction.[105]

In Fig. 11, given four notes x, y, z, a, where x and a are a perfect fourth apart, another four notes b, c, d, e can only belong to the same musical system if y and c and z and d are a fourth, a fifth or an octave apart.

Aristoxenus is thinking in terms of tetrachords bounded by fixed notes, which he treats like auditory shapes or forms that can be compared to other auditory shapes or forms.[106] There is a loose resemblance to Euclidean geometry here: tetrachords are replacing shapes; concordance (*sumphōnia*) replaces equality (*isotēs*), and membership in a musical system replaces similarity

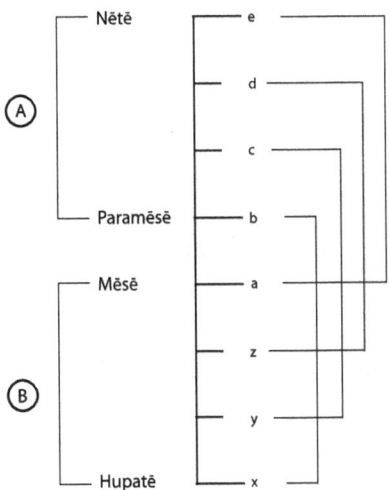

Figure 11 A tuning is musical only if all the notes of two successive tetrachords are concordant. That is: A and B will belong to the same musical tuning if $x \to b$, $y \to c$, $z \to d$, and $a \to e$ are fourths, fifths or octaves. If this condition does not hold, A and B may still be part of the same tuning if they are both concordant with a third tetrachord (this possibility is not indicated in the diagram).

(*omoiotēs*). Just as Euclid claims that two figures are similar if their sides and angles are equal,[107] so does Aristoxenus assert that two tetrachords are in the same system if each pitch in one is concordant with its counterpart in the other. Of course the similarity should not be pushed too far. Aristoxenus himself says that there is a major difference between geometry and harmonics, since geometry makes no use of perception, while harmonics does.[108] It's not wrong to characterize this passage as asserting that geometry deals in 'idealities', in purely noetic objects, while harmonics must attend to sounds that occur in the sensual sphere. But the distance between geometry and harmonics can also be exaggerated. While harmonics describes a sphere of practice that is essentially perceptual, it is also fundamentally concerned with determining the rules that govern musical audible space – rules themselves are not auditory phenomena in the same way as musical tunings are – and it treats that space as an autonomous sphere that is, at least in its autonomy, akin to the noetic sphere of the geometer's.

III

Potentiality and continuity seem to me to operate as a coherent conceptual pair which allow Aristoxenus to describe musical or well-tuned harmonic systems without appealing to any determining factors that do not belong to musically acculturated perception. But a point of view from which music is explainable *only* in its own terms, such as the one Aristoxenus is striving towards, seems to have been difficult to maintain, since he occasionally struggles to be consistent with it.[109] I turn now to one instance where Aristoxenus presumed the autonomy of musical perception but failed to adequately think with it. In the second book of the *Harmonics* he stated that the perfect fourth was equal to exactly two and a half tones, and he claimed to be able to prove this using the following construction (see Fig. 12):

1. First make two pitches (A and B) a fourth apart.
2. Now find the pitch *g* exactly two tones lower than *B*.
   Two tones is not a concordant interval, and therefore very difficult to hear. But since fourths and fifths are easy to hear, and their difference is a tone, we can find the ditone interval using fourths and fifths:

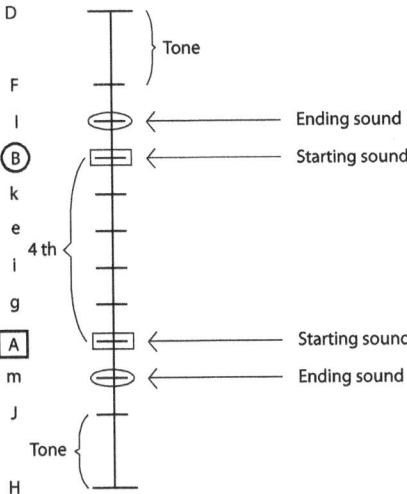

Figure 12 The steps in Aristoxenus' argument that a fourth is equal to exactly two and a half tones.

   a From B, find the pitch a fourth higher: D.
   b Now find the pitch a fifth lower than that: e. This pitch is one tone lower than the B we started with.
   c We need to go another tone down to find the ditone, so we do the same thing again: find the pitch F one fourth higher than E, then find the pitch g one fifth lower than F.

3. Now find the pitch k exactly two tones higher than A, the lower pitch in our original fourth, by doing the same procedure in reverse; find the pitch a fourth lower than A (H), then the pitch a fifth higher than H (i); then the pitch a fourth lower than i (J), and the pitch a fifth higher than J; this is k, and it is exactly two tones higher than A.

    We can be certain that the interval between B and k is the same size as the interval between A and g because we derived both using symmetrical procedures. Aristoxenus says we can think of this as subtracting a ditone from the original fourth in both cases, and since the amount subtracted from the original interval is the same, the amount left over is also the same. The question of the size of the fourth depends on the difference between the ditone and the fourth, so we want to know what the size of this remainder is.

4. Find the pitch l a fourth higher than g.

5. Now find the pitch *m* a fourth lower than *k*.

   We can be sure that the interval between *B* and *l* is equal to the interval between *A* and *m*, because *m* and *l* were produced using symmetrical procedures. But we also know that this interval is the same as the interval between *A* and *g* and between *B* and *k*; we know in addition that this interval corresponds to the difference between a ditone and a fourth. The fourth, in other words, is composed of two tones (the ditone) plus whatever interval makes up *m-A, A-g, k-B* and *B-m*.

6. Listen to the interval between *m* and *l*. Aristoxenus says that it is a fifth. That allows us to conclude that a fourth is equal to two and a half tones.

   A fifth is greater than a fourth by one tone; thus *m-l* is greater than *A-B* by one tone. But *m-A* and *B-l* are the same interval. Since together they make up the difference between the fifth *m-l* and the fourth *A-B*, they make up a tone. Each of them is, then, necessarily half a tone. But *m-a* and *B-l* are the same as *B-k* and *A-g*, so these are also half a tone in size. We know that the remainder when a ditone is taken from a fourth is therefore half a tone and that, consequently, the fourth is made out of two and a half tones.[110]

This demonstration was – and remains – enormously problematic.[111] Because the ratios designating the tone (9:8), fourth (4:3), fifth (3:2) and octave (2:1) were known, mathematically inclined theorists could calculate that the octave was smaller than six stacked tones.[112] An octave was equal to a fourth and a fifth ($3/2 \times 4/3 = 2/1$), and the difference between a fourth and a fifth was a tone ($3/2 \div 4/3 = 9/8$); the octave was therefore equal to two fourths and a tone. But an octave was smaller than six tones (($9:8)^6 > 2:1$), so an octave less a tone was smaller than five tones; two fourths were accordingly also smaller than five tones, which meant that one fourth was smaller than two and a half tones. An additional objection to Aristoxenus' claim could be found in the fact that, at least insofar as the mathematics then used was concerned, there could be no value exactly halfway between the two terms in an epimoric ratio (that is, a ratio in the form $n + 1:1$).[113] Since a tone was expressed as 9:8, a semitone was a mathematically inadmissible entity.

Worse, using only pure intervals corresponding exactly to the mathematical proportions (i.e. a 4:3 fourth, a 3:2 fifth), Aristoxenus' proof does not get the result he claims for it. As David Creese has pointed out, it is entirely possible to perform the operations he prescribes in your head, using the ratios for the major concords and simply multiplying or dividing to calculate the size of the resulting intervals. But when you do this,

> The final interval comes out not as a fifth (3:2), but as something slightly smaller (262 144:177 147) [...] Because of the discrepancy between the arithmetical conclusion that [the final interval] <3:2 and Aristoxenus' statement that 'it turned out that the highest of the notes generated [...] was concordant with the lowest [...] at the fifth', other key elements of his argument which follow from this statement are in disagreement with corresponding elements of the arithmetical version of the procedure.[114]

Creese is a little generous here. If the final interval isn't a fifth, Aristoxenus' argument that a fourth is the same size as two and a half tones is utterly destroyed. Creese points out that the difference between a perfect fifth and the interval you get if you do Aristoxenus' procedure is not imperceptible, either.[115] He concludes that Aristoxenus could never have done this experiment.

I do not believe the demonstration given by Aristoxenus at the end of *El. Harm.* 2 is defensible. But there are tendencies rooted in his vision of harmonics which may provide clues as to how he might have refined the argument. To start, he likely intended to refer only to the rule-governed, autonomous space of musical perception; his identification of harmonics as describing 'what appears to those experienced in music', as well as his exclusion of 'noetic' causes, would almost certainly have led him to reject or at least be unconcerned by any objection grounded in the interpretation of concords as numerical ratios.[116] Mathematical approaches to measurement were not the only ones available. The medical theorist who wrote *On Ancient Medicine*, for example, claimed that medicine stems from the observation that strong foods cause physical distress, while weak ones do not. But it is also true that one can starve if one eats too little or avoids strong foods altogether. Given such a complex situation, we need some kind of measure. The author of *On Ancient Medicine* thinks this measure should come from observation, not calculation:

> You will find measure neither as some number nor as some weight, comparing with which one achieves exactitude, but in nothing other than the perception of the body.[117]

Similarly, the author of the Hippocratic *Regimen* says that you can know the whole theoretical system of medicine, but if you are not present before a patient's body, you cannot make the right decisions for him or her; again, a useful measure must be found by the senses, not imposed by a mind.[118] The author of *On Ancient Medicine* places a high value on long habituation and training; one can only be a medical practitioner if one knows all the elements of the craft that have been compiled over many generations. Not surprisingly, the Hippocratic corpus includes a massive number of case studies; the art is compiled from an evidential base.

In Aristotle, too, there is an extensive discussion of units of measurement. Aristotle prefers the word 'unit' (*to hen*) or 'indivisible unity';[119] but he equates this with measure. Though for the most part he holds measures to be single and indivisible, in the case of music he is forced to admit the existence of two different *dieses*; similarly, he remarks, there are many different letters, and they are the units of speech.[120] Non-numerical measures are perceptible entities – they are the things, he says, 'from which a primary element cannot be taken in perception';[121] he also calls them 'indivisible in perception'.[122] Achieving an exact measurement on the basis of perception was thus entirely conceivable.

If Aristoxenus could have convincingly shown the fourth to be equal to two and a half tones, it would have represented a significant reply to mathematical musicology. While fourths (4:3), fifths (3:2) and octaves (2:1) have easy-to-understand mathematical relationships in that a fourth + a fifth = an octave (4/3 × 3/2 = 2/1), they are all incommensurable with the size of a tone (9:8). That is, as we have already seen, 9:8 does not go evenly into 4:3, 3:2 or 2:1.[123] In Aristoxenian harmonic 'space', however, the fourth would be exactly two and a half tones, the fifth three and a half tones, the octave six tones; the basic concords would therefore be measurable in terms of the same unit. Recall the *Philebus*' insistence that things must be commensurate (*summetros*) to be beautiful; Aristoxenus' approach promises to satisfy this stipulation.[124]

There were therefore compelling reasons for Aristoxenus to have wanted to show the size of the fourth as equal to two and a half tones. How might he have defended this idea, perhaps developing or modifying the argument cited above?

Aristoxenus might have simply asked: is there a harmonic system in which the top note is one fifth away from the bottom? The answer can be reformulated:

is there a system in which the top note is one tone above the note two steps below it? The answer to this question is 'yes'. The 'tonic chromatic', at the very limit of the chromatic range, satisfied this criterion precisely. It would follow that its *puknon* is divided into two semitones, and that the fourth is equal to two and a half tones (see Fig. 13).

Aristoxenus might also have observed something just like the 'experimental' procedure he describes, leading more or less to the result he predicts. A lyrist tuning his instrument to a tonic chromatic tuning could have started with two pitches one fourth apart, then generated the two inner notes using the method Aristoxenus describes, then produced the two outer notes as he recommends.[125] But the lyrist would probably have completed his tuning by ear – tweaking the system thus far produced so that it adhered to what his perception wanted.[126] This last step disqualifies Aristoxenus' demonstration in another way, of course, since it would quite literally have involved fudging the results at the last step. But would this have bothered him? Perhaps not: that final tweaking could have confirmed the primacy of perception, and if a musician altered his tuning this could have appeared to confirm Aristoxenus' insistence on the centrality of musical perception; only when the lyre was in tune, and not before, would the fourth be equal to two and a half tones and the concordances perfectly symmetrical.[127]

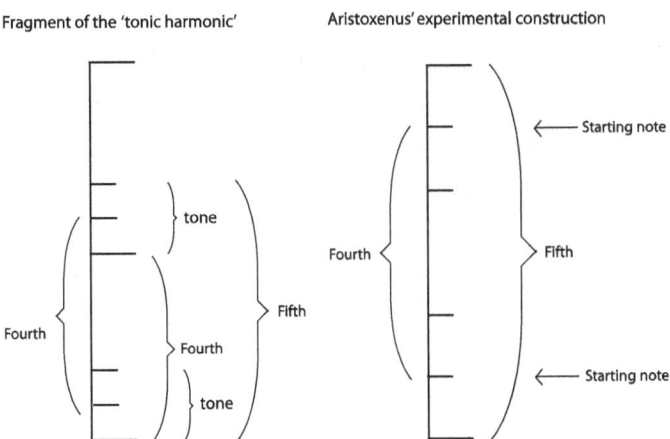

Figure 13 Aristoxenus' experimental construction (on the left) beside a fragment of the tuning called the 'tonic chromatic'.

IV

There is a difference between the object Aristoxenus describes – that is, music – and the goals and procedures of his theory.[128] This is most obvious in the capacities he requires of the theorist:

> The subject matter requires two things: ears and thought. With our ears we determine the sizes of intervals, and with thought we theorize about potentialities.[129]

It isn't clear just how precise the ear of the theorist needs to be – very precise, probably.[130] I think it's inevitable, however, that a theorist like Aristoxenus cannot be understood, on his own account, to be doing the same thing as even the most virtuosic performer or expert composer. Although the theorist aims to make statements that are perfectly in accord with 'what appears to those experienced in music', that is, with the facts of acculturated musical perception, Aristoxenus says that the theorist begins with what can be heard in order to progress towards things that 'can in no way be perceived'.[131] These imperceptible theoretical objects are perhaps the postulates we have been discussing, none of which are in the strictest sense audible: the criteria to which all harmonic tunings must adhere (such as the necessity of completing a fourth in four steps or a fifth in five); the understanding of notes as potentialities, that is, as implicitly a finite set of 'next notes' determined by the harmonic tuning to which they belong; and the theory of musical continuity this leads to. Well-tuned music is a creature of perception; but the axioms which govern it are not. In the broadest (and blandest) terms, we may assert that an account of perception is not itself a perception; a theory of hearing does not hear. Slightly later, in the course of a critique of 'harmonicists' who seem to have claimed that their use of musical notation was an important part of music theory (a claim Aristoxenus finds colossally misguided),[132] he argues that it is a basic error to assume that the end-point (*peras*) of theoretical effort is to produce something evident (*phaneron*); this makes the 'thing judged' (*to krinomenon*) the goal of theory, not 'the capacity to judge' (*to krinon*).[133] In this sense at least the *Harmonics*, although aiming to describe perception, pushes beyond it, and makes the sovereign authority not anything perceptible, nor even, I would risk, perception itself; it is rather the soul and its capacity for

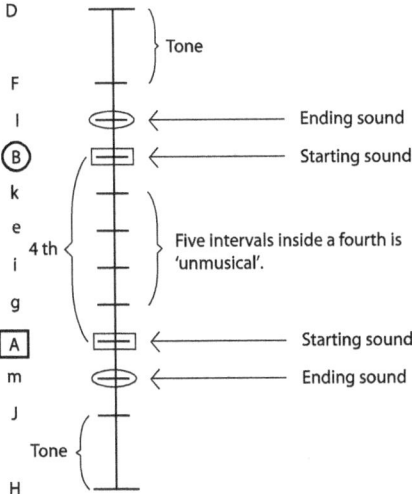

Figure 14 Aristoxenus' construction produces a series of small intervals which cannot be sung through in a 'musical' way as he defines 'musical movement'.

thought that governs here (though, to be sure, it needs perception, and a good one at that).

Indeed, Aristoxenus would appear to be deeply inconsistent unless we understand a rigid distinction between theory and the musical ear.[134] Consider the 'proof' of the size of the fourth. Though I have suggested that it is intended to be constrained by the rules of harmonic space, its reliance on a method in which one finds pitches two tones above and below the starting pitches using the method of concordance results in a series of intermediary pitches which cannot be taken, in aggregate, as belonging to any single harmonic system. The construction produces five intervals within the central fourth, for example (see Fig. 14). Two of them are only 'scaffolding', to be sure, but the voice must nevertheless sing them before it reaches the pitches Aristoxenus is interested in. He really is working in a non-musical tonal space, at least at first.

Similarly, in designating the range of *lichanos* and, via that, of each of the genera, he again introduces a series of intervals and relationships that he acknowledges to be 'unharmonic'.

> The lowest chromatic *lichanos* is higher than the lowest enharmonic *lichanos* by one sixth of a tone, if indeed the chromatic diesis is bigger than the enharmonic diesis by 1/12 of a tone. For it is necessary that the third portion of something be bigger than the fourth portion by 1/12. And the two

chromatic dieses exceed the two enharmonic dieses by double that amount, that is, the sixth, which is an interval smaller than the smallest of the sung intervals. Such intervals are not musical, for we call unmusical what cannot be placed in its own position in a tuning.[135]

Aristoxenus gives himself the liberty, in other words, to work with non-musical acoustic material even as he denies musicians the ability to do so.[136] We might conclude that he does not treat himself as part of the perception-system he describes, that he addresses music as a system of appearances occurring within perception, but from a standpoint that encompasses more than perception.

A question we could ask at this point is why a theory of music is needed at all. Perhaps it goes without saying that musicians usually benefit from some body of esoteric knowledge and practical lore that can provide guidelines and furnish meanings for what they do, or, equally valuably, can provide constraints and restrictions to be struggled against in the search for a subjectively or socially true form of expression. Certainly Greek musicians interfaced actively with theory since at least the late sixth century, when the composer Lasus of Hermione wrote the first *peri harmonias*, and it's entirely possible that some (if not all) of the theorists Aristoxenus criticizes had some practical or professional stake in music performance.[137] In general terms, in other words, music theory needs no *apologia*; its functions are multiple, its historical role significant.

But the question of a theory's influence on music is different from the question of how it conceives its own relation to practice. Did Aristoxenian music theory predict itself? To put this a different way: why should music as Aristoxenus describes it in the *Harmonics* need a theory? On the face of it, if Aristoxenus' description is accurate music doesn't need a theory at all: it just *is*, by nature, autonomous, law-abiding and commensurate with itself. In learning to become musical, one acquired this perceptual system, and in performing, one actualized it. Of course some practical instruction would be required, some sense of how to sing and why must be imparted: but it's in no way clear that anything like Aristoxenus' laws or his definitions of potentiality and continuity would be needed for practical purposes. Indeed, Aristoxenus' claim that those singing musically *just can't not* complete a fourth in four steps or a fifth in five steps implies that it isn't even a choice: singing musically entails doing this, if not automatically then at least autonomously, according to the internal dictates of the musically acculturated ear. I see nothing in the *Harmonics* suggesting that Aristoxenus intended to discipline or police musical practice: the whole project seems to be one of description. This description might make no difference to actual musical practice or to the self-conception of musicians. Given that, the question I ask here is: what was it that drove Aristoxenus to pursue this description as he did?

I cannot know Aristoxenus' mind. But his theoretical tendencies make good sense when they are set beside the constellation of theoretical texts that were produced in the fourth century around Plato and Aristotle on the subject of sound, hearing and music. As I have already suggested, Aristoxenus' work on music fits well within this context. We have seen that several post-Platonic authors separated perception from its material stimuli and treated it as a distinct sphere: what occurred there expressed but did not repeat physical stimuli; it provided material for but was not identical to thought. Aristoxenus' investigations into harmonics extended this position by arguing that musical perception was not only autonomous but also lawful and commensurable with itself. The result was, to be sure, a description of music: but it has equally momentous consequences for the psychology of perception, since it shows that perception can be as regulated or disciplined as philosophy had always insisted the mind should be. His claim in *Harmonics* II that 'there is a wondrous order (*taxis*) to the system of song'[138] seems to bear as much on the question of perception as on the theory of music. Aristoxenus' account insists that in music, at least, there is lawfulness and an epistemological ground; its preeminence among perceptibles may be less important than the fact that *any* area of perception can be so reliable. Here, I think, Aristoxenian musicology might have made a real contribution to fourth-century philosophy: it might have been taken as finding in music an aesthetics that was both autonomous and rigorous, instantiating a logic within the senses.

Chapter 5

> A word may be in order here to forestall a popular fallacy, namely the supposition that musical motion is actual because strings or pipes or the air around them move. Such motion, however, is not what we perceive. Vibration is minute, very fast, and if it comes to rest sound simply disappears. The movement of tonal forms, on the contrary, is large and directed toward a point of relative rest, which is no less audible than the progression leading up to it [...] Musical motion, in short, is something entirely different from physical displacement. It is a semblance, and nothing more.[1]

So Suzanne Langer, writing in 1953. Much of the passage could have come from Aristoxenus. He, too, distinguished musical motion rigorously from physical movement, especially those physical movements that make sound. 'The semblance of a thing,' she writes, 'is its direct aesthetic quality.'[2] Langer doesn't mean that musical motion isn't real; just that it isn't material, with which Aristoxenus would agree completely. 'The setting forth of pure quality or semblance,' she writes, 'creates a new dimension, apart from the familiar world';[3] although artistic semblance can be called 'illusion', it is in fact hyper-real, a sphere of symbols whose meaning emerges as a unique and powerful aesthetic experience.

This much they have in common. But when Langer takes her next step Aristoxenus would refuse to follow.

> The realm in which tonal entities move is a realm of pure *duration*. Like its elements, however, this duration is not an actual phenomenon. It is not a period – ten minutes or a half hour, some fraction of a day – but is something radically different from the time in which our public and practical life proceeds. It is completely incommensurable with the process of common affairs. Musical duration is an image of what might be termed 'lived' or

'experienced' time – the passage of life that we feel as expectations become 'now' and 'now' turns into unalterable fact. Such passage is measurable only in terms of sensibilities, tensions, and emotions; and it has not merely a different measure, but an altogether different structure from practical or scientific time.

The semblance of this vital, experiential time is the primary illusion of music. [...] Music spreads out time for our direct and complete apprehension, by letting our hearing monopolize it, organize, fill, and shape it, all alone. It creates an image of time measured by the motion of forms that seem to give it substance, yet a substance that consists entirely of sound, so it is transitoriness itself. *Music makes time audible, and its form and continuity sensible.*[4]

For Langer, music is defined by its temporality not merely because it happens in time, not just because a performance lasts, say, 45 minutes and cannot be experienced other than as a sequence of events (Langer calls arts like this, arts that take time, 'occurrent arts'). What Langer means, rather, is that temporality is music's business, its intent and import. 'The purpose of all musical labor,' she writes, 'is to create and develop the illusion of flowing time in its passage.'[5] This illusion of time contains a profound truth: it discloses the 'inner temporality' of life, the 'tensions and resolutions' that we undergo in lived duration. Music is, therefore, 'the articulate symbol of feeling'[6] in as much as feeling has its own temporality: indeed, some thinkers working in the line of thought opened by Langer, such as Brian Massumi, have gone so far as to assert that feeling or affect is inherently temporal.[7]

Writing a little earlier than Langer, Victor Zuckerkandl made a comparable set of claims. Beginning from the perfectly Aristoxenian idea that musical expression is an autonomous sphere distinct from both the physical and the cognitive, he arrived at the conclusion that music 'is temporal art in the special sense that in it time reveals itself to experience.'[8] A melody is 'a temporal whole, a whole whose parts are given as a sequence, as temporal succession,'[9] and its most profound message to us is

> the erroneousness of the view that the past can be given only as a memory, the future only as foreknowledge [...] every melody declares to us that the past can be there without being remembered, the future without being foreknown – that the past is not stored in memory but in time, and that it is not our consciousness which anticipates time but that time anticipates itself.[10]

There is no sign that Aristoxenus thought like this. Nor should we expect him to: as Zuckerkandl pointed out, the temporal disclosure of music is a modern phenomenon, perhaps even one of the signal achievements of modern musical thought.[11] Indeed, some have argued that musical time as we know it is a permutation of distinctly modern forms of historical time. Reinhart Koselleck has argued that around the middle of the eighteenth century history was 'temporalized': that is, it was distended (if I can put it that way) such that events appeared to be irreducibly different from each other, and a space was felt to exist between past, present and future. Previous to this, Koselleck claims, these dimensions were felt to overlap and even to coincide at particularly charged moments of crisis. Karol Berger connected changing conceptions of time in early modernity to an alteration in the way the melodic line was conceived: in Bach it had a circular, unifying function, while in Mozart it manifested as teleological motion, looking optimistically to some future resolution.[12]

A priori, then, we would not expect to find an understanding of song as the disclosure of temporality in Aristoxenus. Aristoxenus does acknowledge that music takes place in time. But he goes no farther than acknowledging that music is 'occurrent', as Langer puts it, that it happens in the temporalized setting of coming-to-be and passing-away. For Aristoxenus, temporality is not the essence, inmost truth, or ultimate fact of music, nor does music *disclose* temporality. To the contrary: while music occurs in time, music theory works to display fundamental constraints that govern musical expression and limit its capacity for radical change. The autonomous and law-abiding nature of song as Aristoxenus characterizes it could be described as having the effect of reducing contingency or binding time; music is strict and rigorous, profoundly constrained and essentially predictable, the expression not of inner temporality but of lawfulness, expressed in time to be sure, but not identical with it.[13] I suggest that this music theory binds time. (See the Introduction for an explanation of what 'time binding' means in this context.)

What follows traces how Aristoxenus binds time in in his methodology and in his theory of rhythm (section I); I add a discussion of melodic forms that may not, in fact, be Aristoxenian at all but casts some light on the matter (section II). I then argue that he attributes the same process of time-binding to the *non*-theoretical ear, which experiences music as 'feeling' or 'character' (section III). That leads me, in the last section, to a discussion of Aristoxenus' interpretation of music history. Here, too, I claim, he saw a minimum of change: music was instantiated in an affective community which existed across generations and constrained music-historical change.

I

An explicit acknowledgment of the temporality of music comes at the end of a methodological section in *Harmonics* 2, where Aristoxenus insists that harmonicists must have a good memory.

> It is clear that the understanding of what has been put into song involves following along every change in what happens with ear and mind – for song happens in the sphere of becoming [*genesis*], just like the other parts of music. The understanding of music comes out of two things: perception and memory. One must perceive what happens, and one must remember what has happened. There is no other way to follow along with the things that happen in music.[14]

The expression 'for song happens in genesis' articulates the fact that song occurs in time, an idea that could only have been doubted by theorists who identified harmony with number; we have seen that Aristoxenus is unsympathetic to that approach. But the call for memory here should be understood in the context of his generally Aristotelian epistemology, according to which one acquires general concepts on the basis of a sequence of perceptions, each happening in temporal sequence, which are then grouped and connected through the medium of memory,[15] then converted into a concept. Memory compiles the data of a musical performance and allows it to be treated as part of a harmonic or rhythmic system. Thus, for example, when an aulete plays three notes in sequence, memory allows them to be compared, collated and set next to each other in an imaginative space; and thought, working not with the pitches but with the idea that the notes are related by potentiality, recognizes what other possible notes might be played by the aulete if he stayed in the same tuning; a further step would be to formulate higher-order levels of constraint, such as the statement that four notes in sequence will usually complete a perfect fourth (and when they don't, the fifth note will complete a fifth). This passage may be said therefore to acknowledge the temporality of music but only as a starting point and only in the very weak sense that music shares a modality of being with all the other things that occur in temporal sequence.

Here is another crucial methodological claim, also in the second book of the *Harmonics*:

> One must recognize that understanding music concerns a part that stays the same and a part that changes. This is the case with all music and in every part, to put it simply. First: we perceive the differences between genera because the containing notes are fixed but the inner notes change. Again: when an interval is the same we call one *hupatē* and *mesē*, and another *parhupatē* and *nētē*, and yet while the size is the same the *potentials* of the notes are different. Again: when there are many forms of the same-sized intervals, i.e. the fourth, the fifth, and the rest. Likewise when a modulation sometimes arises from the same interval, and sometimes not. We see many similar things happening in rhythmic matters, too. Even when the ratio by which we define the genera of rhythm stays the same, the size of the feet changes according to the power of the tempo, and though the sizes stay the same the feet may be unequal. Likewise the same magnitude can be a foot or a group of feet. It's clear, too, that the differences of division and form arise because there is a single, abiding size. Generally speaking, *rhythmopoeia* causes many and varied movements, but the feet with which we designate rhythm are simple and always the same. Since music has such a nature it is necessary to train the mind and perception in these matters so that one can judge both what stays the same and what changes.[16]

In different tunings, the fixed notes are always the same but the moving notes change, and the theorist must discern the differences in order to describe, assess and relate different tunings to each other. Likewise with intervals: the same size of interval can have different functions in different regions of a tuning (as we have seen), and the theorist, ranging over the whole system, must be able to discern this. Aristoxenus is concerned with identifying the frames within which change and stability are balanced: the task of the theorist is to identify what changes and what stays the same.

Aristoxenus doesn't say so here, but it seems reasonably clear that the next step is to get at the underlying constraints which both allow and limit fluctuation in and between performances. Consider the case of rhythm. In the passage just cited, Aristoxenus' comments are sparse, even Laconic. But we can expand on these brief remarks, thanks to the survival of a few fragments of Aristoxenus' rhythmic writing. A single, brief excerpt exists of the *Elementa Rhythmica*; there is also a summary from Michael Psellus (eleventh century CE), some short sentences and paragraphs in MSS in Naples and Paris, and a quotation in Porphyry's commentary on Ptolemy's *Harmonics*.[17] It's clear from these sources that Aristoxenus' theory of rhythm was analogous to his harmonics. Time played the role primarily of supplying rhythm with building blocks, and theory articulated the constraints.

The *Elementa Rhythmica*'s analytical framework is a strict Aristotelian hylomorphism. Rhythm is a form (*schēma*) imposed on a material (which the *Elementa Rhythmica* calls the *rhuthmizomenon*).[18] Aristoxenus observes that neither form (*schēma*) nor rhythm (*rhuthmos*) come into existence on their own; just as forms are always immanent in some material, so do rhythms only ever occur as the rhythming of a 'rhythmed' (*El. Rhyth.* 2.6). 'The same expression (*lexis*),' he writes, 'when it is disposed into times (*chronoi*) that differ from one another, takes on certain differences, as many as there are differences in the nature of rhythm.'[19] This is hard to understand: how can the same set of words be arranged into different times? One possibility is that Aristoxenus is referring to the kind of experiments in metathesis practised, later, by euphonist critics and rhetorical theorists: in rearranging the words of a stretch of Homeric verse, one can destroy the rhythm, or change it into a different one altogether.[20] Another possibility is that he meant that the order of the words stays the same, but the time-length of the syllables changes; in this case the rhythm would change depending on whether or not I say a long syllable over a temporal span lasting two or three times that of a short syllable. Regardless of which of these is true (I think the first option is best), what matters most is that verbal expression on its own isn't rhythmic: it needs to be arranged for rhythm to emerge. In parallel with his claims about harmonics, Aristoxenus denies that every arrangement is rhythmic. Certain fundamental laws must be observed, and non-rhythmic diction will be arranged in a schema that does not observe them.

To 'receive' rhythm, something must already be divided up into parts. This division plays an active role in the production of rhythmic presence. 'Rhythm cannot come into existence,' Aristoxenus writes, 'without something which will be given rhythmic form and which cuts up time (*temontos ton chronon*).[21] It must have already cut up or divided time because time does not cut itself up (*ho men chronos autos hauton ou temnei*; *El. Rhythm.* 2.6). Aristoxenus says that he has already explained this assertion, but that part of his text is now lost, so we are left without illumination. Some assistance may be provided if we consult Aristotle's discussion of time in *Physics* IV and in *On Memory*. I have already noted that for Aristotle, continuity is a property of certain kinds of succession such that two limits make a unity.[22] Time is continuous thanks to the peculiar nature of the 'now': the 'now' is the limit (or 'point') at which 'before' and 'after' meet and are unified.[23] If there were only one 'now', we would not be aware of time.[24] We need either two 'nows' or a changing 'now' for time to appear to us. Aristotle understands the now thanks to which time is continuous to be analogous to the point by which a line is made continuous, but he adds a crucial *caveat*: the now, unlike the point, is always changing. The 'now', just by virtue of being a 'changing point', always marks a section of time, and it is through the perception of this section that movement becomes measurable.[25] So it is thanks to the perception of two versions of the same now and the span in between them, which is referred by perception to imagination, and from imagination to memory, that one acquires an idea of time – or rather a mental form of time, the 'movement of time' that is spoken of in *De memoria* as requisite for one to be able to have the experience of memory.[26] In this analysis, knowing time involves a kind of sampling, a reaching into the 'flux' at two points and preserving the section that results as an idea or form or thought of time. Aristotle defines time as the 'number' (*arithmos*) of movement (*kinēsis*), particularly as this concerns 'before and after'.[27] He says he means that time is the number in movement that we count. Returning to Aristoxenus, we could speculate that just as we mark off time as a span between nows, so does something in song divide time by the articulation of certain perceptible changes.

As the *rhythmizomenon* is made out of easy-to-know parts by which time is divided, so is the foot the medium by which rhythm becomes knowable by perception.[28] Aristoxenus measures feet in terms of syllables which are themselves measurable by *chronoi* or 'times'. An iamb, consisting of a short and a long syllable, can therefore be described as a ratio in the form of 1:2 (one *chronos* : two *chronoi*). Aristoxenus claims as well that every foot is divisible into two parts: the 'strong' part is called *up*, and the weak part is called *down*.[29] This dichotomy allows even the most complex rhythmic patterns to be represented schematically as a series of binary up–down alternations.

At this point it may be evident just how far Aristoxenian rhythmic theory goes in making time predictable. 'Up–down' creates a level of abstraction at which *all* feet are the same; and even feet are highly abstract, stabilizing entities. According to Martin West, none of the major musical forms before the fifth century BCE were arranged according to feet: the Indo-European heritage underlying Greek rhythmic material, as well as all of the oldest Greek material, organized expression by *period*, larger units originally determined only by syllable count and later marked by identifiable cadences at beginning and end.[30] Strophic song (associated especially with the Lesbian tradition) and Doric choral music (in Sparta and, later, throughout the Greek world) alike were structured by cola or 'limbs' considerably longer than metrical feet: even the epic 'hexameter' is in fact 'better regarded as consisting of two cola divided by the medial caesura. The cola [...] occur independently in other meters [...] Many of the repeated phrases of epic are designed to fill one or other colon.'[31] Rhythmic analysis based on the classification of feet breaks these larger units into much smaller forms, defined not by their relationship to the natural movement of speech but by means of a quantification of their internal structure – a double abstraction, since the feet are abstractions of verse-forms, and the ratios are abstractions of feet.

Nor is the link between temporal quantity and rhythmic analysis obvious. As Devine and Stephen put it in *The Prosody of Greek Speech* (1994):

> It is clear that the poet and his audience do not assess metricality on the basis of the actual durations they hear in each utterance, for the relatively trivial reason that every utterance, like every snowflake, is in fact unique. [...] The categories of language to which meter is sensitive must clearly be more general and more abstract than the precisely quantified phonetic measurements of nonce utterances, if meter is to be able to function as a system shared by an entire speech community.[32]

Metrical structure is an ideality not identifiable with typical speech events; feet come into being when speech rhythm is broken down into units distinct from prosodic structure and understood according to a highly abstract schema in which 'long' syllables have twice the value of 'short' ones. The quantitative nature of Greek meter, in other words, depends on the abstraction and stabilization of ever-fluctuating events.

Aristoxenus supplemented abstraction with regulation: not all possible feet were rhythmic. Specifically, he claimed that whether a foot is rhythmic or not depends on the nature of the relationship between the 'up' and the 'down'. Only the following relationships count:

1. The two parts of a foot must be commensurate. This means that they must both be measurable in terms of a common temporal unit (otherwise they are *irrational* and not rhythmic).[33]
2. Iambic genera of feet are divided into a ratio of 2:1.
3. Dactylic genera of feet are divided into 2:2 or 3:1 or 1:3. 1:3 and 3:1 are not rhythmic.
4. Paeonic genera of feet are divided into 4:1, 1:4, 3:2 or 2:3. 4:1 and its reciprocal are not rhythmic.[34]

One passage seems to describe irrational feet as non-rhythmic because they have an *unknowable* relationship between the parts.[35] In a similar mode, Aristoxenus claims that non-rhythmic arrangements of *chronoi* are 'foreign to perception'. This might be an extension of Aristotle's assertion that matter without form is unknowable; but arrangements of times that are 'non rhythmic' are not really unknowable or unperceivable, since Aristoxenus himself is able to identify them. What he must mean here, rather, is something akin to what he claims in the harmonic writings: non-rhythmic organizations are those that the trained perception cannot recognize as containing rhythm.

I have delved, however inadequately, into Aristoxenus' theory of rhythm in order to make it clear that although it acknowledges that time is the basic building block of rhythm, and that rhythm works with temporal materials, the end result binds this temporality, sectioning temporal expression into units of analysis, abstracting from all possible forms of foot to a single, binary form, and articulating the constraints on rhythmic expression as a set of ratios. We have yet to find an indication that Aristoxenus thought that time was the meaning of music; in fact it is beginning to appear as though the opposite might be the case.

II

One might also look for a sense that music discloses temporality in the analysis of 'tunes', since the constant and ever-changing unfolding of tones in a tune could be read as a symbol of time.[36] The evidence for theories of tune in antiquity is extremely scarce and difficult, and its connection to Aristoxenus is debatable. Nonetheless the result is the same: in what analyses of tunes have survived I believe we again find a tendency to bind time, to work from the occurrent nature of musical expression towards an analytical perspective which transforms what could have been an infinite variety of melodic forms into a very small set of ever-repeating structures.

I am thinking, here, of discussions in which forms of melodic movement are classified. Authors working later than Aristoxenus, but usually synthesizing earlier lore or theoretical material, treat this material under the heading of *'melopoeia'* or 'songwriting', a subject Aristoxenus included as the seventh part of harmonics[37] and wrote four books about,[38] though neither those books nor the relevant writings from his harmonic work have survived in direct form. Cleonides, the author of a pedagogical handbook on harmonics which is broadly Aristoxenian in orientation, offers a list of 'the things through which *melopoeia* is accomplished':

> *Agōgē, plokē, petteia, tonē. Agōgē* is the route of song through the notes in order, *plokē* is placing alternating intervals next to each other, *petteia* is striking the same note many times, and *tonē* is a single note producing a single vocalization over a long time.[39]

Here we have four broad characterizations which could well be described as 'melodic forms': stepwise motion (*agōgē*), intervallic motion (*plokē*), repetition of a single note (*petteia*) and the singing of a single note for more than one time-unit (*tonē*). This could be treated as a complete catalogue of the forms of motion one might find in a composed piece of music.

A second discussion of *melopoeia* shares some of Cleonides' terminology. This occurs in the twelfth chapter of a large second-century CE work by Aristides Quintilianus, who synthesizes a vast amount of earlier material in the service of his own original theory. Aristides treats *melopoeia* as the seventh part of harmonics in a division which is taken straight out of Aristoxenus.[40] He divides *melopoeia* into *lēpsis* ('choice'), in which a selection of ranges is made (Aristides says there are three ranges in which a piece can be set: *nētoeidēs* (high), *mesoeidēs* (medium) or *hupatoeidēs* (low));[41] *mixis* ('mixture'), in which modes, genera and ranges are mixed or combined; and *chrēsis* ('use'), which is a use of the previously named materials and 'a kind of working out of the melodic expression' (*melōidias apergasia*).[42] It is here that Cleonides' terms appear.

> [The working out of the melody] has three forms: *agōgē, petteia, plokē*. There are three forms of *agōgē*: straight, bending back, and circular. 'Straight' is making a upward sequence through the notes in order; 'Bending back' is returning to the lowest note; 'circular' is going up through the conjunct tetrachord and returning through the disjunct (or vice versa) – it is theorized as part of modulation. *Plokē* is extending a single tone through two or more passed over intervals or notes (whether one starts from the lower of the higher of these), and it works out the song. *Petteia* is how we recognize which of the notes are to be avoided and which chosen and how many for each, and from where we should begin and where we should end. It establishes the *ēthos*. *Melopoeia* is different from melody [*melōidia*]: the latter is the articulation of a song, while the former is a productive capacity.[43]

At a first glance much here seems parallel to the briefer notice in Cleonides. Both emphasize use. Both define *agōgē* in very similar ways: Cleonides' definition, as what we would call 'stepwise' motion, might be said to be fleshed out in Aristides, who distinguishes between rising or falling stepwise motion, rising *and* falling stepwise motion, and motion which rises (or falls) through the disjunct or conjunct tetrachord and returns through the other. Similarly Cleonides describes *plokē* as setting intervals next to each other, while Aristides says it involves intervallic motion, in which the voice does not proceed stepwise but rather by making 'jumps' or 'leaps'. Thus far the two authors appear to agree.

But in the case of *petteia*, they seem to be describing different kinds of things.[44] In Cleonides the word appears to describe playing (striking) the same note many times. This seems like the description of a melodic form, albeit a minimal one. One can imagine listening to a performance, or reading a score, or even planning out a composition, and, when one hears or reads or envisages a sequence of the same note being struck repeatedly, designating that '*petteia*'. In Aristides, on the other hand, we are told that it involves selecting what notes to avoid, specifying which notes to return to frequently, where to start and where to end. To this Aristides adds the claim that it is from *petteia* especially that *ēthos* is derived.

If we were to evaluate definitions for the quality of their metaphors (and there is no *prima facie* reason why we *should* do so), Aristides' discussion would come out on top. *Petteia* was the name for a game in which stones were dropped or placed on a playing surface, and it was connected to the idea of distribution.[45] Aristides' treatment of the word in music can be connected to these ideas: here it designates a set of decisions about which notes to prefer and which to avoid. Now, as it happens, Aristides' concept, though not the word, can securely be associated with Aristoxenus: in a passage quoted in the pseudo-Plutarchean *De Musica*, Aristoxenus attributed the origin of the enharmonic genus to Olympus, who one day began playing in such a way as to frequently return to the diatonic *parhupatē*, leaving out *lichanos*. He liked the *ēthos* this produced, and made it the basis of the spondeion-scale: that, in time, was supplemented with a new note below the diatonic *lichanos* and became the enharmonic proper (see Fig. 15).

> But Olympus, as Aristoxenus says, is understood by musicians to have been the inventor of the enharmonic genus. For everything before him was either diatonic or chromatic. And they think the invention happened like this: Olympus was noodling about in the diatonic, and he was bringing the song often back to the diatonic *parhupatē*, sometimes from *paramesē*, sometimes from *mesē*, and skipping the diatonic *lichanos*. He recognized the beauty of the character [*ēthos*] produced, and marveling and accepting the system of notes created by analogy with this, he created using [this system] in the Dorian [*tonos*, i.e. key or range; he does not mean 'scale species' here]. For he had not touched on things specific to the diatonic, nor to things specific to the chromatic, but already on things specific to the enharmonic.[46]

Aristides' notion of *petteia* seems to be describing the same thing. Olympus is said to prefer certain notes, to frequently return to the diatonic *parhupatē*, and to leave out *lichanos*; this selection and preferment produces an *ēthos* which Olympus likes. He then systematizes this into a new kind of tuning. The word *petteia* is never used, but I would bet that Aristides' discussion – including the word – is connected to this story somehow and is probably therefore Aristoxenian in origin.

It might just be possible to explain the confusion in Cleonides as well: both Aristides' definition and the story told by Aristoxenus involve selecting notes

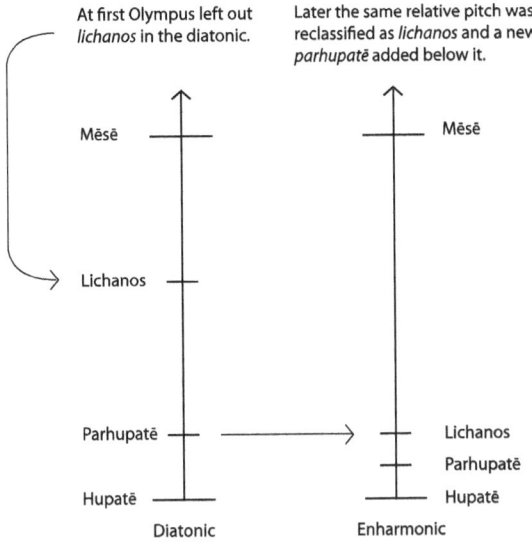

Figure 15 How the enharmonic tuning was made.

and choosing which notes to return to frequently. In Aristoxenus' tale, Olympus returns often to diatonic *parhupatē*: if this return was accomplished with sufficient frequency, the result could well appear to be a single repeated note with melodic departures and returns to it. That repeated note would in effect become a modal 'tone-centre'. Could Cleonides simply be reporting the result of Aristides' definition, that is, what appears to be a single, repeated note, perhaps now erroneously re-interpreted as a 'melodic form?'

Agōgē, the final word shared by Cleonides and Aristides, appears in the extant fragments of both the *Elements of Harmonics* and Aristoxenus' work on rhythm. In his work on rhythm it is the term for the absolute sizes of different feet of the same genus (two feet with the same ratio of 2:1 may have different *agōgai*).[47] In the harmonic writings, Aristoxenus sometimes uses it in this sense, and sometimes in a sense that has to do with pitches, not times. In Book Two, for example, he insists that the study of continuity (which I have discussed earlier) must not be conducted in the manner of those who divide the octave into many micro-intervals; such an approach seems to 'belittle the *agōgē* of song'.[48] Aristoxenus is not talking about what we would call tune. He is simply referring to the constraints that beset a voice singing in a musical manner, above all the fact that one cannot not complete a fourth in four steps, or a fifth in five. We have seen in Chapter 4 what the implications of this are. Here we may observe simply that the *agōgē* of song is little more than the notes of a song expressed as a scalar sequence. Indeed, the very end of *Elementa Harmonica* I, just before the text breaks off, announces – as a kind of axiom – 'let *agōgē* be the movement of the voice through continuous notes on either side of which (except for the ones at the limits) there is an incomposite interval; and let it be straight (*eutheia*) which goes in a single direction'.[49] This seems to be the beginning of the definition set out by Aristides.[50] Again it is not the description of melodic contour, but a simple definition of scalar movement, useful primarily for the representation and analysis of tunings.

A somewhat garbled collection of short essays, known today as the *Anonyma Bellermaniana de musica scripta* (Anon. Bell., for short) discusses *agōgē* separately from 'melopoeia'.

> *Agōgē* is a continuous path from the lower notes up, or a movement of notes from a lower one to a higher, and *analusis* is the opposite. One must sing (*melōidein*) *agōgai* and *analuseis* stretching them out, and not shortening the notes; for resting on them and vocalizing them in a more extended way delights more precise judgment by the ear.[51]

The comment that one should sing *agōgē* and *analysis* slowly suggests that these are practical instructions for how to articulate tunings during a practice session, or when one is playing for a teacher or a judge.[52] Here again, though, *agōgē* refers to a scalar expression of the basic tuning and little more. I doubt the word's original contexts had anything to do with what we call 'tune'.

Under the heading of *melopoeia*, two of the essays in the *Anon. Bell.* also contain a considerably more expanded list of potential melodic forms. This list appears to combine melodic and rhythmic shapes, distinguishing, for example, between '*eklēpsis*' and '*enkrousis*' in that the latter takes place in half the time of the former.[53] The Bellerman texts conclude with a series of exercises, perhaps for aulos,[54] and the whole may have been intended for performers learning not to theorize but actually to perform. As a modern musician learns a scale by playing it in ascending or descending order, then by thirds, then in ascending arpeggios (etc.), so may these ancient figures be understood as components of practice, or even as clichés recognizable to a knowledgeable audience.[55] The existence of a system such as this one, with *melopoeia* being used to describe performative patterns rather than compositional parameters (as Aristides, Cleonides and Aristoxenus use it), could be the provocation for Aristides' statement that '*Melopoeia* is different from melody: the latter is the articulation of a song, while the former is a productive capacity'.[56] Someone was using the word *melopoeia* in a manner that did not fit with the Aristoxenian architectonic. That tradition might be reflected, albeit very hazily, in the catalogue of melodic patterns preserved by the *Anon. Bell.*

I have gone into these passages at some length (though I have certainly not addressed all the issues they raise) because they might be taken as candidates for places where the temporality of melody is addressed. But my conclusion is negative. If we are looking for an approach that attends to the ever-changing flow of a song, the irreducible residuum of change in any performance, this is not it. To the contrary: here all is reduced to a small set of elementary forms. In a manner not unlike what we saw in the case of Aristoxenus' rhythmic theory, time has been 'solved', contingency reduced almost out of existence.

III

The tendency I have traced so far is as follows: a complex variety of events, inevitably occurring in time, is transformed into a set of rules which makes music's expression law-abiding and predictable. This is what *theory* does. In Chapter 4 I argued that there is an important difference between theory and the 'musically acculturated ear' in Aristoxenus' approach, and perhaps it is the case that non-theoretical listening recognized time more robustly. In fact, however, time is also bound in non-theoretical experience, at least as this appears to be detailed in Aristoxenus. What the musically acculturated ear experiences is not a tune but a feeling or flavour which he calls *ēthos*.[57] Consider his description of how the ear recognizes the difference between enharmonic and chromatic tunings, a passage I discussed earlier. Musical perception, he says, is not based on 'the equal and the unequal', that is, on the exact measurement of intervals; it relies, to the contrary, on 'the like and the unlike', that is, on the perception of classes according to similarity or family resemblance. These classes are recognized by their *ēthos*:

> [The imagination (*phantasia*)] calls one tuning 'chroma' and another 'harmony' after considering its similarity to a single form, not the size of

single intervals. I say it posits the form of a *puknon* whenever the two smaller intervals are less than the one above them – for in all *pukna* there is the sound of compression, even though they are not all the same – and it posits the form of the chromatic for so long as the chromatic *ēthos* appears.[58]

Here Aristoxenus appears to be saying that perception just feels the difference between genera as a difference in 'character' (*ēthos*). (I suggested in Chapter 4 that a theorist, who can and does measure, can specify that the puknon is identified any time the first two intervals in a tetrachord cover a range smaller than the third, and that chromatic *pukna* are larger than harmonic *pukna*.)[59] It's not especially preposterous to suppose that the ear knows a tuning or a rhythmic composition by its 'character' or 'feeling', without measuring the sizes of intervals, since plenty of people are capable of musical sensitivity without the ear training that allows you to distinguish different intervals. But how, exactly, can such distinctions be made?

Once again, the fragmentary condition of Aristoxenus' corpus fails us. If he answered the question, the answer is lost. Nonetheless I venture a guess at what he might have said. This guess depends on an assumption about the way Aristoxenus' subjects were related to each other: the 'elementary'[60] subjects of harmonics and rhythmics are also highly abstract, treated independently of the complete musical expressions in which they would normally be encountered, and the full understanding of these elementary subjects will have depended ultimately on some kind of a theory of the whole.[61] The *Elements of Harmonics*, though treating an element of music that it calls 'first' and 'elementary',[62] also insists that it is not 'independent' (*autarkēs*) of the other parts of music, 'as some believe'.[63] Almost certainly the other parts of music are rhythm and diction; these, with harmony, make up the characteristic *troika* of musical composition in Aristoxenus. 'Higher' (*anōterō*) subjects[64] are concerned with how harmonic material is used, and they belong to a 'more perfect' embodiment of musical knowledge. What these statements suggest is that musical perception, though it can be studied in analytical abstractions like those produced by harmonics or rhythmics, was in fact meant to be taken as an integrated whole, with the complete meanings even of basic elements like tunings coming into full view only when the complete composition or song is taken into account.

Here we must turn to a series of claims in 'Plutarch's' *De musica*, which either directly cite Aristoxenus or seem to contain ideas similar to his; a few ideas in this run of text not paralleled elsewhere in Aristoxenus would, if they also can be attributed to our author, provide an important gloss on the discussion of *ēthos* we have cited from the *Harmonics*.[65] In this passage the argument is made that the elementary subjects of harmonics or rhythmics are not sufficient to support a rigorous musical criticism. Harmonics can go no farther than the study of genera, intervals, systems, notes, modes and modulations; it is incapable of teaching a person to judge the appropriateness of a modulation.[66] Likewise the study of rhythm.[67] Rather, the 'power of appropriateness' is instrumental in bringing about the appearance of *ēthos*.[68] To really assess *ēthos* and appropriateness, you need to know both the *ēthos* for the sake of which a specific combination of elements is proposed, and the elements themselves (that is tuning, rhythm and expression).[69] The ultimate criterion of criticism is 'the *ēthos* of the expression which the performer wants to take in hand and express; has it been given in a manner appropriate for the traditional composition?'[70] That is: the judge must assess the combination of elements for appropriateness in the context of a known tradition of performance which is, furthermore, presumed to be stable. I will come back to this final point in the next section of this chapter.

Aristoxenus and others were concerned with the role of appropriateness in governing musical composition. Clement of Alexandria records a passage in which Aristoxenus suggests that the enharmonic genus is appropriate to the Dorian, and the diatonic to the Phrygian.[71] A similar question about appropriateness is being asked when 'Plutarch' raises the issue 'whether, as in the *Mysians*, a poet appropriately chose the Hypodorian *tonos* [i.e. key or range] in the opening, or the Mixolydian and the Dorian in the ending, or the Hypophrygian and the Phrygian in the middle'.[72] In a related vein, Aristides claims that there are three styles (*tropoi*) of songwriting: the dithyrambic, the nomic and the tragic,[73] and adds that the styles are associated with specific ranges – 'the nomic style is high, the dithyrambic is middle, and the tragic is low'.[74] Similarly, in the *Harmonics* Aristoxenus says that it is important to study the range of the singing voice because different tonal systems are placed in different places in this range; such placements are governed by a sense of appropriateness and can profoundly affect the song (*melos*).[75]

'Plutarch' offers a glimpse of how the principles of combination and appropriateness could play out in the analysis of a composition and the determination of *ēthos* in a discussion of Olympus' 'nome of Athena':

> We say that the cause of this [i.e. *ēthos*] is synthesis or mixture or both. Like when the enharmonic was placed in the Phrygian key and mixed with the *paiōn epibatos* by Olympus: this produced the *ēthos* of the beginning of the nome of Athena. If the melopoeia and the rhythmopoeia are taken next, but the rhythm alone is artfully changed to bring out the trochaic instead of the paionic, this establishes the enharmonic genus of Olympus. Even when the Phrygian key and the enharmonic genus are retained, and the whole system too [i.e. the genus or the scale-species], [changing the rhythm] produces a great change of *ēthos*. For the so-called 'harmony' in the nome of Athena is quite different in *ēthos* from the opening.[76]

The first section of the piece used the enharmonic tuning (that is, a tetrachord with the sequence of intervals ¼ tone – ¼ tone – 2 tones), pitched in the key (*tonos*) called 'Phrygian', with the *paiōn epibatos* rhythm. In the second movement, which was called the 'harmony', everything stayed the same except the rhythm, which had a more trochaic feel. The result, however, was a total change in the *ēthos*.[77] Intriguingly, 'Plutarch' reports that, even though Olympus set the opening of the nome in the enharmonic genus, when the trochaic rhythm was introduced 'this established the enharmonic' – almost as though the feeling of the tuning was brought out best by the trochaic rhythm and was somehow obscured when the *paiōn epibatos* was used.

This discussion of *ēthos* as a consequence of the *whole* composition helps to explain how the ear perceives *ēthos* without measuring intervals, as we are told in the harmonic works. For when a musically acculturated ear encounters a tuning, it does not encounter it in isolation, at least not normally. Even a musician tuning a lyre does so with a specific song or performance in mind, and it is to that that she adjusts the strings so that the tuning has the feeling the song demands. We recognize a tuning because it fits with the composition; it is to the relations between the parts that our ear actually responds. The ultimate question, as we have seen, is this: to what degree are all the components appropriately combined to produce the feeling associated with the piece? When, as in the *Elements of Harmonics* or the *Elements of Rhythm*, Aristoxenus focusses on a single component, his claims about *ēthos* are correspondingly limited. *Harmonics* Book Two complains about auditors who expect him to lecture on the moral value and political uses of tunings because they have heard him say that he will discuss whether music has consequences for *ēthos* only in the most limited way,[78] while in passages associated with him in 'Plutarch's' *De musica* there are outright denials that harmonics (or rhythmics) can help one judge the *ēthos* of a piece, as we have seen.[79] He needed to make these protestations because his own argument seems to have represented a significant divergence from other theories. In the next paragraph, we will see Aristoxenus attempting to finesse the findings of Plato's *Republic*, where there seems to be a tight relationship posited between tunings and characters; similar ideas were expressed by Aristotle at the end of the *Politics*.[80] Heraclides Ponticus, too, appears to have asserted that there were only three original modes (the Dorian, the Aeolian and the Ionian), and that these modes reflected the moral nature of the *ethnoi* who used them. This is a variant of *ēthos* theory that again focusses on tunings.[81] For Aristoxenus, in contrast, *ēthos* corresponds to the 'total impact' of a piece; it is his name for the feeling generated by a successfully, that is appropriately, composed whole.

Aristoxenus may have used his own theory of *ēthos* to interpret Plato. The *Republic* associated musical *ēthos* with specific tunings; the Dorian was a manly and courageous mode, while the Phrygian reflected a noble but peaceful character.[82] Aristoxenus seems to have had comments to make.

> Of these tunings there is one that is lamentatory, and one that is relaxing. Plato appropriately blamed these and chose the Dorian as well-fitted to warlike and prudent men. He wasn't at all unaware, as Aristoxenus says in the second of his books on music, that there was something that was useful for the protection of the state even in them: Plato had studied musical knowledge deeply, since he was a student of the Athenian Draco and Megillus the Acragantine. He honored the Dorian above the others because it was very august, as I said before. He wasn't unaware that many Dorian *partheneia* had been made by Alcman, Pindar, Simonides and Bacchylides, and also *Prosodia* and *Paians*, and even that tragic lamentations had been sung in the Dorian mode, not to mention some erotic pieces. Songs to Ares and Athena and *Spondeia* were enough for him: these are sufficient to fortify the soul of a prudent man. Nor was he ignorant about the Lydian or the Iastian, for he knew that tragedy used that *melopoeia*.[83]

Numerous difficulties present themselves in this passage.[84] It's unclear what Aristoxenus said and what 'Plutarch' is saying: it could be that Aristoxenus said Plato *was* ignorant of all that followed (in which case 'Plutarch' would be expressing a disagreement with him), or that Aristoxenus said he *wasn't* ignorant of these things (then 'Plutarch' would be agreeing with him). Ultimately it's impossible to be sure, but 'Plutarch' nowhere else disagrees with Aristoxenus; he simply uses his material, sometimes very close to *verbatim*.[85] It's unclear, too, on whose authority it is said that Plato thought the only music he needed was the nome of Ares, the nome of Athena, and spondeia – or why, given the criticisms of aulos music in the *Republic* and of instrumental music in the *Laws*,[86] he is now said to be happy with pieces we think were composed for solo aulos.

I think the easiest reading of this passage is to take Aristoxenus as defending Plato against the charge of ignorance; Plato knew full well that the Dorian was used in maiden-songs, and so forth. But Aristoxenus did disagree that scalar structures could be said to have concrete moral characters. Instead he believed that *ēthos* came from the total composition. How could his defence of Plato in our passage be squared with this significant disagreement? Perhaps the fact that he attributed to Plato a preference for the nomes of Ares and Athena, as well as for spondeia: these might have used the tunings the *Republic* stated a preference for.[87] Socrates' discussions of these tunings were merely abstractions from the compositions (so, I think, Aristoxenus might have been implying). This possibility is further supported by the sequence of ideas a little earlier in the text, where the *Republic*'s strictures are mentioned again. Here 'Plutarch' cites Plato's rejection of the Lydian mode as too lamentatory: he then immediately cites Aristoxenus' *On Music* to the effect that Olympus was the first to use the Lydian when he played the lament for the Python.[88] 'Plutarch' found this claim in the first book of Aristoxenus' *On Music*, the second book of which contained the remarks on Plato I have been discussing. Could Aristoxenus have been arguing that Plato's rejection of the Lydian as lamentatory was actually based on that section of the Pythian nome? If I'm right, Aristoxenus' point was that it wasn't the Dorian or the Phrygian that were solemn or relaxed, but rather the pieces in which these tunings were used. Plato, Aristoxenus could well have been saying, simply took the part (the tuning) and gave it the characteristics of the whole.

Such a theory could be taken as binding time in that it replaces flux with constrained change. *Ēthos* is not a sense of musical flow but a single, solid-state affective condition. The discussion of *ēthos* which I have been following concludes with a methodological passage in which time is a central topic of concern. Since the correct evaluation of a song's *ēthos* depends on being able to assess the interactions between harmony, rhythm and language,

> it is necessary for perception and thought to run along together [sc. with the music] in the judgment of the parts of music, and perception must not take the lead (as is done by overly quick faculties of perception and those which get carried away) nor follow behind, which happens to slow and hard-to-move faculties of perception. It sometimes happens in some that perception both runs ahead *and* falls behind, because of some anomalous nature. But these things must be attempted if the perception is going to run along [with the musical performance].[89]

Because Aristoxenus (or his paraphraser) uses the verb *homodromein*, 'run along', to describe the action of perception and intellect, he has been interpreted as acknowledging that music 'unfolds in time'.[90] No actual expression of music can occur otherwise than as a temporal sequence. It's therefore methodologically exigent that a theorist be able to follow along, both hearing and thinking in sync with the musical expression. Theory's results, however, are quite different from its preliminary method. Though the musical expression is in time, the next paragraph makes it clear that the precise synchronization of perception and intellect facilitates a process of abstraction in which the critical listener experiences the performance as something more than temporal movement.

> It is always necessary that these basic things fall upon the ear together, I mean pitch and time and the syllable or letter. It comes about that we recognize the harmony from the movement of the notes, and the rhythm from that of the time, and the thing said from that of the syllable or letter. Since they go forward together, it is necessary to follow along with the perception. But this is also clear: if the ear cannot distinguish each of the elements I have named, it will not be able to follow each of them along and to see as a unity (*sunoran*) what has been done in error in each case and what not.[91]

The key sentence here is the one in which Aristoxenus asserts that harmony, rhythm and *lexis* are *known from* the movement of notes, time and syllables.

He does not say that they are identical with these temporal unfoldings but rather that the object of judgment can be derived from them, which is to say that it is other than they are, though it has expression within them. One must be able to 'take in at a glance' or 'see as a unity' what has been done well, and what not, in harmony, rhythm and diction and in their combination. Temporal attention, in other words, leads to cognition of the harmonic, rhythmic and linguistic systems that underlie or constrain temporal 'unfolding'; this is done in the service of discerning the *ēthos* of a piece. We are back to describing the requirements for successful theory here, but theory's work, ultimately, is to assess the elements contributing to what is experienced as musical not by theory but by the musically acculturated ear (as had also been the case in the *Harmonics*). Here, in order to know whether a piece has succeeded, that is, whether it 'feels right' to an experienced audience, one must, as it were, extract from the temporal flow a sense of its elements and their combinations; only this will allow one to assess the single thing (still temporal, but trivially so) that is musical *ēthos*.

IV

Ēthos also played a role in Aristoxenus' approach to musical history.[92] Consider the following, a discussion of the location of *lichanos* in the enharmonic tuning:

> That there is a way of composing which requires *lichanos* at the ditone, and that this is not the most insignificant but actually the most beautiful of compositional styles is not at all clear to many of those who now apply themselves to music, though it would be if they were exposed to it. But to those who are accustomed (*suneithismenois*) to the first and the second of the ancient styles what I have said is sufficiently clear.[93] For those who are used (*sunētheis*) only to the currently prevailing style of composition quite reasonably rule out the ditone *lichanos*: almost everybody currently playing uses sharper *lichanoi*. The reason for this is that they always want to be sweet (*glukainein*), and the sign that this is true is that they are always aiming for it; for they spend nearly all their time working in the chromatic, and whenever they come to the enharmonic they lead it closer to the chromatic and they destroy its *ēthos*.[94]

The passage is built around a *schema etymologicum*, a pun that is more than a pun: the reason there is debate about the location of *lichanos* in the enharmonic, and the reason the enharmonic's characteristic *ēthos* has been destroyed, is that many musicians are accustomed (*sunētheis*) only to a contemporary style of composition in which chromatic tunings are characteristically favoured. (Pseudo-Plutarch says the chromatic was originally avoided in tragedy;[95] the real Plutarch says it was introduced in that genre by Agathon.)[96] Those who have been acculturated (*suneithismenoi*) to the 'old' styles of music are used to the sound of *lichanos* at the ditone and have no difficulty with it. The 'character' of a tuning is connected, here, to the culture of the hearer. I think this is important: just as harmonics was to be grounded in the experienced musical ear, so is the study of historical tunings connected to the nature of that experience. You discern and appreciate the *ēthē* you're used to; musical character and musical culture literally have the same root.[97]

Aristoxenus is referring to contemporary musicians and their audiences here; the loss of memory of the older styles with their slightly lower *lichanos* is clearly in contrast to his own knowledge of such tunings. The theorist, in fact, may have a wider acculturation than many practicing musicians, since he is expected to know about multiple styles and their attendant tunings. In a crucial methodological section (which I discussed at the end of Chapter 4) Aristoxenus claims that in order to pursue harmonic theory one must train both one's mind (so that one can theorize about *dunameis*) and one's perception (*aisthēsis*). There he uses the same verb, *ethizō*, as he does in this passage on the ditone *lichanos*, to refer both to the training of perception and of thought.[98] But Aristoxenus claims to have more than just a highly experienced ear. Thanks to his cultivation of thought as well, he will be able to describe and judge what musicians do and audiences enjoy. In a passage in 'Plutarch's' *De Musica*, probably of Aristoxenian provenance, it is said that 'all learning about music that doesn't take into account the purpose (*to tinos heneka*)' of the elements of music is 'acculturation', *ethismos*.[99] Nothing wrong with *ethismos*, of course; everyone needs it, including the theorist. But without the additional ability to reason about ends and uses, one is not in a position to evaluate what one hears.

There appears to be a strong association in Aristoxenus between beauty and the strict enharmonic with *lichanos* at the ditone.[100] If contemporary musicians are always trying to make things 'sweet', the old music with the low lichanos had a beautiful *ēthos*: in the story about Olympus' discovery of this tuning it is exactly this beauty that attracts him to it (see earlier). Aristoxenus claims that in inventing the spondeion scale and linking it to the Dorian, Olympus initiated 'Greek and beautiful music'.[101] Elsewhere in 'Plutarch' someone – I think it's Aristoxenus – says that archaic rhythmic innovations always stayed within the ambitus of the beautiful mode of expression. Change does take place, but it is highly limited, constrained by the demands of the *ēthos*. Terpander, we are told, innovated by introducing 'a certain beautiful style' (*kalon tina tropon eis tēn mousikēn eisēgage*).[102] Polymnestus innovated after him, and likewise Thaletas and Saccadas: but all of them maintained (*echomenos*) and did not stray from (*ouk ekbainontes*) the 'beautiful type' (*tou kalou tupou*). Is his use of 'beauty' to be taken absolutely (so that the 'most beautiful' style is simply the best, and all others would just be uglier, worse, ideally avoided), or socially (so the 'most beautiful' was the best for its immediate audience), or is it meant in a strictly musical-immanent sense, where beauty would have a technical meaning and might be associated with one style of singing among others? Barker argues that it is impossible to say 'beautiful' without implying a hierarchy of values at which it is at the top: the word, he thinks, is inherently teleological and moral in implication.[103] That is of course impossible to gainsay – so long as beauty is being used in a realm governed by moral philosophy. But the general trajectory of Aristoxenus' work is to establish a coherent and closed discourse in which judgments are regulated by musically immanent considerations. There is no compelling reason to think that in his discussions of musical traditions a similar attempt at autonomous theory did not prevail.[104]

Aristoxenus has a reputation for being a musical conservative, a fan of the old styles and highly critical of tragedy and the so-called 'new' music.[105] In an anecdote reported in Themistius, when someone asked Aristoxenus what would happen if he dedicated himself to the 'ancient style', he replied 'you will sing less frequently in the theatres, for it is not possible to please everyone and be faithful to the past'.[106] We have already discussed Aristoxenus' claim that the enharmonic with *lichanos* at the ditone was the best tuning, but that it had fallen out of use because of a preference for chromatic sounds. A similar complaint, attributed by Barker to Aristoxenus,[107] claims that people go so far as to deny that they can even *hear* the enharmonic diesis (more or less a quarter-tone), and that since it can't be achieved using a rational tuning method it isn't musical. The passage has harsh criticisms of these musicians, whoever they are, who abandoned the 'most beautiful of the genera'.[108] Aristoxenus also appears to have compared the history of music to the barbarization of certain old Greek colonies:

> Aristoxenus, in the *Mixed Sympotics*, says: 'We have done the same as the Poseidonians who live in the Tyrsenian gulf. It happened to them to barbarize and become Tyrsenian after having been Greek, and they changed their language and the rest of their ways of life, but they still practise a single one of the Greek festivals, in which they come together and remember their old names and laws, and then after mourning together and lamenting, they break up and go back to their homes. Things are similar with us, he says: the old music has barbarized in the theatres and descended into great disrepair, and few of us still remember what it was like'.[109]

I don't doubt that Aristoxenus did underscore the difference between the 'old' music and theatre music, especially tragedy, but I would like to place heavier emphasis on the evidence suggesting that beneath or beside his criticism there was a systematic description of even more recent musical styles.[110] In fact I think that Aristoxenus' treatment of music history may have been akin to his treatment of musical expression: he saw it as a series of different articulations constrained by a stable system rooted in acculturated perception. Just as, according to Berger, melodic development as a progressive temporal unfolding is linked to the enlightenment view of history as progress, so, in Aristoxenus, is the absence of significant temporality in song linked to a view of history as mostly stable. 'Old' music and 'theatre' music were distinct musical styles, each with its own ethical aura, so to speak, and its own relatively stable historical development. When Aristoxenus claimed that theatre music had led people to forget what music used to be like and amounted to a barbarianization that destroyed whatever was 'Greek' in what came before, we have every reason to believe that he meant what he said. He could well have disliked tragedy, even thought it was 'worse' than older music; but his analysis of music history nonetheless treated both theatre music and 'old' music seriously, as distinct and even incommensurable styles, defined by their own communities of affect and embodied in their own sets of compositional constraints.

'Plutarch' tells us that Aristoxenus investigated the *ēthos* of tragic music:

> The Mixolydian is associated with suffering and well fitted to tragedy. Aristoxenus says that Sappho first discovered (*heurasthai*) it, and the tragic

poets (*tragōiopoioi*) learned it from her – but after they appropriated it they yoked it to the Dorian, since that gives off grandeur and worthiness, while the other gives off suffering, and tragedy is mixed out of these two.[111]

Tragedy has long been associated with complex affect: Gorgias' *Encomium of Helen* attributed to poetry the capacity to cause 'a fearful shudder, tearful pity, and a pain-loving desire'.[112] The last affect in Gorgias' triad is especially interesting: it names a feeling long associated with musical responses (think of the desire Apollo feels when he hears Hermes playing a lyre for the first time, or of Odysseus' response to the Sirens' song),[113] but qualifies that with an adjective that is distinctly paradoxical – 'pain-loving'. Such a complex, almost contradictory affect – to long for grief – could well be a description of the unusual joy of tragedy, a joy that arises from the spectacle of terrible suffering. Aristotle discerned similar affective contents – and con*flicts*: Tragedy brings about pity and fear (and thus purges them). What we find in Aristoxenus seems to be the application of similar ideas within his own framework: the combination of two distinct musical forms produces the characteristic feeling of tragedy, which would constitute an entirely different melopoietic realm: ethnically impure, as it were, and ethically or affectively diverse as well. It would be incommensurable with the 'beautiful' 'Greek' style represented by Olympus' nomes.

If Aristoxenus thought a single figure was responsible for the transition from the 'beautiful and Greek' style of *melopoeia* to the 'new' and 'theatrical' style, it could well be Lasus of Hermione. Lasus, a composer and theorist who came to Athens and composed dithyramb there in the late sixth century, around the time the Greater Dionysia was consolidated as a major musical festival, is described by 'Plutarch' as follows.

> Lasus of Hermione changed the rhythms into the dithyrambic *agōgē*, and he imitated the polyphony of the *auloi*, using more and widely scattered notes. Doing so, he brought the pre-existing music to a changed state (*eis metathesin tēn prouparchousan ēgage mousikēn*).[114]

This isn't obviously Aristoxenus, but it relates a historical detail that may have been of some interest to our author (and some of the language is enticing, as we will see later). Elsewhere in 'Plutarch' we are told that the difference between the old musical style (from Olympus to Stesichorus) and the newer ones amounted to a difference between the taste for rhythmic complexity (old) and the taste for harmonic complexity (new).[115] Lasus' innovations clearly implied an increase in harmonic complexity. 'Plutarch''s claim that he led the previously existing music into a transformation could mean that he, like Olympus, had developed a new musical style and *ēthos*.

Because musical styles are cultures, even cognitive habits – they are the product of 'growing accustomed' which makes one able to experience certain *ēthē* – one is, in a way, a prisoner of one's upbringing. (Aristoxenus would not say 'prisoner': he did not see it as a bad thing.) Consider the story of Telesias, who according to 'Plutarch' tried late in life to take up a new style of composition:

> That correction or destruction comes from your way of life and your studies (*para tas agōgas kai tas mathēseis*) was made clear by Aristoxenus. For he says that among those of his own age it happened that Telesias of Thebes was raised, when he was young, in the most beautiful music, and he learned the songs of the best-reputed, including those of Pindar and Dionysius of Thebes and Lampros and Pratinas, and of the rest as many as were poets good at the lyric sound [*kroumatoi*]. He also played the lyre well, and he worked hard and was up to scratch in the other parts of music. But when he had gone past the prime of his life he was so badly deceived by complicated and theatrical music that he looked down on those beautiful ones on whom he had been raised, and he memorized the songs of Philoxenus and Timotheus, and of these the most elaborate and the ones that had the most novelty in them; but when he wanted to make songs, and he tried both styles, that of Pindar and that of Philoxenus, he couldn't get it right in the Philoxenian style; the cause was his most beautiful way of life from childhood.[116]

This story does not say that Telesias could not compose in Philoxenus' style because it was bad (though it does imply that this style *is* bad). It says that he could not compose in this style because he was deeply practised in *another one*: his training provided him with what Barker called 'aesthetic instincts' that were fundamentally different from those of Philoxenus and Timotheus.[117] There is a curious pun at work at the beginning of this passage: the 'correction or destruction of music' comes about from *agōgē*, a word which can mean both 'way of life' and 'the scalar articulation of a harmonic system' (see earlier). In effect, what is implied by the pun (if you choose to hear it) is that tuning and way of life are intimately connected. The qualification that matters here is education – what one studies as a young musician determines how one plays, and also, via the synonymy of *agōgē*, how one is.[118] The emphasis is not on 'environmental' or cultural *paideia*, but on the deliberate acquisition of musical intuitions through training. Such a thesis would have been no great stretch for a former student of Aristotle. According to Aristotle, the productive capacity of an artist was a form installed in her/his soul through repetitive exposure to certain perceptions: these perceptions were compiled by memory and eventually transformed into 'experience' or 'art'.[119] Telesias was too experienced in one style to work in another.

There is a story which suggests that Aristoxenus agreed with Aristotle on the importance of repeated exposure to one's musical and affective disposition. The tale concerns a man who was so afraid of the war-trumpet or salpinx that he fell into a panic whenever he heard the instrument. This was particularly inconvenient because one usually heard the salpinx when it was played in a hoplite division; soldiers who panic at a sound meant to encourage and co-ordinate them are not likely to find many friends. Aristoxenus cured the man, we are told, by 'introducing him to the aulos bit by bit, and made him able to tolerate even the salpinx by means of this introduction'.[120] Although this is presented as part of a discussion of the medical use of music,[121] it is better treated as an example of how habituation or repetitive exposure can induce knowledge and culturally appropriate behaviour. Aristoxenus trained the man to be able to sustain the sound of the salpinx by inoculating him to the sound of a substitute; the aulos.[122] Such stories are best treated with scepticism as to their historical veracity in the strictest sense: it was a common ancient practice to wrap interpretations in fabricated narratives for illustrative purposes. But in emphasizing the role of acculturation in the formation (or in this case the reformation) of hearing, the tale seems to me to communicate an important insight into Aristoxenus' approach.

I think the material gathered in this chapter suggests that Aristoxenus characterized music history as constrained change within relatively stable aesthetic and affective traditions. New styles did emerge, but these were treated as stable systems, which came to exist alongside older ones. 'Plutarch's' language in his description of Lasus' innovation is that he 'led music into a change' (*eis metathesin ēgage*). When Olympus invented the 'beautiful and Greek manner', he is said by 'Plutarch' to have 'augmented music by leading in [*tōi eisagagein*] something which had not been created or known by those before him'.[123] Note the repetition of forms of *agō*, and the repeated idea that innovation brings music into different conditions or places. Should we connect this language with the pun on *agōgē* in the tale of Telesias? Musics would be distinguished by their tunings and tempos (*agōgai*) and the training and lifestyle (*agōgē*) of their makers, the most creative of whom actually led music into new forms or introduced new tonal materials to it (*eisēgagon*, in both cases). Metaphorically, the idea of 'leading in' or introducing a new music evokes the idea that different musics occur within or are associated with different musical spaces, a metaphor which has analogues in other metaphors associated with Aristoxenus' comparisons of musical styles: recall his observation that a singer who adopted an older style of music would end up not singing in theatres. Though the story is about the tastes of the audience, it figuratively links the genre with its characteristic performance space. Metaphorical or not, such a topographical differentiation of musical styles might indicate a sense in which Aristoxenus' view of musical history could acknowledge the co-existence of mutually incommensurable styles, all perhaps genetically linked but ultimately occupying different cognitive, perceptual and cultural spaces.

This chapter has followed a winding course through topics related to musical time. Beginning with Aristoxenus' methodological claims, then passing in review his treatment of rhythm and the topic (which may not in fact be Aristoxenian) of melodic contour, then turning to his model of *ēthos* and its consequences for musical history, I have argued that Aristoxenus attempted to describe the temporal unfolding of music as law-governed and therefore minimally contingent. Time is 'bound' here, its disruptive or unsettling aspects – those aspects that led the *Timaeus* to link temporality with embodiment and sensation – mitigated to the maximum possible degree. Here again we see a vision of music as highly ordered or even, as Aristoxenus put it in the *Harmonics*, as preeminently ordered among aesthetic phenomena.

Let me conclude Part Two with a speculation, that is, with an attempt to reflect the scattered fragments of Aristoxenus' work as a unity. In performance as in history, musical culture is a collective sharing of affect through the medium of senses trained by both direct instruction and passive habituation. Both recognizing and enjoying musical compositions and the structures which subtend these depend, ultimately, on collective belonging, on the coincidence of performance and reception traditions so that what makes sense to a listener is exactly the sort of thing that a musician is inclined to express. If this image is consistent with the passages from Aristoxenus which have survived, it raises the question again of the role of the theorist. As musical meaning, *ēthos* just works, so long as the piece is appropriately constructed and all the parties to a musical event are adequately acculturated. This would appear to be just as true of musics (such as theatre music) which Aristoxenus disliked as of musics which he liked (such as the archaic nomes of Olympus).

Aristoxenus' consistent concern was to develop a theory of music that was amenable to philosophy. Indeed, after the tale about Telesias which I have just discussed, 'Plutarch' goes on to assert that anyone wanting to 'use music beautifully (*kalōs*) and judiciously (*kekrimenōs*)' should not only study the 'ancient style', but should also 'supplement music with other forms of learning, and establish philosophy as his teacher'; philosophy is able 'to judge what measure is appropriate and useful for music'.[124] Expertise in music – for example knowing how to play and sing, even knowledge of harmonics, rhythm and the art of words – does not qualify one to judge; you need to be able to tell what the music is for.[125] *Ēthos* is a final cause: tunings, rhythms and words are only means to that end.[126] The possibility exists, here, that those without philosophical training, including, one can assume, most working musicians, are incompetent to judge what they do. Indeed, they are liable to make theoretical errors such as focusing only on the enharmonic;[127] or abandoning it completely;[128] or dividing the octave into very small intervals and insisting that all tunings conform to this division;[129] or even altering the size of fourths and fifths.[130] Philosophy can correct and regulate these musical errors.

Note, however, that the kind of mistakes which 'Plutarch' flags here are not compositional or performative. It is nowhere implied that auletes who haven't studied philosophy play badly, just that they theorize incorrectly. It's tempting to ask who these bad theorists are; how did they fit into the social fabric of fourth century BCE music? But from our perspective what matters most is just that they're not philosophers, which here means theorists who recognize the full range of compositional options and evaluate them only in terms of their complete combination in a musical *ēthos*. (Once Aristoxenus claims that none of the earlier theorists have dealt with 'all' music because they were not familiar with all the different tunings in each different genus, and that as a result they had not acculturated (*suneithisthai*) themselves to make all the necessary distinctions.[131] This could amount to claiming that musicians do not theorize well because they only know their own style – a claim comparable, it seems to me, to the tale of Telesias.) The dispute here is over who gets to theorize, not over what music is, how it should be made, or by whom. It's not incompatible with these passages in 'Plutarch' to conclude that Aristoxenus had nothing to correct musicians on except their tendency to try to explain themselves. The explanations, Aristoxenus suggests, should be left to him, or at least to those who practice harmonics as he conceives it.

Indeed, musicians don't really need to philosophize, since composition and performance are determined and constrained by cultural traditions which are actualized through technique but altered only extremely rarely, and only to create new traditions, such as happened with the innovations of Lasus. The autonomy of music as a form of already-forged auditory culture, however, also has a consequence for the philosophy of music, in that it leaves it with nothing to do other than listen and describe. We could remark, as I did at the end of Chapter 4, that in fact theory has often played a crucial role at the heart of musical practice, either as dictating what can or should be played, or as guiding pedagogical practice, or just as a foil to creative energies. Nothing in the Aristoxenian texts suggests this was what he thought his work was for. But if Aristoxenus' approach has no clear application to the regulation of musical practice, it does seem to have some philosophical value: it confirms that there is a form of sensuality which is rule-governed, autonomous and stable, not just in harmonics but in culture as a whole.

That he establishes music as an autonomous perceptual sphere primarily because that is what philosophy wants helps to explain the rather extreme rigidity with which he presents his theory of harmonic construction. Aristoxenus insisted, as we have seen, that a voice moving musically must complete a fourth in four steps or a fifth in five. The consequences are unequivocal: any vocal performance which does not conform to this rule is not musical. Aristoxenus' doctrine of modulation may have allowed for a degree of flexibility in dealing with apparently unmusical tunings (it is lost, and we are once again left grasping at straws), but even that has limits, and it's not difficult to imagine musical styles and practices which would end up on the wrong side of the rule. Similar consequences could have prevailed in the analysis of *ēthos* as well: since the question seems to be 'is the *ēthos* of the expression appropriate to the traditional composition' (1144e), or 'did the composer act appropriately in using different materials at different spots in the composition' (1142f), there is always the possibility for a negative answer; at which point a performance or a composition would effectively be disqualified from the set of 'things that are musical', of no further interest to the theorist other than as examples of musical error. As music exegesis, such an approach leaves much to be desired. But this is not exegesis; it is a philosophy of music, a construction of music for philosophy.

Indeed, I submit that it is a construction of music *as* philosophy, as a locus of exactly the ordered perception Plato's writing seemed aimed at helping to produce. In music Aristoxenus finds what Plato had been looking for: a rule-governed, autonomous region of perception. Treated both as an established fact and as the embodiment of cultural norms, shot through with both a sense of history and of immediate, non-contingent value, implicitly juxtaposing itself with Platonic desiderata and in some sense fulfilling them, Aristoxenus' model of music seems to me to be comparable to the notion of auditory culture as it is understood and lived today.

Conclusion

Taking their cue from the suggestion that the modern study of what has come to be called 'auditory culture' draws one of its sources of inspiration from the philosophy of the ancient world, these pages have sought for signs that Plato and Aristoxenus might articulate a perspective akin to the contemporary study of sound, at least among scholars who are interested in the cultural and technological formation of hearing as a learned practice. I have not made many explicit connections between the ancient and the modern discourses, in large part because the details are very different. What they share is the belief that hearing can be trained or acculturated and therefore deserves to be treated as a cultural artifact, and a model in which meaning – auditory or musical, as the case may be – is constituted by and within an acculturated community. I pointed to Plato's discussions of music as clues to understanding his writing project, which aims, I asserted, at changing readers' orientation to the senses and thus creating a new sensory culture. I then turned to Aristoxenus, where, I suggested, we find a full-blown theory of music as an ordered form of acculturated perception guiding both musical expression and reception that exists in history as a relatively stable affective and expressive tradition.

Readers who have stayed with me this far may have begun to feel dissatisfied with my proposal that Plato and Aristoxenus somehow constitute a single phenomenon. Not only do the two bodies of work demand such radically different approaches, but they seem to present perspectives that are almost the opposite of each other. The largest and most significant difference lies in the fact that Plato's writing grounds its orientation to music and the senses in a theory of being. This is true even when the theory of being changes, as it arguably does between the *Cratylus* and the *Republic*, on the one hand, and the *Timaeus* on the other; music's ability to hurt or harm souls is grounded in some idea of what the senses are and how they are related to the world in which we find ourselves.

Plato's writing evinces a tendency to ground music in some sonic materiality. The most explicit theory of perception to be found in Plato's work (in the *Timaeus*) makes no meaningful distinction between the audible world and the sense of hearing; in this model, both sense and what is sensed are creatures of the world of movement and change, brought into being as the tumultuous consequence of creation. The specific process of hearing described by Timaeus in that dialogue is also, in essence, a process which reinforces the idea that sound and hearing belong to the same sphere. Hearing, to put it simply, is 'becoming-like'. Thus smooth sounds cause the liver, which appears to be the crucial sound–soul interface, to become smooth itself, a process that is pleasurable because things like to be restored to their natural state (according to Plato the liver is naturally smooth). Similarly with music: audible consonances like the fourth and fifth are valuable in the *Timaeus* primarily because they represent a sensible way to teach the soul about the better harmonies of the heavens; the soul gets better by becoming like what it hears (though to be sure its trajectory is eventually beyond the senses). Similar identities are posited in other dialogues: in the *Cratylus* the movement and confusion of appearances leads to movement and confusion in the minds of the name-makers, with the consequence that language itself encodes movement and confusion within it; and in the *Theaetetus* perceptions fail as a basis for knowledge because they are as unstable and unreliable as what flows through them to the soul.

Aristoxenus, on the other hand, vigorously denies the relevance of any such considerations to the theory of music. No reference to the nature of the sonic stimulus is needed, he claims, to make sense of music, since the object of musical knowledge is musical perception and that alone. Indeed, his 'theory of perception' is that the nature of audible stimuli is irrelevant to the study of music; only trained perception needs to be taken into account. I have suggested that the viability of this claim relies on assumptions that are similar to, if not identical with, ideas about perception in which there is a fundamental difference between the sound or 'external stimulus' and the hearing. For many post-Platonic philosophers there were differences in kind between the movements that influenced the ear and the event of hearing itself. Because of these differences, it is possible to develop a psychology of perception (as in Aristotle) or even, as in Aristoxenus, an autonomous aesthetics of music grounded only in the nature and training of the ear; one can disregard the material nature of the stimulus to study the cognitive result in isolation. As far as the interpretation of sensation is concerned, Plato and Aristoxenus seem to exist in fundamentally different worlds.

Another (not unrelated) difference lies in what we might call the modal orientation of the two bodies of work relative to the idea of auditory culture. I have suggested that Plato's writings are built in order to contribute to the reform of the way his readers comport themselves vis-à-vis the senses through which the texts are communicated. As far as the training of the senses is concerned, his is a *deontology*, a discourse concerned above all with how the senses *should be*.

Aristoxenus' theory of music, by contrast, is an *ontology*: it is a description of what music *is*. The few glimmers of a normative model of music, such as his apparent preference for what he called the 'beautiful and Greek' music of Olympus over the tonally complex music of the theatre, are grounded, as I have argued, in a rigorously descriptive approach to musical perception. All music alike is to be treated via an assessment of the harmonic, rhythmic, and compositional rules that govern it, and this descriptive methodology lies at the core of his theoretical undertaking.

These differences are real, and they are large. Plato and Aristoxenus, as I said in the Introduction, do not go well together. But they have a kind of awkward intimacy, for all that, as though they were standing back to back. Aristoxenus' ontology, though grounded in principles that are fundamentally different from what we find in Plato's writing, looks in some ways like an answer to Plato's psycho-sensual deontology. When Aristoxenus finds stability in perception, this is not an outright denial of claims such as we find in the *Timaeus*. Rather, it is something more like a refinement: the *Timaeus* suggested that a comparative perceptual calm *could* be achieved, and Aristoxenus asserts that it *has been* achieved in the specific, constrained area of acculturated musical perception. Aristoxenus is a conservative not primarily in the sense that he thinks old music is better (though he does seem to think this), but in the much more rigorous sense that his model treats musical history as largely structural and unchanging in its most basic elements; this position could be said to depend on the implicit and unacknowledged retention of a sense of what should be within the description of what is: what is *is what should be*. That is why it changes so little: nothing resists change like the perceptible facts, especially when those facts are also norms.

The compound picture that emerges from the juxtaposition of these two figures evinces dissonances not unlike what we find in modern discussions. For every musician or music theorist who has attempted to derive their claims about musical material from the physical nature of sound (recall, for example, that Rameau and Schoenberg both appealed to the overtone series as the basis for harmony), there are aesthetic theorists who deny the relevance of the physical basis of sound as a constraint on musical expression (a few relevant figures in the twentieth century would be Susanne Langer and Roger Scruton). Neuroscientists interested in music have theorized a continuity between the structures of musical sound and the cognitive events which occur in those who listen to it,[1] while avant-garde composers and sound artists have more than once built musics designed to create or radicalize differences between a musical expression and its audition. And, of course, there are critics and audiences who find in music an already-perfected art form, a culture established and good; but there are also critics, composers, and audiences who imagine future musics, musics that could be better than they are today. Vast differences prevail between now and the fourth century BCE, of course, but in both we see similar overlaps and tensions between the deontic and the ontic, monism and dualism, sonic materialism and cultural conditioning.

It could be that these antinomies arise from something more profound, something rooted in the idea and experience of auditory culture itself: both ancient and modern ideas of auditory culture emphasize that they start from an active or passive learning process and then become habitual. Such a progression, however, could be said to lead to the conflation of just the differences I have detailed earlier. When learned processes of perception are routinized and become habitual, the result is (1) that what we first experienced as a set of deontic claims ('you should hear things this way') are recategorized as ontic claims ('things are this way; I know because I can hear it'); and (2) perceptions are assimilated to things (since however much we understand that there is a difference between the cognitive acts of listening and hearing, on the one hand, and the physical and physiological processes that catalyze them, in most contexts we act and think as though there is no difference; when a bird sings I just hear a bird, though I could be prompted to focus on my act of listening).[2] The same may even be true when we listen to music for which we have been well-prepared. Thanks to my upbringing I hear the heavenly emotions of Holst's *Jupiter* or the deeply righteous groove of Sun Ra and his Arkestra without much difficulty or resistance; unless I am doing something very artificial and focused I do not hear 'sound' as a distinct object in these pieces (though of course I still *hear*), and still less do I normally reflect on the fact that I have been prepared all my life just to understand this music. These things are simply 'music' to me, because I have been raised and trained to know them as such. It takes expressions for which we are unprepared for 'music' to be replaced, again, by sound – though often it is sound in its negatively-valued garb as 'noise' that actually emerges in such situations. We could say that in (1), above, we move from an orientation typical of Plato to one characteristic of Aristoxenus, while in (2) we move from Aristoxenus back to Plato. It might be, in other words, that the asymmetries between Plato and Aristoxenus are in some sense constitutive of auditory culture, though they are not commonly acknowledged.

Notes

Introduction

1. Sterne 2003: 96.
2. Sterne 2003: 92.
3. See Feher et al. 2009.
4. Kane 2015: 8. Sound studies and auditory culture are now huge fields, with multiple journals and several handbooks. Canonical are Feld 1990; Schafer 1994; Johnson 1995; Corbin 1998; Kahn 1999; Howes 2003; Picker 2003; Rath 2003; Sterne 2003; Ihde 2007; Schwartz 2011. Valuable as starting points, as summas, or for their introduction of new tools are Damousi and Hamilton 2016; Fineman 1988; Bull and Back 2003; Rice 2003; Erlmann 2004; Howes 2005; LaBelle 2010; Pinch and Bijsterveld 2012; Sterne 2012; Cecchetto 2013; Toner and Classen 2014; Kane 2016; Kapchan 2017; Schulze 2018. In the study of antiquity, see Bettini 2008; Lachenaud 2013; Butler 2015; Emerit, Perrot and Vincent 2015; Gurd 2016; Butler and Nooter 2018. I beg forgiveness for the many works this necessarily selective list has left out.
5. Mauss 1979: 104.
6. Mauss 1979: 104. That notion is expressed most consistently in the *Laws*, a dialogue to which I will turn in Chapter 3.
7. Mauss 1979: 120.
8. Hadot 1995, 1998.
9. Patočka 2002.
10. Foucault 1988. See Patočka 2002: xixn7 for acknowledgement of his influence by both Foucault and Derrida.
11. See Dillon 2012 for critical discussion of the old belief that Aristoxenus was hostile to Plato. The worst issue was a charge of plagiarism: we owe to Aristoxenus the claim that most of the *Republic* was lifted from Protagoras' *Antilogics* (Wehrli (1944) fr. 67).
12. Barker 2012a: 302–304.
13. Barker 2012a: 299, comparing Aristox. *Harm.* 69.1–5 with Pl. *Phlb.* 17a–d. See also Barker 1991b.

14 See Barker 2012b: 16–17, and my discussion in Chapter 4. Gibson 2005: 112–126 has an overview of the extensive points of contact between Plato and Aristoxenus on the theory of musical *ēthos*. Caution is appropriate: most of the really compelling evidence for the existence of agreement between Aristoxenus and Plato comes from the Pseudo-Plutarchean *De Musica*, and for this reason alone definitive philological demonstration is likely to be elusive. It is not easy to tell in this text where the fragments of Aristoxenus begin and where they end, and it is rarely certain whose words we are reading, or how much of what is not directly attributed to Aristoxenus is nonetheless derived from his work, though recent years have seen a tendency (in which I share) to treat more and more of the dialogue as Aristoxenian.

Aristoxenus also shows interest in speculations over the meanings of individual letters, which were crucial to Plato's *Cratylus* – he seems to have been an early explicator of Lasus' asigmatic experiments, attributing the avoidance of *sigma* to the impression that it was 'hard on the mouth' and ill-suited to the aulos, while the *rho* was 'good natured'. Wehrli fr. 87. See Porter 2007; Gurd 2016: 105–107.

15 See especially Pl. *Leg.* 3.700a–701b.
16 See Pl. *Resp.* 3.397b–402d.
17 Pl. *Resp.* 399a–c.
18 There is, actually, an exception to this: it comes in a passage where Aristoxenus makes claims about Plato's musical preferences that are not attested in Plato's texts. See below, Chapter 5.
19 Wright 1978: 2, 25. Perlman, who is citing here, paraphrases slightly.
20 Burnham 1993: 77.
21 Perlman 2004: 4. The last quotation is from Christensen 1993: 305.
22 See Robbins 2002.
23 See Suidas III.236 Adler, with Porter 2007; Gurd 2016: 107.
24 See Anderson 1966; Lord 1978; Wallace 1991, 2004, 2015: 52–63; Brancacci 2005; Wallace 2015: 52–63.
25 See Huffman 1993, 2005; Barker 2007: 263–307.
26 A study that exhaustively traces Aristoxenus' influence on later musical writings, particularly the handbook literature, would show, I think, that it was extensive but that he was not the only authority from which musical pedagogy drew. (The handbook literature, most of which is collected in Jan 1895, should not itself be taken as representing professional music pedagogy. On the latter, see Hagel and Lynch 2015; Hagel 2018.)
27 Small 1998; Becker 2008.
28 Eggebrecht 2010 and Scruton 1987 both arrive at a far more encompassing view of understanding; for them it expands to include the set of all possible reactions

(though both limit what is a 'possible reaction'). The notions of musicking and art worlds demand a modification: it is not clear that 'understanding' is the right word for what a bartender is doing during a jazz performance, although it is clearly an important part of the total scene – and is likely done in a slightly different way while the music is going on from when it is not (nothing is more annoying than clinking glasses during a bass solo).

29 On functional differentiation see Luhmann 1977.
30 See Wilson 2002; Csapo 2004.
31 'By the last decade of the fifth century, Athens was in serious competition for top talent. [...] It was perhaps the rising demand and cost for good performers that induced the Athenian state to assume the fees of poets, actors and, possibly, pipers. [...] The increased frequency, scale and distribution of theatrical entertainments now afforded musicians a comfortable living' Csapo 2004: 209–210. See Pickard-Cambridge, Gould and Lewis 1988: 279–321; Lightfoot 2002.
32 Luhmann 1993: 51–72.
33 Zuckerkandl 1956: 77.
34 Zuckerkandl 1956: 262.
35 Berger 2007, developing ideas found in Koselleck 2004.
36 Gadamer 2004.
37 Kuhn 2012.
38 Foucault 1980.
39 Rancière 1999, 2004.
40 The best account is Barker 2007. Hagel 2010 is a superb history of musical practice with significant contributions to make about the theoretical material as well. West 1992: 218–253 covers the theoretical material more briefly.
41 The handbooks are collected in Jan 1895.
42 On the earliest notation systems, see Stefan Hagel 2010; Barker 2016, with a survey of his and others' earlier opinions on the matter. Aristoxenus' negative assessment of the value of notation for harmonic theory occurs at *Harm.* 2.39–40.
43 See, for example, Aristid. Quint. 1.12, 'Plut'. *De mus.* 1144A.
44 A warning: in the case of the fourth and the fifth, modern ears accustomed to twelve-tone equal temperament may prefer intervals slightly smaller than what many ancients may have liked.
45 Barker 2007 takes this as a central theme.
46 In fact there is no essential reason this should be so, and a set of tunings reported by Aristides Quintilianus (1.9) as having been known to Plato do not obey this principle. But Aristoxenus presumes that it cannot be violated; and the 'tunings' reported by Aristides could well be abstract representations of the total set of

pitches used by pieces which modulated. See Hagel 2010: 370–371 for a convincing demonstration of the systematicity underlying them.

47 See Chapter 5.

48 See Chapter 5.

49 It seems worth emphasizing that the modern word 'melody', which can be a synonym for 'tune', and the ancient word *melōidia*, which means 'the singing of a song', are semantically distinct enough to deserve being called 'false friends'. See Aristid. Quint. 1.12, a passage I will return to briefly in Chapter 5. To avoid confusion, I resist the practice of translating *melos* as 'melody', and I avoid translating *melopoeia* as 'melodic composition', referring to it as 'song writing' or 'melic composition' instead. Presumably discerning the same danger, Mathiesen 1999: 24 also uses 'melic composition'.

50 A word on my use of secondary sources. The scholarship on Plato is simply unmanageable; I have tried to account for the most recent and most relevant work in the notes. In the body of the text I have tried to think for myself, but I am not the first person to read Plato, and there will inevitably be overlap between my readings and those of others. When I am aware of such overlap I have signalled it; where I have learned from or make explicit use of the interpretations of others I have also indicated that. I have especially benefited from Moutsopoulos 1959; Barker 2007; Pelosi 2010. With such an author and such a bibliography I am painfully aware that I will neglect the work of too many. The case of Aristoxenus is rather different; he has been studied by fewer people, but the landscape is dominated by titanic figures. Centrally important are Laloy 1904; Bélis 1986; Mathiesen 1999: 294–354; Barker 2007: 33–262.

Chapter 1

1 Diog. Laert. 3.5; Olympiodorus *In Alcib.* 2.31–61; *Anon. Proleg.* 3; Apul. *De dog. Plat.* 1.2.184; Gell. *NA* 19.11; Ael. *VH.* 2.30; Macrob. *Sat.* 2.2.5; 'Plut'. *De Musica* 1136f and the material gathered in Riginos 1976: 44–45. Riginos is healthfully sceptical ('the reports of Plato the poet are influenced by what he says in his own writings and have no historical basis'; 48).

2 The best general introductions to the production and performance of tragedy in Athens are Pickard-Cambridge, Gould and Lewis 1988; Wilson 2000. I draw most of the information in this section from there.

3 Arist. *Poet.* 1449a18.

4 See Wilson 2000: 198–264.

5 See Wilson 2000: 83, with bibliography.
6 'We do not know on what basis the archon allotted choruses, and in particular what personal factors may have been involved. Where a new poet was concerned, the help of influential or experienced friends might well have been invaluable'; Halliwell 1980: 42.
7 'By the end of the fifth century Attica had at least five annual theatrical festivals, at least fifteen or sixteen by the mid-fourth, and a minimum of eighteen or nineteen in the late fourth century'; Csapo 2004: 208. See his bibliography in 208n5 and Pickard-Cambridge *et al.* 1988: 1–56 on the 'lesser festivals'. Also Scodel 2001; Paga 2010; Csapo *et al.* 2014; Vahtikari 2014: 231–390.
8 'Even the rural Dionysia secured top talent and possibly new works'; Csapo 2004: 209; evidence in 209n10.
9 So, at least, concluded the authors of the scholia to Ar. *Nub.* 530–533, where it is claimed that *Knights* (424) was the first play produced by Aristophanes under his own name: everything earlier, including the *Acharnians*, was produced by Callistratus. See also *Wasps* 1015–1022, with Mastromarco 1979; Halliwell 1980; MacDowell 1982. Halliwell's contribution is particularly intriguing (though criticized by MacDowell) for its hypothetical reconstruction of the earliest phases of a dramatist's career. 'Part of the apprenticeship,' he surmises, 'entailed contributing to the plays of others – a collaboration which may have been an established way of encouraging new dramatists, and which is not to be thought of as purely literary but rather as experience in the creation of a dramatic script for production. By 427 Aristophanes was in a position to provide a whole play for performance, and it was one which may have gained him some patrons even before it was publically produced. The task of applying for a chorus was given to Callistratos, who probably also had a large hand in the preparations for the productions [...] The poet did not attain to full *kōmōididaskalia* until 424, but the impression given by *Knights* 541–4 is of a gradually increasing involvement by the author in his own productions' (43–44). The earliest phase of this progression takes on added significance when it is placed beside Diogenes Laertius' report that Plato began by composing lyric poetry – *parts* of a tragedy, in other words, that might have been intended for incorporation into complete dramas.
10 So the author of the scholion on Ar. *Ran.* 67.
11 Plato's association with Agathon is suggested by Agathon's friendship with Socrates (Pl. *Symp.*). Euripides' contacts with Agathon are the matter of the plot in Ar. *Thesm.*; this then inspired legends in late antiquity, collected in *TrGF* 5.1 T 79–82.
12 Diog. Laert. 3.5; Ael. *VH* 2.30.
13 Perhaps not totally, if the report is true that he acted as choregus, with the Syracusan Dion providing the cash: Diog. Laert. 3.3–4.

14 Chroust 1965, with H. Tarrant 1993: 11–17, 58–107. Tarrant identifies Aristophanes of Byzantium as the first to use analogies with other genres, and especially tragedy, as a tool for thinking about Plato's literary form. See also Haslam 1972; Cameron 1978. Charalabopoulos 2012 is considerably more literal: he claims that Plato was writing *actual* drama, meant to be performed, and that there are traces of Dionysian culture in the aura of the Academy.

15 Diog. Laert. 3.56.

16 Arist. *Poet.* 1449a.14–19.

17 Olympiodorus *In Alcib.* 2.156–162 (Olympiodorus 1956); compare *Anon. proleg.* 1.29–35 (Westerink 1956); *Phaedo* 85a–b, with Richter 2009: 94–98.

18 On the intimate relationship between frustration and seduction, see Baudrillard 1980; Proust 1988 and below.

19 Diog. Laert. 3.37.

20 Pl. *Apol.* 34a and 38b, *Phd.* 59b, where he's noted as absent.

21 Pl. *Resp.* 3.392d–395d. The distinction is applied to Plato's texts in the *Anon. Proleg.* 20; Diogenes Laertius criticizes it as appropriate to tragedy rather than philosophy (3.50).

22 On fictional worlds, see Doležel 1998.

23 This has become a critical commonplace, but see Stokes 1986; Arieti 1991; Sayre 1995; Rowe 2007a; Charalabopoulos 2012.

24 Pl. *Phdr.* 277e–278b.

25 Pl. *Phdr.* 275d–e.

26 Pl. *Phdr.* 278b–e.

27 Havelock 1963; Derrida 1969.

28 Pl. *Ep.* 7.341c. For Plato's complex relation with writing, see Rowe 2007b; Fisher 1966; McAdon 2004; Long 2008; McCoy 2009; Rapp 2014; Al-Maini 2015.

29 See Kotzé 2015: 56n63 for a good recent bibliography. Also Edelstein 1966; Lewis 2000; Knab 2006; Burnyeat 2015.

30 Pl. *Cra.* 440a–b.

31 Pl. *Tht.* 152a. See Cooper 1970; Burnyeat 1976; Frede 1987; Silverman 1990.

32 Pl. *Tht.* 152 b–c.

33 Pl. *Tht.* 152d.

34 Pl. *Tht.* 153a–154b.

35 Pl. *Tht.* 165c.

36 Pl. *Tht.* 159c–161d.

37 Pl. *Tht.* 169d–171c.

38 Pl. *Resp.* 530d.

39 Pl. *Resp.* 531a.

40 Pl. *Resp.* 531c.

41 See Zaslavsky 1981; Scodel 1987; Stewart 1989; Tarrant 1990; McCabe 1992; Brisson 1998; Racinero 1998; Roochnik 2001; Weiss 2005; Burnyeat 2009; Reydams-Schils 2011; Werner 2012; Balot 2013; Bryan 2013.
42 Pl. *Resp.* 514a–517a.
43 Pl. *Resp.* 514a–b; 517b–518d.
44 Pl. *Resp.* 517a.
45 Pythagoras T14 Most-Laks: 'it is said that when Pythagoras was asked to speak to children he spoke in a childlike way, and in a manner fitted to women when he spoke to women, and in an adolescent way when he spoke to adolescents. For it is a mark of wisdom to find the style of wisdom appropriate to each'. Compare Aristoxenus fr. 43 Wehrli (= Pythagoras T15 Most-Laks).
46 On Plato's myths, which have a vast bibliography, see Brisson 1998; Partenie 2009; Collobert, Destrée and Gonzalez 2012.
47 Brann 2004: 88. On the *Republic* she remarks that 'the conversation [is] contained within a revealing structure and marked by significant turns and pregnant omissions, all designed as invitations to speculative interpretation' (93).
48 An excellent and authoritative overview may be found in Rayner and Pollatsek 2012.
49 See Iser 1978.
50 Rapp 2014: 8.
51 Pl. *Tht.* 189e–190a.
52 Ionescu 2014 makes exactly the point I am trying to articulate here.
53 An observation made incisively by Brann 2004.
54 Plat. *Prot.* 326a–b. On the general tendency to see music this way, see Woerther 2008, though few scholars working on music in Plato do not recognize it.
55 Brann 2004: 150. See Pelosi 2010: 1, with reference to the *Phaedo:* 'we should be using music to bring light to philosophical questions'.
56 See Lynch 2017.
57 Barker 2005b: 41, on Pl. *Resp.* 401b–d.
58 See Halliwell 2014 on how Platonic philosophy and music are connected; a different account from mine, but not to be ignored. Also Rowe 2007b: 33, who argues that Plato's dialogues are affective like drama, but for the better. This is essentially the Neoplatonist interpretation as well: 'why, when elsewhere Plato criticized complex things – he attacks aulos playing because it uses complex and many-holed instruments, and kithara playing as involving different strings, and comedy because of the different characters, and likewise tragedy – attacking things for this reason, why does he himself make use of such a written form, a dialogue composed of complex and variegated characters? To this one should say that the variety of characters is not the same in comedies and tragedies as it is in Plato. For in those, the good and bad characters remain the same, but in Plato if it's possible

to find good and bad characters it's also true that you can find them changing from bad to good, instructed and purified, and stepping away from their material life. The result is that the variety in other genres is different from the variety in his writing'. *Anon. proleg.* 4.14 (Westerink 1956). Moutsopoulos 1959 remains an invaluable resource on this and all subjects having to do with music in Plato.
59 Pl. *Phd.* 60d–61c.
60 Pl. *Resp.* 591c–d. See Lynch 2017.
61 Pl. *Leg.* 617a–d.
62 Pl. *Leg.* 811c–e. See Chapter 3.
63 Pl. *Leg.* 817b. cf. 858c–859b.
64 Pl. *Leg.* 691a.
65 Pl. *Leg.* 722d–e.
66 Barker 2009 suggests that *nomos* as a term for musical composition 'was a late fifth-century usage, perhaps adopted by conservative critics' (291) to describe a musical style that may be at least a century older. Power 2010: 215–224 is a superb overview of the term in its musical contexts and beyond.
67 Pl. *Soph.* 253b.
68 Andrieu 1954: 288–289. This is a maximalist interpretation: the variety with which even double point and *paragraphos* were executed in the MSS, which Andrieu characterizes as 'flottante' (and which I believe a systematic study of Platonic papyri and codices would show to be extremely variable) suggests that Plato's authorial MSS may have had even fewer indications of speaker change, requiring readers to determine not only who speaks, but also when.
69 Pl. *Soph.* 253b.
70 Discussing the parallel passage at *Phaedo* 100a.3–5, Bailey 2005: 95 argues that 'Plato was thinking of a robust analogy between the way pitches form unities when related by certain intervals, and the way theoretical claims form unities when related by explanatory co-dependence'. Compare Gentzler 1991; Richter 2009; Lippman 1963: 23 (music, or harmonics, is the science of what mingles and what does not in connection with sound, and philosophy pursues the same kind of science with respect to classes).

Chapter 2

1 *Resp.* 616d–617b. See Junge 1948; Cornford 1952; Wersinger 2006; Pollard 1965.
2 12 DK A21 (All references to fragments with the tag DK are drawn from Diels and Kranz 1969).

3   See Csapo 2008; Steiner 2011.
4   Eur. *Ion* 1074–1086; *El.* 464–469. See also Soph. *Ant.* 1146–53 and Csapo 2008.
5   44 DK A 16.
6   Zhmud 2012: 344.
7   See Burkert 1972: 261–269, 386–399; Barker 2007: 278–286.
8   See, for example, *Regimen* 1.8, with Burkert 1972: 262–263, and compare Pl. *Symp.* 186c–188a.
9   Pl. *Resp.* 546b–d.
10 Arist. *De caelo* 2.9.
11 The physical doctrine, if not the astronomy, may be traceable to Archytas, a slightly older contemporary of Plato, or to the mathematicians Archytas cites as predecessors. See 47 DK B1.
12 47 DK B1. That this may speak to the theme of heavenly music was suggested by Huffman 2005: 61.
13 Aristotle had another objection to the idea of heavenly music, and he thought this one was far more lethal: anything as immense as the heavens would make sounds so loud that they would cause massive destruction. Witness, he suggested, the damage that thunder can do: it can split rocks and trees (*De cael.* 290b.30–290a.4).
14 Pl. *Ti.* 37b. Strictly speaking the thing in this sentence that is moving silently is the world soul's *logos*, perhaps 'reason' here. This passage makes it clear, however, that the soul, which has a share in reason and harmony, is indiscernible to perception (*aoratos*, literally 'invisible'); I think we infer that the harmonic movements of the world soul are correspondingly unheard and, in a strict sense, unhearable. Hearing is crucial to this account, however: see my discussion in the next chapter.
15 Pl. *Tht.* 189e–190a.
16 See Nichom. 3; Ptol. *Harm.* 3.4–16. Much more sophisticated is Arist. Quint. 3.18–24.
17 Cic. *Resp.* 6.18–19.
18 Macrob. *In Somn.* 2.4.15; cf. Aristid. Quint. 3.20.
19 Ptol. *Harm.* 3.8–15.
20 Aristid. Quint. 3.20 (where we cannot hear the heavens because we are contaminated, as it were, by our bodies) and 3.103.
21 Hom. *Od.* 2.39–54, 158–200.
22 See, for a still valuable overview, Pollard 1965: 137–145.
23 Burkert 1972: 357.
24 Theon 146.8. There is an excellent overview in Holford-Strevens 2006: 22–23.

25 Plut. *Quaest. Conv.* 749b–747a; Macrobius *Comm. in Scip.* 2.3.1. See Holford-Strevens 2006: 43n53 for other explanations.
26 Plot. *In R.* 2.238–9 Kröll.
27 *Noeran harmonian,* Plot. *In R.* 2.239 Kröll.
28 See Holford-Strevens 2006: 19.
29 Plot. *In R.* 2.239 Kröll. See Moro Tornese 2013 for an overview of Neoplatonist readings of music in Plato.
30 See, for example, McClain 1978: 47–55.
31 Compare Long 2007: 72, where Socrates sings 'dialectical songs' with his interlocutors: 'this music, which at once calls us beyond ourselves yet remains firmly grounded in the sensuous, finite and temporal, has the capacity to harmonize the tension between this world and that other'. See also Petraki 2008.
32 Pl. *Symp.* 215a–c.
33 Pl. *Symp.* 215e–216a.
34 Pl. *Resp.* 399c–d.
35 Pl. *Resp.* 399e.
36 On Alcibiades see Gribble 1999; Stuttard 2018; and Sansone 2018, an excellent study of Plato's characterization of Alcibiades' rhetorical style.
37 Plut. *Alc.* 2. This episode was discussed in seminal articles by Wilson 1999; Martin 2003.
38 Pl. *Symp.* 210a–211d.
39 Pl. *Symp.* 218c–219d.
40 Pl. *Phdr.* 235c–d.
41 Pl. *Phdr.* 242d–e.
42 Pl. *Phdr.* 238d, 241e. The last four words of his speech do appear to fall into a dactylic rhythm; 241d.
43 Pl. *Phdr.* 237a.
44 See Pl. *Phdr.* 243a–c.
45 Pl. *Phdr.* 242b–c.
46 Pl. *Phdr.* 253e.
47 Belfiore 2006: 195.
48 Belfiore 2006: 195–204.
49 Belfiore 2006: 196, discussed by Carpenter 1997: 25–26.
50 See Franklin 2013.
51 Belfiore 2006: 205.
52 Belfiore 2006: 205–206.
53 Seaford 1976; Belfiore 2006: 199, relying on Seaford 1976: 213 and 213n29. The evidence for the pedagogical function of Satyrs is not overwhelming,

but it turns around myths concerning the education of Olympus by Silenus or Marsyas.
54 De Romilly 1982: 109.
55 See Gurd 2012: 130n30.
56 Compare Moore 2014, who finds allusions to Pindar in the *Phaedrus*.
57 Pl. *Phdr.* 275d–e.
58 There is excellent discussion in Ford 2002: 244–249.
59 Pl. *Phdr.* 276e–277a.
60 Pl. *Phdr.* 259e–262c.
61 Pl. *Phdr.* 270b–272b.
62 Pl. *Phdr.* 252d–253c.
63 Pl. *Resp.* 398e–399c.
64 See below, Chapter 3.
65 On music in the third book of the *Republic* see especially Barker 1991b, 2007; Schofield 2010: 308–311.
66 Pl. *Resp.* 397a.
67 Pl. *Resp.* 399c–e.
68 Pl. *Resp.* 402c.
69 Glaucon and music: Pl. *Resp.* 398e. Glaucon desiring more flavourful food: Pl. *Resp.* 372c.
70 Arist. *Poet.* 1447b.
71 See Nightingale 1995.
72 Pl. *Ion* 533d–534a.
73 Indeed, the magnet here is called 'Heracleian' after the Dactyl Heracleos: see Blakely 2006: 139–152.
74 Pl. *Resp.* 400b–c and Aristoph. *Cl.* 651.
75 As was pointed out by Farness 1988: 27–28.
76 Pl. *Resp.* 597a–d.
77 Pl. *Resp.* 597e, 598e–599a.
78 Pl. *Resp.* 604b–607a.
79 Pl. *Resp.* 605c–606b.
80 Pl. *Resp.* 605b.
81 Pl. *Resp.* 394e–395c.
82 Pl. *Resp.* 395c–d.
83 Pl. *Resp.* 395d–396e.
84 Pl. *Resp.* 397a–b. And see above.
85 That is, the *Symposium*, *Phaedo*, *Parmenides* and *Euthydemus*.
86 Brilliantly discussed in Johnson 1998 (with older bibliography): see also Gurd 2012: 34–39.

Chapter 3

1. On the *Cratylus*, see Williams 1994; Genette 1995; Barney 1998; Rosenmeyer 1998; Joseph 2000; Keller 2000; Barney 2001; Silverman 2001; Sedley 2003; Colvin 2007; Wood 2007; Smith 2008; Thomas 2008; Ademollo 2011; Trivigno 2012; Tarrant 2013; Ewegen 2014, nearly all of which assume language to be the main subject of the dialogue.
2. An example of the kinds of etymological procedure Socrates engages in can be provided with his explication of the name 'Poseidon': 'It seems to me that Poseidon was so named by the first who called him this because the nature of the sea held him as he walked, and prevented him from making progress, but was like a bond (*desmos*) for his feet (*podōn*). So he called the god who governed this capacity Poseidon, because he "bound the feet" (*posi-desmon*). But he added the *e* for the sake of making the word more attractive. Or maybe he didn't say this, but instead of the first *s* he said *ll* (*polleidōn*), to indicate that the god knew (*eidotos*) much (*polla*). Or maybe he was called "the shaker" (*ho seiōn*) because of the earthquakes, and the *p* and the *s* were added later.' Pl. *Cra.* 402e–403a.
3. See, for example, Pl. *Cra.* 404d–e.
4. See Genette 1995: 25.
5. Pl. *Cra.* 411b–c.
6. Pl. *Cra.* 397d.
7. Pl. *Cra.* 408e (sun), 410b (air and ether).
8. Pl. *Cra.* 401c–d.
9. Pl. *Cra.* 402a–d.
10. Pl. *Cra.* 404d.
11. See, for example, Pl. *Cra.* 401d–402b.
12. Pl. *Cra.* 426d–e.
13. Pl. *Cra.* 427a–b.
14. See Pl. *Cra.* 385a–391a.
15. Pl. *Cra.* 428d–435a. This is not the end of Socrates' engagement with Cratylus: the next phase concerns the viability of Heracliteanism and of sensuality as an epistemological tool.
16. Pl. *Cra.* 440a–b. Cited above, Chapter 1.
17. Pl. *Cra.* 440c.
18. A bibliographical note here would be ridiculous, given the importance of the *Timaeus* to so much subsequent thought. Overviews of its reception may be found in Neschke-Hentschke 2000; Moro Tornese 2013.
19. Pl. *Tim.* 27d–28a.
20. Pl. *Tim.* 28a. Subsequent references will be in the body of the text.

21 E.g. Pind. *Ol.* 1. 114.
22 Taylor 1928: 27–28. See also Lisi 2007; Silverman 2010; Reydams-Schils 2011; Johansen 2013.
23 See the masterful discussion in Power 2010: 187–200.
24 At Pl. *Ti.* 48b. See below.
25 See Comotti 1991: 15–18, which is dated but still valuable (though I do not agree with all details). On the form of the citharodic nome particularly, see Power 2010: 224–234. For the multi-part nature of at least some nomes, see Pollux *On.* 4.66, 84; 'Plut'. *De mus.* 1134a-b, 1142f–1143a-c.
26 Pl. *Ti.* 35b–36d. I use the explanation of Barker 1989: 59n17.
27 44 DK 6A. There is a sceptical discussion of whether Philolaus actually calculated the *leimma* as 256:243 in Barker 2007: 267–271. Barker 2007: 320 also points out that Timaeus nowhere explicitly says that the series is rising in pitch, though this seems the best inference.
28 So Taylor 1928: 147. On the monochord see Creese 2010.
29 This is a structural feature that the *Timaeus* shares with the *Republic*: as I noted above, Socrates had completed his description of what he called the most healthy republic in Book Two, while the rest of the dialogue is an attempt to rebalance things in response to Glaucon's desire for a modicum of luxury (Pl. *Resp.* 372a).
30 See Pelosi 2010: 18–19.
31 Pl. *Ti.* 43c4–d2, with Zeyl 2000 *ad loc.* Compare Pl. *Phlb.* 33d, where sensual experiences cause a 'tremor' in the soul. And see Fletcher 2016.
32 See Pelosi 2010: 66–113; Fletcher 2016.
33 See Taylor 1928: 303–4.
34 Pl. *Resp.* 507a–509c.
35 On perception in the *Timaeus*, see Brisson 1999; Johansen 2004, chapter 8; Lautner 2005; Wolfsdorf 2013, 2014.
36 The assonance in the English happily reproduces Timaeus' wordplay on *braduteran* and *baruteran*.
37 See Pelosi 2010: 98, 155–171; Barker 2000; Lyon 2016.
38 Lyon 2016 translates *plēgē* as 'percussion' and takes the feminine adjectives in the second half of the passage as agreeing with it: this has the consequence of making Timaeus' theory of sound almost the same as the broadly accepted modern one, in which the frequency of pressure waves produces pitch and the amplitude causes volume, while the temporal envelope causes timbre.
39 *prosenechthentos*, 59 DK A106.
40 60 DK A1.
41 68 DK A128.

42 68 DK A135.55.
43 On Archytas, see Huffman 2005, especially 129–148. Huffman thinks Archelaus and Democritus could have influenced him, and also perhaps Zeno and Lasus (132–137).
44 47 DK B1.
45 47 DK B1.
46 Moutsopoulos 1959: 231 and 237 are characteristically elegant. See also Pelosi 2010: 106–107, 171–180.
47 Taylor 1928: 576 comments, 'the "dying away" of a note depends not on the slowing down of the *rapidity* of the corresponding vibrations but on the diminishing of their *amplitude*'.
48 Lyon 2016: 263.
49 See Lyon 2016: 265, 263.
50 See above, Chapter 1.
51 On music in the *Laws* see Moutsopoulos 1959: 98–121, Rocconi 2016, the essays collected in Peponi 2013, and Folch 2016.
52 Pl. *Leg.* 893b–896a.
53 Pl. *Leg.* 896d–e.
54 Pl. *Leg.* 898a–b.
55 Pl. *Leg.* 898d–899d.
56 Pl. *Leg.* 659d.
57 Pl. *Leg.* 644c–d.
58 Pl. *Leg.* 653d–e.
59 Pl. *Leg.* 789c–d. Does Archytas again lurk in the background here? He designed a clapper for infants: Huffman 2005: 19.
60 Pl. *Leg.* 791a.
61 Pl. *Leg.* 788a–c.
62 Pl. *Leg.* 788a.
63 Pl. *Leg.* 788a.
64 Pl. *Leg.* 723a.
65 Pl. *Leg.* 722d–e.
66 Pl. *Leg.* 795e–796e.
67 Pl. *Leg.* 796e–798a.
68 Pl. *Leg.* 799a–803b.
69 Pl. *Leg.* 799a–b. See also 657a–b; 797b–c.
70 Pl. *Leg.* 801a–d.
71 Pl. *Leg.* 802b–c.
72 Pl. *Leg.* 802c.
73 Pl. *Leg.* 802d.

74 Pl. *Leg.* 802c–d.
75 Pl. *Leg.* 800c–d.
76 Pl. *Leg.* 700b–701a.
77 The standard descriptions of this phenomenon are West 1992: 357–374 and Csapo 2004.
78 Calame 1994; Henrichs 1994, 1996; Weiss 2018.
79 Pl. *Leg.* 815e–816e.
80 Pl. *Leg.* 669b.
81 Pl. *Leg.* 670b.
82 Pl. *Leg.* 670d–e.
83 Pl. *Leg.* 669c.
84 Pl. *Leg.* 669d.
85 Pl. *Leg.* 669e.
86 See Porter 2007; Gurd 2016.
87 Pl. *Leg.* 817b.
88 Pl. *Leg.* 811c–d.
89 Pl. *Leg.* 811d–e.
90 Pl. *Phlb.* 17b–e.
91 Pl. *Phlb.* 26a. Huffman 2001 finds Philolaus behind this account.
92 Pl. *Phlb.* 26d.
93 Pl. *Phlb.* 25e–26a.
94 Pl. *Phlb.* 32a–b.
95 Pl. *Phlb.* 64d–e.
96 Pl. *Phlb.* 55e–56a.
97 Pl. *Grg* 463b. *Gorgias* discusses music at 485d, 501d–502d, 504a–b.
98 Pl. *Phlb.* 56a. Music is a recurrent theme in the *Philebus*: see 33a–47a, on pleasure and pain, grounded in a quasi-Hippocratean theory of the harmony of elements; 48aff, on tragic and comic pleasure; 51d on auditory pleasure. I have learned from Moutsopoulos 1959: 64–65; Pelosi 2010: 137; Barker 1987; Borthwick 2003.
99 Frede 1992; Gordon 1999.

Chapter 4

1 Wehrli fr. 1; Suda s.v. Aristoxenus. On music in Tarentum, see Castaldo 2010. The fundamental works on Aristoxenus (already cited at the end of my Introduction), all of which are equally indispensable – but which by no means agree in either

detail or overall picture – are Laloy 1904; Bélis 1986; Mathiesen 1999: 294–354; Barker 2007: 33–262. See also Gibson 2005; Levin 2009.
2 Wehrli fr. 1; Suda s.v. Aristoxenus (Wehrli 1944).
3 Wehrli fr. 1; Suda s.v. Aristoxenus.
4 Wehrli fr. 11a–41.
5 Wehrli fr. 47–50.
6 Wehrli fr. 51–60.
7 Wehrli fr. 61–68.
8 On music-theoretical subjects, see Wehrli fr. 69–94. On instruments, Wehrli fr. 94–102.
9 Wehrli fr. 103–112.
10 Wehrli fr. 113–116.
11 For the *El. Harm.*, I consult Aristoxenus 1954; the translations of Macran 1902 and Barker 1989 are both very useful.
12 Fragments collected in Pearson 1990.
13 I consult the edition of Ziegler and Pohlenz 1953; the best commentary is still Weil and Reinach 1900.
14 Partially collected in Jan 1895.
15 In Book One, see *Harm* 1.2–8; in Book Two, see 2.35–38. They differ primarily in the fact that Book Two includes 'songwriting' or *melopoeia* as a final part of harmonics.
16 Aristox. *Harm.* 1.29; 2.54.
17 See below.
18 So argued Barker 1989: 122–123 and Barker 2007: 113–135, who thinks Book Two represents a reconsideration – that is, in effect a second draft – of Book One (Barker 2007: 165 gives a synoptic view of the passages that can be found in both books, as well as notice of what is new in Book Two, and points out that the main emphasis of Book Two is 'methodological and conceptual issues'). Mathiesen 1999: 295–297 calls *Harm.* 1 '*De principiis*' and thinks the relationship between this and Book Two is 'highly systematic' (299). See Gibson 2005: 39–40 for a survey of earlier discussions.
19 *El. Harm.* 1.2.
20 There is one 'proof' in Book Two, but it relies on the ear in a fundamental (if misguided) way that is never repeated in Book Three, a methodological change I think should be taken as decisive. I discuss this proof below.
21 Aristox. *Harm.* 1.4; See also 1.20; 1.21. For a full list see Aristoxenus 1954: 185, under *phusis*.
22 Aristox. *Harm.* 1.18.
23 See Barker 1978; Gibson 2005: 23–38; Barker 2007: 105–112; Mathiesen 1999: 303–304; Bélis 1986 speaks of 'pistes' running from Aristotle to Aristoxenus.

24 Arist. *Eth. Nic.* 1140a.1–24. See Barker 2007: 160–162, who argues that harmonic systems 'are not artificial but natural, and we discuss them rather than creating them' (160); at 149 nature is taken to mean 'a consistent and unified kind of being, unfolding itself in time like a plant from a seed'. On Aristotle and art, see Angier 2010. See Arist. *Metaph.* 980b–982a and *An. Post.* 100a.3–10 for the difference between art, experience and knowledge.
25 Arist. *Ph.* 192b.13–15. See Barker 2007: 159–160.
26 Compare Arist. *Ph.* 193b.22–194b.9. Bélis 1986 concludes, compellingly, that 'music is, if we are to believe Aristoxenus, both a work of nature and a work of art, or, better: in harmonics both nature and the artist are at work' (199).
27 Compare Pl. *Phlb.* 27a, where Socrates asserts that the difference between poiesis and genesis is no more than verbal.
28 Aristox. *Harm.* 2.43.
29 Aristox. *Harm.* 2.44. See Bélis 1986: 193–194.
30 Aristox. *Harm.* 1.8–10. Compare 1.15.
31 See Chapter 3, above, and also below.
32 Aristox. *Harm.* 1.9. Macran translates, compellingly, 'in the light of sensuous cognition'. The sentiment is repeated at 1.12.
33 Aristox. *Harm.* 2.32. See Barker 2007: 141–143.
34 The standard account of mathematical musicology is Barker 2007: 263–410. On the impossible origins of the discovery, see Burkert 1972: 375n23.
35 Suidas s.v. Aristoxenus (Wehrli fr. 1).
36 But see below.
37 Bélis 1986: 76: 'a sound is only high or low to the degree that it is perceived'.
38 Aristox. *Harm.* 1.5. Barker 2007: 142 concludes from this that 'if melody is essentially an *aisthēton*, then its patterns must be discovered within the perceptual data themselves [...]; and in that case they must be identified empirically, not through speculations about their hidden causes, let alone through mathematical reasoning'.
39 Aristox. *Harm.* 2.32–33.
40 Arist. *An. Post.* 100a–c.
41 See Chapter 3.
42 This could also be compared to the ideas of Pierre Schaeffer, who insisted on the 'acousmatic' nature of musical listening, at least in *musique concrète*, and of Roger Scruton, who has invoked Schaeffer to support the idea that musical listening must be strictly distinguished from any listening for the material causes of musical sound. See Schaeffer 2017: 64–69; Kane 2016; Scruton 1999: 2–3.
43 Xenocrates ff. 1–7 (Xenocrates 1982).
44 Porphyry, *In Ptol. harm.* 30D.27ff. = Xenocrates f. 87 (Xenocrates 1982).

45 Arist. *De an.* 419a.32. On Aristotle and sound see Modrak 1987; Barker 1991a; Towey 1991; Pelosi 2006.
46 Arist. *De an.* 419b.9–420a.3.
47 Arist. *De an.* 420a.20–420b.5. See Barker 2002b: 27–28 (with whom I am not in complete agreement on this point).
48 Arist. *De gen.* 787a.5–23.
49 My suggestion in this paragraph is that Aristotle treats pitch as a function not of 'vibration' or the locomotive velocity of a sound (the two most popular factors in earlier Greek sources), but of the speed with which the air is set into motion, that is, the speed with which the form which is transmitted through the air, is created: 'morphogenetic velocity'. This is not in agreement with others. Polansky 2007: 296–297 thinks Aristotle derived pitch from vibrational velocity; Hicks 1907: 387 attributes to him a theory of 'quality' supposedly also present in Theophrastus (I discuss Theophrastus below). But I believe the discussion in *De gen.* is decisive.
50 Arist. *De an.* 424a.18–25.
51 This is exactly the import, I think, of Arist. *De an.* 417b.28–418a.6.
52 See Arist. *De an.* 417a.15–21.
53 Arist. *Post. An.* 71b.22–23.
54 Arist. *Post. An.* 72a.6–25.
55 Arist. *Post. An.* 99b.36.
56 Arist. *Post. An.* 100a.2–4.
57 Erroneously attributed to Aristotle by Porphyry. On authorship, see Barker 1984b: 94–95 and Gottschalk 1968, who proposes Strato (accepted by Gibson 2005: 29; see also Barker 2015: 225n252). On peripatetic music theory in general, see Anderson 1980.
58 'Arist'. *De audib.* 800a.1–11.
59 'Arist'. *De audib.* 800a.14–803a.1.
60 'Arist'. *De audib.* 803b.19–29.
61 'Arist'. *De audib.* 803b.34–40.
62 'Arist'. *De audib.* 804b.40–804a.8.
63 Barker 2004a asserts closer affiliations between Theophrastus and Aristoxenus than had previously been assumed; I follow him here. See also Sicking 1998; Baltussen 2000; Fatuzzo 2009; Rocconi 2009: 195–198.
64 Sextus Empiricus' summary of Peripatetic epistemology, for example, lumps Aristotle and Theophrastus together. See Theophrastus fr. 301A (I cite from Fortenbaugh and Gutas 1992). Theophrastus fr. 265 has an overview of his psychological works.
65 Theophrastus fr. 282.
66 Theophrastus fr. 275B, 277B–C.

67 Theophrastus fr. 277B.
68 Theophrastus fr. 273–274.
69 Theophrastus *Sens. passim.*
70 Theophrastus fr. 716. See Barker 1985, 2007; Fatuzzo 2009: 411–436; Raffa 2018.
71 Theophrastus fr. 716.
72 Theophrastus fr. 716.62.5–10.
73 Raffa 2018: 45–61.
74 Theophrastus fr. 716.61. Compare Ath. 14.628c, citing Damon to the effect that dance comes about 'when the soul is moved' (37 DK B6). Barker 2007: 434–435 connects the movement of the soul in Theophrastus with the *Timaeus*, compellingly. Barker 1985: 314 remarks on the word *trepei* here that it is 'allied to the noun *tropos*, commonly used in musical sources to mean 'style', and often linked with or substituting for *harmonia*. The singer must be able to produce a melody in the right *tropos*'. Aristoxenus uses *tropos*, too, quite frequently: see Aristoxenus 1954: 183. See also Woerther 2007: 68–69, 119–122 on the connections between *tropos* and *ēthos*.
75 Theophrastus fr. 716.64–65.
76 Recent attempts to historically situate Theophrastus' interlocutors in Barker 2004b; Barker 2007: 422–428. Laloy 1904: 182–184 suggestively associates this with Aristoxenus' claim that musical vocal movement is 'intervallic'.
77 See Theophrastus fr. 277b.36–37.
78 Theophrastus fr. 716.65.
79 Theophrastus fr. 719AB.
80 Theophrastus fr. 440A–B–C.
81 Barker 2007: 149.
82 Aristox. *Harm.* 2.36.10–16. See Barker 1984a, 1991a, 208–213, Barker 2005a: 176–183, 2007: 184–192; Gibson 2005: 44ff.
83 Aristox. *Harm.* 2.47.30–48.3. Nothing in Cleonides (*Eisagōgē* 11, 14) suggests other than this. See the Introduction for an explanation of the note names. Barker 2007: 185–186 collects Aristoxenus' statements on *dunamis*.
84 There is a major difference, however, between the analogy I have made between modern scale degrees and Aristoxenus' notion of *dunamis*, and that is that in the modern (digitally enforced) system the *absolute* difference between (say) C and E is supposed to be always the same, though it may vary in practice slightly. Aristoxenus' notion of *dunamis* is meant to deal with a musical situation in which the distance between C and E may well change from piece to piece or performer to performer. See just below.
85 Arist. *Metaph.* 1046a.11.
86 Barker 2007: 188.

87 Aristox. *Harm.* 3.66–72.
88 Aristox. *Harm.* 1.8.
89 Aristox. *Harm.* 1.10–11.
90 Aristox. *Harm.* 2.47.
91 Aristox. *Harm.* 2.47–48.
92 Aristox. *Harm.* 2.53.
93 Aristox. *Harm.* 3.69.1–11. This, as Barker 1984a: 46 has pointed out, seems to evoke Plato's discussion of infinitude in *Phlb.* 16b–17e.
94 Aristox. *Harm.* 2.48.
95 Aristox. *Harm.* 2.33.
96 At Aristox. *Harm.* 2.33 Aristoxenus says that hearing 'measures the sizes of intervals'. This seems to contradict 2.48, where he appears to explicitly deny that the hearing measures at all. Perhaps the contradiction disappears when we compare the agents in the two passages. At 2.33 it is 'us' (*krinomen, theōroumen*); in 2.48 it is 'the coming into appearance associated with perception' (*tēn tēs aisthēseōs phantasian*). The latter, I think we are safe in assuming, coincides with the perceptions of those experienced in music which is the object of harmonics. 'Us', on the other hand, refers to harmonicists, who, as I will suggest below, are a different group, and who may indeed use their ears differently, including actually measuring intervals.
97 Aristox. *Harm.* 1.28; the notion is systematically defended in 2.53. Mathiesen 1999: 317 connects Aristotle to Aristoxenus here, though briefly.
98 Arist. *Ph.* 4.227a.10–17. See Bélis 1986: 153.
99 Aristox. *Harm.* 1.27.
100 Aristox. *Harm.* 1.27.
101 See Moore 2012: 315, 325.
102 Aristox. *Harm.* 1.18.18–19.17.
103 Aristox. *Harm.* 2.54.
104 Aristox. *Harm.* 2.54.
105 Aristox. *Harm.* 2.54–55.
106 Barker 1984a, in the only major recent commentary on Aristox. *Harm.* 3, has shown that Aristoxenus always thinks in terms of tetrachords bounded by fixed notes.
107 Euc. *El.* 1.6 hor. 1.
108 Aristox. *Harm.* 2.33. Compare Pl. *Resp.* 6.510c–511a and Arist. *Ph.* 2.194a.
109 See, for example, the incisive remarks on Aristoxenus' attempt to handle 'pitch', *tasis*, in a manner consistent with his principles in Barker 2007: 148.
110 Aristox. *Harm.* 2.57–58.

111 For an overview see Creese 2012; the proof is devastatingly criticized in Ptol. *Harm.* 1.23–24.
112 Ptol. *Harm.* 1.25–27; Euc. *Sect. Can.* 157–158, 161. There is an excellent overview in Barbera 1977.
113 Euc. *Sect. Can.* 152–153, 163. Boethius De *institutione musica* 3.1 attributes a proof of this claim to Archytas (47 DK A19).
114 Creese 2012: 50.
115 Creese 2012: 58.
116 'His demonstration is neither mathematical nor empirical. Rather, it is cast in a totally new spatial logic that mathematical objections cannot address, and although it is possible to test the demonstration on a monochord with reasonable results, the empirical validity is less important than the demonstration's conceptual idealization' (Mathiesen 1999: 329).
117 Hippoc. *VM* 9.
118 Hippoc. *Regimen* 1.11.
119 Arist. *Metaph.* 1052b.15.
120 Arist. *Metaph.* 1053a.15–20. See Bélis 1986: 70; Gibson 2005: 'Aristotle's grasp on the concepts of Pythagorean musical theory is less than perfect' (25).
121 Arist. *Metaph.* 1053a.5–6.
122 Arist. *Metaph.* 1053a.22–23.
123 Gibson 2005: 'it is clear that the implications of a ratio-based definition of intervals preclude a unit of measurement', because of the disturbing incommensurabilities between the concords and their derivatives (25).
124 See Kucharski 1959 on Aristoxenus and the *Phlb.*
125 See Huffman 2005: 419–420 on Archytas and lyrists' tuning methods.
126 See Barker 1989: 50–51.
127 It seems relevant to recall here that for Aristoxenus the musical movement of the voice is exclusively of one kind: the voice seems to rest on pitches and to jump to the next pitch. Anything other than this is the movement of speech, not song (Aristox. *Harm.* 1.8–10); the more precisely the voice stops on pitches and jumps between them, the more clearly is the song said to be articulated (Aristox. *Harm.* 1.10), and any adjustments to a lyre's tuning, which by definition involve some glissando-type sound, would be excluded from musical perception. (Aristoxenus says that in singing physical adjustments of the sounding body are inapparent; *Harm.* 1.10). Tuning is not (yet) music, on this account; see Aristox. *Harm.* 1.11.
128 See Barker 2007: 230, suggesting the unlikelihood that Aristoxenus thought the harmonics would be useful for musicians.

129 Aristox. *Harm.* 2.33. See Barker 2007: 168–175. Relevant as well is Brancacci 2008: 101–124. At 114 he connects Aristoxenus' epistemology to Speusippus' idea of knowledgeable perception.
130 'A thoroughly expert ear', says Barker: Barker 2012b: 11.
131 Aristox. *Harm.* 2.33.
132 Aristox. *Harm.* 2.39–41.
133 Aristox. *Harm.* 2.41.
134 Barker 1991a: 'the crucial task of harmonics, as he conceived it, is to go beyond the essentially preliminary compilation of facts to their systematic coordination in a scheme of scientific understanding' (188).
135 Aristox. *Harm.* 1.25.
136 Compare Wehrli fr. 93, with Aristox. *Harm.* 2.46.8–16, where long series of small intervals cannot be moved through melodically.
137 See the illuminating discussion in Barker 2014: 59–70.
138 Aristox. *Harm.* 1.5.

Chapter 5

1 Langer 1953: 108. Likewise Schaeffer 2017: 64–69; Kane 2016; Scruton 1999: 2–3.
2 Langer 1953: 50.
3 Langer 1953: 50.
4 Langer 1953: 109–110. Emphasis in the original.
5 Langer 1953: 120.
6 Langer 1953: 50.
7 Massumi 2002.
8 Zuckerkandl 1956: 200.
9 Zuckerkandl 1956: 229.
10 Zuckerkandl 1956: 235.
11 Zuckerkandl 1956; 262, cited above.
12 Berger 2007. On music and time, see Alperson 1980: 407 ('On the one hand it has been claimed, especially since Kant, that music is an art of time, if not *the* art of time. On the other hand, it has been claimed that music has what has often been called 'musical time', which has somehow to be distinguished from some other kind or kinds of time.'). Also Epstein 1995; Adlington 2003.
13 It may be relevant here that a persistent motif running through his work on harmonics is a preference for metaphors linking music to ideas of stasis or stillness. Pitches are places, says Aristoxenus, where voices 'rest' (*histēsin*); between

two pitches, what moderns call an interval, is a 'standing apart' (*diastēma*); combinations of intervals, which we might call tunings or scales, are 'standings together' (*sustēmata*).

14 Aristox. *Harm.* 2.38–39. Glossed by Mathiesen 1999: 323 as 'music is a phenomenon passing through time, not a frozen moment in time'. Compare Barker 1989: 155n37: 'the laws of harmony are, centrally, laws of sequence, and are not fully captured in the abstract representation of frozen structures'. Similarly Barker 2007: 172: 'Harmonics is not the study of static or abstract structures'. A careless reading might lead one to overstate the alternatives: the laws of harmonics are laws of sequence in that they govern sequence, not in that they are the same as it. Very simply, they are not themselves sequences. Compare Laloy 1904: 109 ('Melody is a whole, and this whole is not given us in space but in time') and take it together with 181 ('neither a melodic line nor the line of an arabesque are anything other than the material translations of a certain system of relationships which attention perceives through the medium of sense'). Bélis 1986: 143, citing Aristot. *Phys.* 7.247b.10–13 ('the initial acquisition of knowledge is not generation: in our opinion reason knows and thinks by rest and stillness') remarks: 'a stable and organized collection of sounds; such is *melos hērmosmenon*' (Bélis 1986: 144).

15 See Arist. *Pr. An.* 100a–b and above.

16 Aristox. *Harm.* 2.33–34. Compare Barker 2007: 170–175, which I diverge from slightly.

17 Collected in Pearson 1990. See Koster 1972; Rowell 1979; Mathiesen 1999: 334–344 and Calvié 2014b, 2014a, 2014c, 2016.

18 Aristox. *Rhythm.* 2.3. See Gibson 2005: 88–90.

19 Aristox. *Rhythm* 2.4. It is a difficult passage, but I find Pearson's interpretation misleading.

20 The former is done by Heracleodorus, as reported by Philodemus *On Poems* 1.38–9 (p. 226 Janko); the latter by Demetr. *Eloc.* 189; see Janko 2000: 227n2 for a brief overview with further bibliography.

21 Aristox. *Rhythm.* 2.6 (Pearson).

22 Arist. *Ph.* 227a.11–12.

23 Arist. *Ph.* 220a.14–21.

24 Arist. *Ph.* 219a.32–219b.1.

25 Such, I take it, is the point of Arist. *Ph.* 219a.21–31.

26 Arist. *Mem.* 452b23–453a3.

27 Arist. *Ph.* 219b.2–3.

28 Aristox. *Rhythm.* 2.16.

29 See Lynch 2016.

30 West 1982: 1–5.

31 West 1982: 35.
32 Devine and Stephens 1994: 45.
33 Aristox. *Rhythm.* 2.20–21.
34 Aristox. *Rhythm.* 2.30–35.
35 *Fragmenta Neapolitana* 10–12, ed. Pearson.
36 See Gurd 2016: 22–24.
37 Aristox. *Harm.* 2.35–38.
38 Wehrli ff. 92–93, which are not richly informative.
39 Cleonides 14.
40 Aristid. Quint. 1.12.
41 This is Aristoxenian; see *Harm.* 1.7.
42 Briefly discussed as Aristoxenian by Mathiesen 1999: 324.
43 Aristid. Quint. 1.12.
44 Pointed out by Barker 1989: 431n145.
45 So Barker 1989: 431n145, with Pl. *Resp.* 6.487c, *Leg.* 7.820e; Arist. *Rhet.* 1371a.3; Aesch. *Supp.* 13.
46 'Plut'. *De musica* 1134e (Wehrli fr. 83), reading *ēdē* rather than *oude* in the last clause. See Ziegler and Pohlenz 1953 *ad loc.* Compare Winnington-Ingram 1928; Hagel 2010: 397–413; Barker 2011. In what follows I rely on 'Plutarch' almost exclusively. He cites Aristoxenus from a work which 'discussed certain musical styles or harmoniai, and followed their invention by historical or pseudohistorical figures, and their development and use in society past and present' (Gibson 2005: 109).
47 See frag. Neap. 15 Pearson. In *On the Primary Chronos* he treats it as though it means 'tempo'.
48 Aristox. *Harm.* 2.53.
49 Aristox. *Harm.* 1.29. This passage has been much altered by critics. I translate Macran's text, which is quite different from Westphal's. Barker 1984a: 147n129 thinks this discussion is part of the 'analysis of melodies' themselves, with reference to Aristides Quintilianus 1.9, where *melōidia* is divided into *agōgē* and *plokē*. Note that in Aristid. Quint. we have only two categories, and that they are associated with *melōidia*, not *melopoeia*.
50 Aristoxenus seems to exclude *melopoeia* from harmonics in Book One (Aristox. *Harm.* 1.2; see Barker 1989: 126n4; *contra* Barker 2007: 139–140, where it is said that 'the two books do not flatly contradict each other' (140)).
51 *Anon. Bell.* 79.
52 So now Hagel 2018: 145–146, who compellingly locates these texts as part of musical pedagogy. On the Anonymous Bellerman texts, see also Hagel 2008; Pöhlmann 2018.

53 See Najock 1972: 161–182, 68–69.
54 See Hagel 2008.
55 See Hagel 2010: 309–310 for an instance where one of the *Anon. Bell.'s* figures appears in a notated piece of music from late antiquity.
56 Arist. Quint. *De musica* 1.12.
57 On *ēthos* see W. D. Anderson 1966; Barker 2005b, 2007: 178–180, 242–259; Woerther 2007; Ferrario 2011; Raffa 2011; Rocconi 2012.
58 Aristox. *Harm.* 2.48.15–49.1. Compare Litchfield 1988: 54.
59 That the difference between the enharmonic genus and the chromatic genus is heard as a feeling or *ēthos* is relevant to another passage in his harmonic writings, this time in Book One, where Aristoxenus is again measuring out spaces in a tetrachord. Here he wants to establish the range within which *lichanos* 'moves', that is, the 'space' within which it is to be found in all possible tunings. This range, he asserts, is exactly one tone. It is found never closer to *mesē* than a tone (in the diatonic genus), and it is never farther away than two tones (in the enharmonic genus). It is controversial, he says, that the lower limit is two tones away from *mesē*, since some contemporary musicians want it to be a shade higher, again preferring the consequent *ēthos* (Aristox. *Harm.* 1.23). I discuss this passage below.

A related claim seems to be made about rhythm in the Oxyrhynchus papyrus known by the romantic name of '34.2687'. (On this papyrus fragment, see Reinach 1898; Koster 1972; Mathiesen 1985; Calvié 2014b.) This text contains a discussion of the ways in which rhythms can be mixed within a composition (the papyrus' name for this is *rhythmopoeia*). Thus, for example, the author approves of the following rhythmic structure:

–∪–|–∪–|–∪–|–∪–|–∪–
∪–∪–|∪–∪–|∪–∪–
–∪–|–∪–|–∪–|–∪–

This run of verse contains two sequences of –∪– divided by an iambic trimeter (∪–∪–, three times). The beginning of the column of text is lost, but it's likely that he is claiming that –∪– and ∪–∪– are appropriate to each other (1.34). He goes on to say, however, that such alternations do not typically go on for very long. A few columns later a parallel claim is made: a paion epibatos (– – | – – –) can be composed out of spondaic or trochaic components. He continues: 'Such a usage (*chrēsis*) should not be continuous. For the *ēthos* of such a *rhythmopoeia* is completely alien to that of the paion and the things named earlier' (P. Oxy 34.2687 col iv. 6–12 (ed. Pearson)).

Our author adds that in general one should avoid compositions that perception rejects. This seems to me to be more or less the same claim we witnessed in the

Harmonics: different constructions have different feelings (*ēthē*); one can bend but not break the borders between them, and the ultimate arbiter is musical perception.

In 2014 Laurent Calvié argued on the basis of a very close consideration of the papyrus' language and theoretical assumptions that it cannot be Aristoxenian. Calvié's most compelling arguments derive from his belief that the Oxyrhynchus fragment's terminology is considerably less precise than what we have in the surviving fragments of the *Elementa Rhythmica*. Although I don't think Aristoxenus is quite as precise, terminologically speaking, as Calvié claims, his critique is strong enough that the only way to preserve the fragment for Aristoxenus, as far as I can see, is to suggest that it does not come from his rhythmic theory but from a discussion of *rhythmopoeia* akin to the *melopoeia* discussions we have preserved in 'Plutarch' and Aristides Quintilianus. At any rate it may be that the burden of proof now lies on those wishing to vindicate the fragment for Aristoxenus.

60 See Aristox. *Harm.* 1.1.
61 See Aristox. *Harm.* 1.1–2; 2.32, with my comments below.
62 Aristox. *Harm.* 1.1.
63 Aristox. *Harm.* 2.32.
64 Aristox. *Harm.* 1.8, 1.2.
65 The passage is 'Plutarch' *De musica* 1142b–1144e. Weil and Reinach 1900: xviii attribute the whole section to Aristoxenus (see their comments *ad loc.* for direct parallels). So that readers can see, at least schematically, the reasons for suspecting an Aristoxenian source, I offer the following breakdown.

    1142b–c: Aristoxenus is named (= F 76 Wehrli).

    1142d–e: parts are perhaps comparable to Aristox. *Harm.* 2.35. Assumed to be Aristoxenian because of context by Weil and Reinach 1900; Barker 1984b: 238n210.

    1142f–1143b: similar to Aristox. *Harm.* 2.31–32, 35–38.

    1143b–c: a style of analysis similar to the one contained at 1134f; 1134f is explicitly ascribed to Aristoxenus.

    1143d–e: repeated sentiments from 1142ff–1143c (compare Aristox. *Harm.* 2.31–32).

    1143e–f: compare Aristox. *Harm.* 1.2 (= Testimonium 99 da Rios) (Aristoxenus 1954). The general tendency of the two passages may be quite different, however.

    1144a–c: compare Aristox. *Harm.* 2.38–39.

    1144c–1144e: repeated sentiments from 1142ff–1143c (compare Aristox. *Harm.* 2.31–32).

66 'Plut'. *De musica* 1142f.
67 'Plut'. *De musica* 1143b–1143d.

68 'Plut'. *De musica* 1143a.
69 'Plut'. *De musica* 1143d.
70 'Plut'. *De musica* 1144e.
71 Wehrli fr. 84. *Harm.* 1.7 suggests that ranges of tunings are governed by appropriateness; See Barker 2007: 243–249; Lomiento 2011 on Aristoxenus' doctrine of appropriateness.
72 'Plut'. *De musica* 1142f. Writing not of range but of tunings, Aristotle remarks on the difficulty Philoxenus had in using the Dorian, and likewise finds the reason to be that Dorian was inappropriate in the context where he wanted to use it. Arist. *Pol.* 1342b9.
73 Aristid. Quint. 1.12.
74 Aristid. Quint. 1.12. Barker 2011: 52 points out that there is a similar kind of analysis in a scholion to Euripides' *Orestes* 1384, which contains a reference to a musical composition called the *harmateion nomos*, the 'chariot nome'. The scholiast says this nome is sung in a high pitch; it was high pitched because it imitated the sound of axels. Collectively the scholia give the appearance of not knowing what the *harmateion melos* in Euripides is, as is clear from the fact that they offer a set of possibilities, some or all drawn from Didymus. This particular line in the *Orestes* has been suspected since Antiquity (Apollodorus Cyrenaicus, in the scholia *ad loc.*, first questioned it); Diggle 1994 bracketed it.
75 Aristox. *Harm.* 1.7–8.
76 'Plut'. *De musica* 1143b–c. See above, n. 65, for the justification of an Aristoxenian source. See also Barker 2012b: 22–23.
77 On *ēthos* and Aristoxenus' doctrine of criticism see Barker 2007: 243–259.
78 Aristox. *Harm.* 2.31.
79 'Plut'. *De musica* 1142f–1143b.
80 Arist. *Pol.* 1340a.15–1340b19.
81 Ath. *Deip.* 624c (= Heraclides fr. 163 Wehrli). See Barker 2009.
82 Pl. *Resp.* 399a–c.
83 'Plut'. *De musica* 1136e–1137a (Wehrli fr. 82). On Plato's theory of *ēthos* see W. D. Anderson 1966: 64–110; Pelosi 2010: 29–67.
84 See Barker 2012a: 301, 2012b: 24–25.
85 See Weil and Reinach 1900: xiii–xx for a discussion of the sources of the *De musica*.
86 Pl. *Resp.* 399d, *Leg.* 669e. Weil and Reinach 1900 *ad loc.* discuss the difficulties with this passage.
87 About the nome of Ares I'm making a guess. The spondeion was an early enharmonic composition associated with the Dorian; see 'Plut'. *De Musica* 1135a (though this passage suggests it was associated with the Dorian range, not tuning).

At 1143b, in a passage I discussed above, we are told that the nome of Athena combines the enharmonic with the Phrygian *tonos*, though *tonos* here must mean 'key' or 'range', since Aristoxenus' usual word for tuning is *harmonia*.

An unfortunate side-effect of this interpretation was that he had to attribute to Plato a liking for aulos compositions; but the criticism of instrumental music is in the *Laws*, which was unfinished at Plato's death and edited together by Philip of Opus; it's not impossible that Aristoxenus didn't know it. See Diog. Laert. 3.37.

88 'Plut'. *De musica* 1136c (fr. 81 Wehrli).
89 'Plut'. *De musica* 1143f–1144a. Weil and Reinach 1900: xviii treat this as Aristoxenian. See Barker 2007: 237–239.
90 See Barker 2005a, 2007: 172–174, 2012a: 306–307.
91 'Plut'. *De musica* 1144a–1144b.
92 On Aristoxenus' theory of history, see Barker 2011, 2012b, 2014.
93 I do not know what the 'first and second musical styles' are: perhaps they correspond, somehow, to the 'spondeion scale' and the true enharmonic discussed by Aristoxenus in the passage quoted at 'Plutarch' 1143a. See Barker 2011; Barker 2014.
94 Aristox. *Harm.* 1.23. See also 2.35.
95 'Plut'. *De musica* 1137e.
96 Plut. *Quaest. Conv.* 645e.
97 Compare *Laws* 802c–d, discussed in Chapter 3.
98 Aristox. *Harm.* 2.33.
99 'Plut'. *De musica* 1142e. On the attribution, see above.
100 'Plut'. *De musica* 1134f (Wehrli f. 83); 1142b (Wehrli f. 76); 1145a, 1142c–d; Aristox. *Harm.* 1.23.
101 'Plut'. *De musica* 1135b.
102 1135c; *tupos* is a term of analysis associated with genre and *ēthos* at Aristid. Quint. 1.12.
103 Barker 2007: 258.
104 Aristoxenus was not the only one working with musical history in this way. He may have garnered more than a little from Glaucus of Rhegium, a late-fifth-century historian who made similar compositional claims, such as, for example, that Stesichorus 'used the *harmatios nomos* and the dactylic form' ('Plut'. *De musica* 1133f), or that Thaletas mixed the paionic and cretic rhythms with Archilochus' *melopoeia* (1134d). Glaucus may be one of the 'musicians' cited at 1134e as a source for the material about Olympus; indeed, Plutarch may have drawn even his Glaucus material from Aristoxenus' report. See Barker 2009: 283.
105 Power 2012 offers an excellent reading of the most important candidates for Aristoxenian authorship in 'Plutarch' *De musica*. See especially 1135a, 1135d, 1137a–c.

106 Wehrli fr. 70.
107 Barker 1984b: 245n242.
108 'Plut'. *De musica* 1145a.
109 Wehrli fr. 124 (Ath. 14.632AB, vol. 3.394–395 Kaibel).
110 See also 'Plut'. *De musica* 1140d–e, where theatre music is called degenerate, and 1136b–c, much less certainly Aristoxenian. Musical conservatism was, after all, a commonly held position.
111 'Plut'. *De musica* 1136d (= fr. 81 Wehrli).
112 *Phrikē periphobos, eleos poludakros kai pothos philopenthēs*; 82 B11.9 DK.
113 *Homeric Hymn to Hermes* 420–423. See Peponi 2012: 96–127.
114 'Plut'. *De musica* 1141c. Heracleides of Pontus also wrote extensively on Lasus (ff. 161, 163 Wehrli). Heraclides did not attribute modal innovation to Lasus (at least in these exiguous fragments); to the contrary, he thought Lasus' adoption of the Aolian was a conservative adherence to one of the original Greek modes.
115 'Plut'. *De musica* 1138b–c.
116 'Plut'. *De musica*, 1142b (Wehrli fr. 76).
117 See Barker 2007: 248.
118 Compare Ath. 624d, citing Heraclides Ponticus (fr. 163 Wehrli), where a similar link between *agōgē* = scale and *agōgē* = way of life may be implied.
119 See Arist. *Pr. An.* 100a–b.
120 Wehrli fr. 6. See Fortenbaugh 2012.
121 Wehrli 1944 2: 48 connects this story with the Aristotelian theory of catharsis; W. Anderson 1980: 87 associates it with Aristoxenus' account of Pythagorean practices of purification (Wehrli fr. 26). On musical catharsis, see Figari 2006. Fortenbaugh 2012: 167 convinces me: 'Should we think, then, of Aristoxenus introducing the Theban to orderly rhythms played on the *aulos*? The Theban understands that the rhythms are associated with war, but they produce composure and confidence, so that in time the Theban is no longer terrified when he hears the sound of the *salpinx*'; 'we are not to think of catharsis' (167n43).
122 Aristoxenus seems to have accepted that music could be used in different ways in different contexts: 'Plutarch' has him asserting that it can calm and soothe the over-heating effects of wine ('Plut'. *De musica* 1146e–f = fr. 123 Wehrli), while Strabo cites him to the effect that learning music can teach and correct souls. We are not very far from the insight of the *Laws* that socio-political design entails musical design. Indeed, Proclus cites Aristoxenus as claiming that the ordered condition of philosophers' souls was expressed in their voices (Wehrli fr. 75). He does not say the philosophers were singing, but he at least establishes a link between psychic and vocal order that would surely imply different social and

psychological systems for different musical forms. Wehrli fr. 117, from Apollonius (the same source as the story of the salpinx-cure) associates Aristoxenus with an aetiology of the paian in Italy which associates its early adoption with therapy of psychological ailments among the local women. See Fortenbaugh 2012: 170–171.
123 'Plut'. *De musica* 1135b.
124 'Plut'. *De musica* 1142d.
125 'Plut'. *De musica* 1144c.
126 'Plut'. *De musica* 1144e.
127 'Plut'. *De musica* 1143e.
128 'Plut'. *De musica* 1145a.
129 'Plut'. *De musica* 1145c.
130 'Plut'. *De musica* 1145d.
131 Aristox. *Harm.* 2.35.

Conclusion

1 See Levitin 2006; Patel 2008.
2 This is the thesis of both Dewey 1980 and James 1976.

Works Cited

Ademollo, F. 2011. *The Cratylus of Plato: A Commentary*. Cambridge: Cambridge University Press.

Adlington, R. 2003. 'Moving Beyond Motion: Metaphors for Changing Sound'. *Journal of the Royal Musical Association* 128: 297–318.

Al-Maini, D. 2015. 'Collection and Division in Plato's Critique of Writing'. *Ancient Philosophy* 35: 41–62.

Alperson, P. 1980. '"Musical Time" and Music as an "Art of Time"'. *The Journal of Aesthetics and Art Criticism* 38: 407–417.

Anderson, W. 1980. 'Musical Developments in the School of Aristotle'. *Royal Musical Association Research Chronicle* 16: 78–98.

Anderson, W. D. 1966. *Ethos and Education in Greek Music: The Evidence of Poetry and Philosophy*. Cambridge, MA: Harvard University Press.

Andrieu, J. 1954. *Le dialogue antique: structure et présentation*. Paris: Les Belles Lettres.

Angier, T. 2010. *Technē in Aristotle's Ethics: Crafting the Moral Life*. London: Continuum.

Arieti, J. A. 1991. *Interpreting Plato: The Dialogues as Drama*. Savage, MD: Rowman & Littlefield.

Aristoxenus. 1954. *Elementa harmonica*. Edited by R. da Rios. Rome: Typis Publicae Officinae Polygraphicae.

Bailey, D. T. J. 2005. 'Logic and Music in Plato's *Phaedo*'. *Phronesis* 50: 95–115.

Balot, K. K. 2013. 'Likely Stories and the Political in Plato's *Laws*'. In *Probabilities, Hypotheticals, and Counterfactuals in Ancient Greek Thought*, edited by V. Wohl. 65–83. Cambridge: Cambridge University Press.

Baltussen, H. 2000. *Theophrastus Against the Presocratics and Plato: Peripatetic Dialectic in the* De sensibus. Boston, MA: Brill.

Barbera, C. A. 1977. 'Arithmetic and Geometric Divisions of the Tetrachord'. *Journal of Music Theory* 21: 294–323.

Barker, A. 1978. 'Music and Perception: A Study in Aristoxenus'. *Journal of Hellenic Studies* 98: 9–16.

Barker, A. 1984a. 'Aristoxenus' Theorems and the Foundations of Harmonic Science'. *Ancient Philosophy* 4: 23–64.

Barker, A. 1984b. *Greek Musical Writings, Volume I*. Cambridge: Cambridge University Press.

Barker, A. 1985. 'Theophrastus on Pitch and Melody'. In *Theophrastus of Eresus*, edited by W. W. Fortenbaugh. 289–324. New Brunswick, NJ: Transaction.

Barker, A. 1987. 'Text and Sense at *Philebus* 56a'. *Classical Quarterly* 37: 103–109.

Barker, A. 1989. *Greek Musical Writings, Volume II*. Cambridge: Cambridge University Press.

Barker, A. 1991a. 'Aristoxenus' Harmonics and Aristotle's Theory of Science'. In *Science and Philosophy in Classical Greece*, edited by A. C. Bowen. 188–226. New York: Garland.

Barker, A. 1991b. 'Plato and Aristoxenos on the Nature of Melos'. In *The Second Sense*, edited by C. Burnett, M. Fend and P. Gouk. 137–160. London: The Warburg Institute.

Barker, A. 2000. 'Timaeus on Music and the Liver'. In *Reason and Necessity*, edited by M. R. Wright. 85–99. Classical Press of Wales.

Barker, A. 2002. 'Words for Sounds'. In *Science and Mathematics in Ancient Greek Culture*, edited by L. Wolpert and C. J. Tuplin. 22–35. Oxford: Oxford University Press.

Barker, A. 2004a. 'Theophrastus and Aristoxenus: Confusions in Musical Metaphysics'. *Bulletin of the Institute of Classical Studies* 47: 101–117.

Barker, A. 2004b. 'Transforming the Nightingale: Aspects of Athenian Musical Discourse in the Late Fifth Century'. In *Music and the Muses: The Culture of Mousike in the Classical Athenian City*, edited by P. Wilson and P. Murray. 185–204.

Barker, A. 2005a. 'The Journeying Voice: Melody and Metaphysics in Aristoxenian Science'. *Apeiron* 38: 161–184.

Barker, A. 2005b. *Psicomusicologia nella Grecia antica*, edited by A. Meriani. Napoli: Guida.

Barker, A. 2007. *The Science of Harmonics in Classical Greece*. Cambridge: Cambridge University Press.

Barker, A. 2009. 'Heraclides and Musical History'. In *Heraclides of Pontus: Discussion*, edited by W. Fortenbaugh and E. Pender. 273–298. New Brunswick, NJ: Transaction.

Barker, A. 2011. 'The Music of Olympus'. *Quaderni Urbinati di cultura classica* 99: 43–57.

Barker, A. 2012a. 'Aristoxenus and the Early Academy'. In *Aristoxenus of Tarentum: Discussion*, edited by C. Huffman. 297–324. New Brunswick, NJ: Transaction.

Barker, A. 2012b. 'Did Aristoxenus Write Musical History?' In *Aristoxenus of Tarentum: Discussion*, edited by C. Huffman. 1–28. New Brunswick, NJ: Transaction.

Barker, A. 2014. *Ancient Greek Writers on Their Musical Past: Studies in Greek Musical Historiography*. Pisa: F. Serra.

Barker, A. 2015. *Porphyry's Commentary on Ptolemy's Harmonics: A Greek Text and Annotated Translation*. Cambridge: Cambridge University Press.

Barker, A. 2016. 'Aristoxenus *Harm*. II, 49.1–50.18 Da Rios: A Recantation'. *Greek and Roman Musical Studies* 4: 90–102.

Barney, R. 1998. 'Socrates Agonistes: The Case of the *Cratylus* Etymologies'. *Oxford Studies in Ancient Philosophy* 16: 63–98.

Barney, R. 2001. *Names and Nature in Plato's Cratylus*. London: Routledge.

Baudrillard, J. 1980. *De la séduction*. Paris: Éditions Galilée.

Becker, H. S. 2008. *Art Worlds*. Berkeley: University of California Press.

Belfiore, E. 2006. 'Dancing with the Gods: The Myth of the Chariot in Plato's *Phaedrus*'. *The American Journal of Philology* 127: 185–217.

Bélis, A. 1986. *Aristoxène de Tarente et Aristote. Le Traité d'harmonique*. Paris: Klincksieck.

Berger, K. 2007. *Bach's Cycle, Mozart's Arrow: An Essay on the Origins of Musical Modernity*. Berkley, CA: University of California Press.

Bettini, M. 2008. *Voci: Antropologia Sonora del Mondo Antico*. Torino: G. Einaudi.

Blakely, S. 2006. *Myth, Ritual, and Metallurgy in Ancient Greece and Recent Africa*. Cambridge: Cambridge University Press.

Borthwick, E. K. 2003. 'Text and Interpretation of *Philebus* 56 A'. *Classical Philology* 98: 274–280.

Brancacci, A. 2005. 'Les *tropoi* de Damon (37 B 2 et B 10 DK)'. In *Agonistes: Essays in Honour of Denis O'Brien*, edited by J. Dillon and M. Dixsaut. 13–21. London: Routledge.

Brancacci, A. 2008. *Musica e Filosofia da Damone a Filodemo: Sette studi*. Firenze: Olschki.

Brann, E. 2004. *The Music of the Republic: Essays on Socrates' Conversations and Plato's Writings*. Philadelphia: Paul Dry Books.

Brisson, L. 1998. *Plato the Myth Maker*. Edited by G. Naddaf. Chicago: University of Chicago Press.

Brisson, L. 1999. 'Plato's Theory of Sense Perception in the *Timaeus*: How it Works and What it Means'. In *Proceedings of the Boston Area Colloquium in Ancient Philosophy 13*, edited by J. J. Cleary and G. M. Gurtler. 147–176. Leiden: Brill.

Bryan, J. 2013. '*Eikos* in Plato's *Phaedrus*'. In *Probabilities, Hypotheticals, and Counterfactuals in Ancient Greek Thought*, edited by V. Wohl. 30–46. Cambridge: Cambridge University Press.

Bull, M., and L. Back, eds. 2003. *The Auditory Culture Reader*. Oxford: Berg.

Burkert, W. 1972. *Lore and Science in Ancient Pythagoreanism*. Cambridge, MA: Harvard University Press.

Burnham, S. 1993. 'Musical and Intellectual Values: Interpreting the History of Tonal Theory'. *Current Musicology* 53: 76–88.

Burnyeat, M. 1976. 'Plato on the Grammar of Perceiving'. *Classical Quarterly* 26: 29–51.

Burnyeat, M. 2009. 'Eikos Muthos'. In *Plato's Myths*, edited by C. Partenie. 167–186. Cambridge University Press.

Burnyeat, M. 2015. *The Pseudo-Platonic Seventh Letter*. Edited by M. Frede and D. Scott. Oxford: Oxford University Press.

Butler, S. 2015. *The Ancient Phonograph*. New York: Zone.

Butler, S., and S. Nooter, eds. 2018. *Sound and the Ancient Senses*. London: Routledge.

Calame, C. 1994. 'From Choral Poetry to Tragic Stasimon: The Enactment of Women's Song'. *Arion* 3: 136–154.

Calvié, L. 2014a. 'The Indirect Tradition of ῾Ρυθμικὰ στοιχεῖα of Aristoxenus of Tarentum'. In *On the Fringe of Commentary: Metatextuality in Ancient Near Eastern and Ancient Mediterranean Cultures*, edited by S. H. Aufrère, P. S. Alexander and Z. Plese. 329–343. Leuven: Peeters.

Calvié, L. 2014b. 'Le fragment rythmique du P.Oxy. 9 + 2687 attribué à Aristoxène de Tarente'. *Revue de philologie, de littérature et d'histoire anciennes* 88: 7–54.

Calvié, L. 2014c. 'Les extraits pselliens des *Éléments rythmiques* d'Aristoxène de Tarente'. *Revue des Études Byzantines* 72: 139–191.

Calvié, L. 2016. 'L'organisation d'ensemble du livre II des Ῥυθμικὰ στοιχεῖα d'Aristoxène de Tarente'. *Greek and Roman Musical Studies* 4: 103–125.

Cameron, A. 1978. *Plato's Affair with Tragedy*. Cincinnati, OH: University of Cincinnati.

Carpenter, T. H. 1997. *Dionysian Imagery in Fifth-Century Athens*. Oxford: Oxford University Press.

Castaldo, D. 2010. 'Aspetti della cultura musicale a Taranto nell'età di Archita'. In *Per una storia dei popoli senza note*, edited by P. Dessi. 137–143. Bologna: ClueB.

Cecchetto, D. 2013. *Humanesis: Sound and Technological Posthumanism*. Minneapolis: University of Minnesota Press.

Charalabopoulos, N. G. 2012. *Platonic Drama and its Ancient Reception*. Cambridge: Cambridge University Press.

Christensen, T. 1993. *Rameau and Musical Thought in the Enlightenment*. Cambridge: Cambridge University Press.

Chroust, A. H. 1965. 'The Organization of the Corpus Platonicum in Antiquity'. *Hermes* 93: 34–46.

Collobert, C., P. Destrée, and F. J. Gonzalez, eds. 2012. *Plato and Myth: Studies on the Use and Status of Platonic Myths*. Boston: Brill.

Colvin, M. 2007. 'Heraclitean Flux and Unity of Opposites in Plato's *Theaetetus* and *Cratylus*'. *Classical Quarterly* 57: 759–769.

Comotti, G. 1991. *Music in Greek and Roman Culture*. Translated by R. V. Munson. Baltimore: Johns Hopkins University Press.

Cooper, J. M. 1970. 'Plato on Sense-Perception and Knowledge (*Theaetetus* 184–186)'. *Phronesis* 15: 123–146.

Corbin, A. 1998. *Village Bells: Sound and Meaning in the Nineteenth-Century French Countryside*. Translated by M. Thom. New York, NY: Columbia University Press.

Cornford, F. M. 1952. *Plato's Cosmology: The Timaeus of Plato*. New York: Humanities Press.

Creese, D. 2012. 'Instruments and Empiricism in Aristoxenus' *Elementa Harmonica*'. In *Aristoxenus of Tarentum: Discussion*, edited by C. A. Huffman. 29–64. New Brunswick, NJ: Transaction.

Creese, D. E. 2010. *The Monochord in Ancient Greek Harmonic Science*. Cambridge: Cambridge University Press.

Csapo, E. 2004. 'The Politics of the New Music'. In *Music and the Muses: The Culture of Mousikē in the Classical Athenian City*, edited by P. Murray and P. Wilson. 207–248. Oxford: Oxford University Press.

Csapo, E. 2008. 'Star Choruses: Eleusis, Orphism, and New Musical Imagery and Dance'. In *Performance, Iconography, Reception: Studies in Honour of Oliver Taplin*, edited by M. Revermann and P. Wilson. 262–290. Oxford: Oxford University Press.

Csapo, E., H. R. Goette, J. R. Green, and P. Wilson. 2014. *Greek Theatre in the Fourth Century BC*. Walter de Gruyter.

Damousi, J., and P. Hamilton, eds. 2016. *A Cultural History of Sound, Memory, and the Senses*. Oxford: Routledge.

De Romilly, J. 1982. 'Les conflits de l'âme dans le *Phèdre* de Platon'. *Wiener Studien* 95: 100–113.

Derrida, J. 1969. *La dissémination*. Paris: Éditions de Minuit.

Devine, A. M., and L. D. Stephens. 1994. *The Prosody of Greek Speech*. New York: Oxford University Press.

Dewey, J. 1980. *Art as Experience*. New York: Perigee.

Diels, H., and W. Kranz. 1969. *Die Fragmente der Vorsokratiker*. Zürich: Weidmann.

Diggle, J. 1994. *Euripidis fabulae*. Vol. 3. Oxford: Clarendon.

Dillon, J. 2012. 'Aristoxenus' *Life of Plato*'. In *Aristoxenus of Tarentum: Discussion*, edited by C. Huffman. 283–296. New Brunswick, NJ: Transaction Publishers.

Doležel, L. 1998. *Heterocosmica: Fiction and Possible Worlds*. Baltimore: Johns Hopkins University Press.

Edelstein, L. 1966. *Plato's Seventh Letter*. Leiden: Brill.

Eggebrecht, H. H. 2010. *Understanding Music: The Nature and Limits of Musical Cognition*. Burlington, VT: Ashgate.

Emerit, S., S. Perrot, and A. Vincent, eds. 2015. *Le paysage sonore de l'antiquité: méthodologie, historiographie et perspectives*. Châtillon: Institut français d'archéologie orientale.

Epstein, D. 1995. *Shaping Time: Music, the Brain, and Performance*. New York: Wadsworth Publishing.

Erlmann, V., ed. 2004. *Hearing Cultures: Essays on Sound, Listening, and Modernity*. Oxford: Berg.

Ewegen, S. M. 2014. *Plato's Cratylus: The Comedy of Language*. Bloomington: Indiana University Press.

Farness, J. 1988. 'Plato's Architexture: Some Problems for Philosophical Interpretation'. *Arethusa* 21: 27–46.

Fatuzzo, C. 2009. 'Il pensiero musicale di Teofrasto'. In *Il sapere musicale e i suoi contesti da Teofrasto a Claudio Tolemeo*, edited by D. Castaldo, D. Restani and C. Tassi. 1000–1022. Ravenna: Longo.

Feher, O., H. Wang, S. Saar, P. P. Mitra, and O. Tchernichovski. 2009. 'De Novo Establishment of Wild-Type Song Culture in the Zebra Finch'. *Nature* 459: 564–568.

Feld, S. 1990. *Sound and Sentiment: Birds, Weeping, Poetics, and Song in Kaluli Expression*. Chapel Hill: Duke University Press.

Ferrario, M. 2011. 'Parola e musica in 'Plutarco' (περὶ μουσικῆς) e in Filodemo'. *Quaderni Urbinati di cultura classica* 99: 73–81.

Figari, J. 2006. 'Musique et médecine dans la philosophie présocratique'. In *Musique et Antiquité*, edited by O. Mortier-Waldschmidt. 121–146. Paris: Les Belles Lettres.

Fineman, J. 1988. 'The Sound of O in Othello: The Real of the Tragedy of Desire'. *October* 45: 77–96.

Fisher, J. 1966. 'Plato on Writing and Doing Philosophy'. *Journal of the History of Ideas* 27: 163–172.

Fletcher, E. 2016. '*Aisthēsis*, Reason and Appetite in the *Timaeus*'. *Phronesis* 61: 397–434.

Folch, M. 2016. *The City and the Stage: Performance, Genre and Gender in Plato's Laws*. Oxford: Oxford University Press.

Ford, A. L. 2002. *The Origins of Criticism: Literary Culture and Poetic Theory in Classical Greece*. Princeton, NJ: Princeton University Press.

Fortenbaugh, W. W. 2012. 'Apollonius on Theophrastus on Aristoxenus'. In *Aristoxenus of Tarentum: Discussion*, edited by C. Huffman. 155-175. New Brunswick, NJ: Transaction.

Fortenbaugh, W. W., and D. Gutas. 1992. *Theophrastus: His Psychological, Doxographical and Scientific Writings*. New Brunswick, NJ: Transaction.

Foucault, M. 1980. *The Archaeology of Knowledge*. New York: Harper & Row.

Foucault, M. 1988. *The History of Sexuality*. Translated by R. Hurley. New York: Vintage Books.

Franklin, J. C. 2013. '"Songbenders of Circular Choruses": Dithyramb and the "Demise of Music"'. In *Dithyramb in Context*, edited by B. Kowalzig and P. Wilson. 217-236. Oxford: Oxford University Press.

Frede, M. 1987. 'Observations on Perception in Plato's Later Dialogues'. In *Essays in Ancient Philosophy*, edited by M. Frede. 3-8. Minneapolis: Minnesota University Press.

Frede, M. 1992. 'Plato's Arguments and the Dialogue Form'. In *Methods of Interpreting Plato and his Dialogues*, edited by J. C. Klagge and N. D. Smith. 201-219. Oxford: Clarendon Press.

Gadamer, H. G. 2004. *Truth and Method*. Translated by J. Weinsheimer and D. G. Marshall. London: Continuum.

Genette, G. 1995. *Mimologics*. Translated by Thaïs E. Morgan. Lincoln: University of Nebraska.

Gentzler, J. 1991. 'Συμφωνεῖν in Plato's *Phaedo*'. *Phronesis* 36: 265-276.

Gibson, S. 2005. *Aristoxenus of Tarentum and the Birth of Musicology*. London: Routledge.

Gordon, J. 1999. *Turning Toward Philosophy: Literary Device and Dramatic Structure in Plato's Dialogues*. University Park, PA: Penn State University Press.

Gottschalk, H. B. 1968. 'The *De audibilibus* and Peripatetic Acoustics'. *Hermes* 96: 435-460.

Gribble, D. 1999. *Alcibiades and Athens: A Study in Literary Presentation*. Oxford: Clarendon Press.

Gurd, S. 2012. *Work in Progress: Literary Revision as Social Performance in Ancient Rome*. Oxford: Oxford University Press.

Gurd, S. 2016. *Dissonance: Auditory Aesthetics in Ancient Greece*. New York: Fordham University Press.

Hadot, P. 1995. *Philosophy as a Way of Life: Spiritual Exercises from Socrates to Foucault*. Translated by A. I. Davidson. Oxford: Blackwell.

Hadot, P. 1998. *The Inner Citadel: The Meditations of Marcus Aurelius*. Cambridge, MA: Harvard University Press.

Hagel, S. 2008. 'Ancient Greek Rhythm: The Bellermann Exercises'. *Quaderni Urbinati di cultura classica* 88: 125-138.

Hagel, S. 2010. *Ancient Greek Music: A New Technical History*. Cambridge: Cambridge University Press.

Hagel, S. 2018. '"Musics", Bellermann's *Anonymi*, and the Art of the *Aulos*'. *Greek and Roman Musical Studies* 6: 128–176.

Hagel, S., and T. Lynch. 2015. 'Musical Education in Greece and Rome'. In *A Companion to Ancient Education*, edited by M. Bloomer. Hoboken, NJ: Wiley-Blackwell.

Halliwell, S. 1980. 'Aristophanes' Apprenticeship'. *The Classical Quarterly* 30: 33–45.

Halliwell, S. 2014. 'Plato'. In *The Routledge Companion to Philosophy and Music*, edited by T. Gracyk and A. Kania. 307–316. London: Routledge.

Haslam, M. 1972. 'Plato, Sophron, and the Dramatic Dialogue'. *Bulletin of the Institute of Classical Studies* 19: 17–38.

Havelock, E. A. 1963. *Preface to Plato*. Cambridge, MA: Harvard University Press.

Henrichs, A. 1994. '"Why Should I Dance?" Choral Self-Referentiality in Greek Tragedy'. *Arion* 3: 56–111.

Henrichs, A. 1996. 'Dancing in Athens, Dancing on Delos: Some Patters of Choral Projection in Euripides'. *Philologus* 140: 48–62.

Hicks, R. D. 1907. *Aristotle, De Anima*. Cambridge: Cambridge University Press.

Holford-Strevens, L. 2006. 'Sirens in Antiquity and the Middle Ages'. In *Music of the Sirens*, edited by L. P. Austern and I. Naroditskaya. 16–51. Bloomington: Indiana University Press.

Howes, D. 2003. *Sensual Relations: Engaging the Senses in Culture and Social Theory*. Ann Arbor: University of Michigan Press.

Howes, D. 2005. *Empire of the Senses: The Sensual Culture Reader*. Oxford: Berg.

Huffman, C. A. 1993. *Philolaus of Croton, Pythagorean and Presocratic*. Cambridge: Cambridge University Press.

Huffman, C. A. 2001. 'The Philolaic Method: The Pythagoreanism Behind the *Philebus*'. In *Essays in Ancient Greek Philosophy 6: Before Plato*, edited by A. Preus. 67–85. Albany NY: State University of New York Press.

Huffman, C. A. 2005. *Archytas of Tarentum: Pythagorean, Philosopher, and Mathematician King*. Cambridge: Cambridge University Press.

Ihde, D. 2007. *Listening and Voice: Phenomenologies of Sound*. Albany: State University of New York Press.

Ionescu, C. 2014. 'Dialectial Method and Myth in Plato's *Statesman*'. *Ancient Philosophy*: 29–46.

Iser, W. 1978. *The Act of Reading: A Theory of Aesthetic Response*. London: Routledge and Kegan Paul.

James, W. 1976. *Essays in Radical Empiricism*. Cambridge: Harvard University Press.

Jan, C. 1895. *Musici Scriptores Graeci*. Leipzig: Teubner.

Janko, R. 2000. *Philodemus: On Poems, I*. Edited by R. Janko. New York: Oxford University Press.

Johansen, T. 2004. *Plato's Natural Philosophy: A Study of the Timaeus-Critias*. Cambridge: Cambridge University Press.

Johansen, T. 2013. 'Timaeus in the Cave'. In *The Platonic Art of Philosophy*, edited by G. R. Boys-Stones, C. Gill and D. El Murr. 90–109. Cambridge University Press.

Johnson, J. H. 1995. *Listening in Paris: A Cultural History*. Berkeley, CA: University of California Press.

Johnson, W. 1998. 'Dramatic Frame and Philosophic Idea in Plato'. *American Journal of Philology* 119: 577–598.

Joseph, J. E. 2000. *Limiting the Arbitrary: Linguistic Naturalism and its Opposites in Plato's Cratylus and The Modern Theories of Language*. Amsterdam: Benjamins.

Junge, J. 1948. 'Die Sphären-Harmonie und die Pythagoreisch-Platonische Zahlenlehr'. *Classica et Medievalia* 9: 184–194.

Kahn, D. 1999. *Noise, Water, Meat: A History of Sound in the Arts*. Boston: MIT Press.

Kane, B. 2015. 'Sound Studies without Auditory Culture: A Critique of the Ontological Turn'. *Sound Studies* 1: 2–21.

Kane, B. 2016. *Sound Unseen: Acousmatic Sound in Theory and Practice*. Oxford: Oxford University Press.

Kapchan, D., ed. 2017. *Theorizing Sound Writing*. Middletown, Connecticut: Wesleyan.

Keller, S. 2000. 'An Interpretation of Plato's *Cratylus*'. *Phronesis* 45: 284–305.

Knab, R. 2006. *Platons siebter Brief: Einleitung, Text, Übersetzung, Kommentar*. New York: Olms.

Koselleck, R. 2004. *Futures Past: On the Semantics of Historical Time*. Translated by K. Tribe. New York: Columbia University Press.

Koster, W. J. W. 1972. 'Quelques remarques sur l'étude de rythmique Ox. Pap. 2687 (9)'. *Revue des études grecques* 85: 47–56.

Kotzé, A. 2015. 'Three Instances of Greek Autobiographical Writing from the Fourth Century BCE'. *Classical World* 109: 39–67.

Kucharski, P. 1959. 'Le *Philèbe* et les *Éléments harmoniques* d'Aristoxène'. *Revue Philosophique de la France et de l'Étranger* 149: 41–72.

Kuhn, T. S. 2012. *The Structure of Scientific Revolutions*. Chicago: The University of Chicago Press.

LaBelle, B. 2010. *Acoustic Territories: Sound Culture and Everyday Life*. London: Bloomsbury.

Lachenaud, G. 2013. *Les routes de la voix: l'antiquité grecque et le mystère de la voix*. Paris: Les Belles Lettres.

Laloy, L. 1904. *Aristoxène de Tarente et la musique de l'antiquité*. Paris: Société française d'imprimerie et de librairie.

Langer, S. 1953. *Feeling and Form: a Theory of Art.* New York: Scribner.
Lautner, P. 2005. 'The *Timaeus* on Sounds and Hearing with Some Implications for Plato's General Account of Sense-Perception'. *Rhizai. A Journal for Ancient Philosophy and Science* 2: 235–253.
Levin, F. R. 2009. *Greek Reflections on the Nature of Music*. Cambridge: Cambridge University Press.
Levitin, D. J. 2006. *This is Your Brain on Music: The Science of a Human Obsession*. New York, NY: Dutton.
Lewis, V. B. 2000. 'The *Seventh Letter* and the Unity of Plato's Political Philosophy'. *The Southern Journal of Philosophy* 38: 231–250.
Lightfoot, J. L. 2002. 'Nothing to do with the *technitai* of Dionysus?' In *Greek and Roman Actors; Aspects of an Ancient Profession*, edited by E. Hall and P. Easterling. 209–225. Cambridge: Cambridge University Press.
Lippman, E. A. 1963. 'Hellenic Conceptions of Harmony'. *Journal of the American Musicological Society* 16: 3–35.
Lisi, F. L. 2007. 'Individual Soul, World Soul and the Form of the Good in Plato's *Republic* and *Timaeus*'. *Études Platoniciennes* 4: 105–118.
Litchfield, M. 1988. 'Aristoxenus and Empiricism: A Reevaluation Based on His Theories'. *Journal of Music Theory* 32: 51–73.
Lomiento, L. 2011. 'Riflessioni critiche sul concetto di 'appropriatezza' nel *De musica* dello Ps. Plutarco (De mus. 32–36)'. *Quaderni Urbinati di cultura classica* 99: 135–152.
Long, A. 2008. 'Plato's Dialogues and a Common Rationale for Dialogue Form'. In *The End of Dialogue in Antiquity*, edited by S. Goldhill. 45–59. Cambridge: Cambridge University Press.
Long, C. P. 2007. 'Socrates and the Politics of Music: Preludes of the Republic'. *Polis* 24: 70–90.
Lord, C. 1978. 'On Damon and Music Education'. *Hermes* 106: 32–43.
Luhmann, N. 1977. 'Differentiation of Society'. *Canadian Journal of Sociology* 2: 29–53.
Luhmann, N. 1993. *Risk: a Sociological Theory*. Walter de Gruyter.
Lynch, T. 2016. 'Arsis and Thesis in Ancient Rhythmics and Metrics: A New Approach'. *The Classical Quarterly* 66: 491–513.
Lynch, T. 2017. 'The Symphony of Temperance in *Republic* 4'. *Greek and Roman Musical Studies* 5: 18–34.
Lyon, E. L. 2016. 'Ethical Aspects of Listening in Plato's *Timaeus*'. *Greek and Roman Musical Studies* 4: 253–272.
MacDowell, D. M. 1982. 'Aristophanes and Kallistratos'. *The Classical Quarterly* 32: 21–26.
Macran, H. 1902. *The Harmonics of Aristoxenus*. Oxford: Clarendon.

Martin, R. 2003. 'The Pipes are Brawling: Conceptualizing Musical Performance in Athens'. In *The Cultures within Greek Culture: Contact, Conflict, Collaboration*, edited by C. Dougherty and L. Kurke. 153–180. Cambridge: Cambridge University Press.

Massumi, B. 2002. *Parables for the Virtual: Movement, Affect, Sensation*. Durham, NC: Duke University Press.

Mastromarco, G. 1979. 'L'esordio "segreto" di Aristofane'. *Quaderni di Storia* 10: 153–196.

Mathiesen, T. J. 1985. 'Rhythm and Meter in Ancient Greek Music'. *Music Theory Spectrum* 7: 159–180.

Mathiesen, T. J. 1999. *Apollo's Lyre: Greek Music and Music Theory in Antiquity and the Middle Ages*. Lincoln, NE: University of Nebraska Press.

Mauss, M. 1979. *Sociology and Psychology: Essays*. Translated by B. Brewster. London: Routledge and Kegan Paul.

McAdon, B. 2004. 'Plato's Denunciation of Rhetoric in the *Phaedrus*'. *Rhetoric Review* 23: 21–39.

McCabe, M. M. 1992. 'Myth, Allegory and Argument in Plato'. *Apeiron* 25: 47–67.

McClain, E. G. 1978. *The Pythagorean Plato: Prelude to the Song Itself*. Stony Brook, NY: N. Hays.

McCoy, M. B. 2009. 'Alcidamas, Isocrates, and Plato on Speech, Writing, and Philosophical Rhetoric'. *Ancient Philosophy* 29: 45–66.

Modrak, D. K. W. 1987. *Aristotle: The Power of Perception*. Chicago: University of Chicago Press.

Moore, B. 2012. *An Introduction to the Psychology of Hearing*. Leiden: Brill.

Moore, C. 2014. 'Pindar's Charioteer in Plato's *Phaedrus*'. *Classical Quarterly* 64: 525–532.

Moro Tornese, S. F. 2013. 'Music and the Return of the Soul in Proclus' Commentaries on Plato's *Timaeus* and *Republic*'. In *Ancient Approaches to Plato's Republic*, edited by A. Sheppard. 117–128. London: Institute of Classical Studies.

Moutsopoulos, É. A. 1959. *La Musique dans l'oeuvre de Platon*. Paris: Presses universitaires de France.

Najock, D. 1972. *Drei anonyme griechische Traktate über die Musik*. Kassel: Barenreiter.

Neschke-Hentschke, A. B., ed. 2000. *Le Timée de Platon: Contributions à l'histoire de sa réception*. Leuven: Peeters.

Nightingale, A. W. 1995. *Genres in Dialogue: Plato and the Construct of Philosophy*. Cambridge: Cambridge University Press.

Olympiodorus. 1956. *Commentary on the First Alcibiades of Plato*. Edited by L. G. Westerink. Amsterdam: North-Holland Publishing Company.

Paga, J. 2010. 'Deme Theaters in Attica and the Trittys System'. *Hesperia: The Journal of the American School of Classical Studies at Athens* 79: 351–384.

Partenie, C. 2009. *Plato's Myths*. New York: Cambridge University Press.

Patel, A. D. 2008. *Music, Language, and the Brain*. Oxford: Oxford University Press.

Patočka, J. 2002. *Plato and Europe*. Translated by Petr Lom. Stanford, CA: Stanford University Press.

Pearson, L. 1990. *Aristoxenus, Elementa rhythmica: the Fragment of Book II and the Additional Evidence for Aristoxenean Rhythmic Theory*. Oxford: Clarendon Press.

Pelosi, F. 2006. 'Aristotele, *De sensu* III, VI, VII: la percezione del suono e la consonanza nella musica greca'. *Quaderni Urbinati di cultura classica* 84: 27–60.

Pelosi, F. 2010. *Plato on Music, Soul and Body*. Translated by S. Henderson. Cambridge: Cambridge University Press.

Peponi, A.-E. 2012. *Frontiers of Pleasure: Models of Aesthetic Response in Archaic and Classical Greek Thought*. Oxford: Oxford University Press.

Peponi, A.-E., ed. 2013. *Performance and Culture in Plato's Laws*. New York: Cambridge University Press.

Perlman, M. 2004. *Unplayed Melodies: Javanese Gamelan and the Genesis of Music Theory*. Berkeley: University of California Press.

Petraki, Z. 2008. 'The Soul "Dances": Psychomusicology in Plato's *Republic*'. *Apeiron* 41: 147–170.

Pickard-Cambridge, A. W., J. Gould, and D. M. Lewis. 1988. *The Dramatic Festivals of Athens*. Oxford: Clarendon Press.

Picker, J. M. 2003. *Victorian Soundscapes*. Oxford: Oxford University Press.

Pinch, T. J., and K. Bijsterveld, eds. 2012. *The Oxford Handbook of Sound Studies*. New York: Oxford University Press.

Pöhlmann, E. 2018. 'Ἀνωνύμου σύγγραμμα περὶ μουσικῆς (*Anonymi Bellermann*)'. *Greek and Roman Musical Studies* 6: 115–127.

Polansky, R. M. 2007. *Aristotle's De anima*. New York: Cambridge University Press.

Pollard, J. 1965. *Seers, Shrines and Sirens: the Greek Religious Revolution in the Sixth Century B.C.* London: Allen & Unwin.

Porter, J. 2007. 'Lasus of Hermione, Pindar, and the Riddle of S'. *Classical Quarterly* 57: 1–21.

Power, T. 2012. 'Aristoxenus and the "Neoclassicists"'. In *Aristoxenus of Tarentum: Discussion*, edited by C. Huffman. 129–154. New Brunswick, NJ: Transaction Publishers.

Power, T. C. 2010. *The Culture of Kitharōidia*. Washington: Center for Hellenic Studies.

Proust, M. 1988. *Du côté de chez Swann*. Paris: Gallimard.

Racionero, Q. 1998. 'Logos, Myth, and Probable Discourse in Plato's *Timaeus*'. *Elenchus* 19: 29–60.

Raffa, M. 2011. 'Il canto di achille (ps. Plut. 'de mus'. 40, 1145d–f)'. *Quaderni Urbinati di cultura classica* 99: 165–176.

Raffa, M. 2018. *Theophrastus of Eresus: Commentary Volume 9.1. Sources on Music (Texts 714–796C)*. Leiden: Brill.

Rancière, J. 1999. *Dis-agreement: Politics and Philosophy*. Translated by Julie Rose. Minneapolis: University of Minnesota Press.

Rancière, J. 2004. *The Politics of Aesthetics: The Distribution of the Sensible*. Translated by Gabriel Rockhill. London: Continuum.

Rapp, J. R. 2014. *Ordinary Oblivion and the Self Unmoored: Reading Plato's Phaedrus and Writing the Soul*. New York: Fordham University Press.

Rath, R. C. 2003. *How Early America Sounded*. Ithaca, NY: Cornell University Press.

Rayner, K., and A. Pollatsek. 2012. *The Psychology of Reading*. New York: Psychology Press.

Reinach, T. 1898. 'Les nouveaux fragments rythmiques d'Aristoxène'. *Revue des Études Grecques* 11: 389–418.

Reydams-Schils, G. J. 2011. 'Myth and poetry in the *Timaeus*'. In *Plato and the Poets*, edited by P. Destrée and F. G. Herrmann. 349–360. Leiden: Brill.

Rice, T. 2003. 'Soundselves: An Acoustemology of Sound and Self in the Edinburgh Royal Infirmary'. *Anthropology Today* 19: 4–9.

Richter, G. 2009. 'Silence as the Greatest Music: the Harmony of Philosophy and Mousike in Plato's *Phaedo*'. *Literature & Aesthetics* 19: 88–113.

Riginos, A. S. 1976. *Platonica: The Anecdotes Concerning the Life and Writings of Plato*. Leiden: Brill.

Robbins, E. 2002. 'Lasus'. In *Brill's New Pauly*, edited by H. Canick and H. Schneider. Leiden: Brill.

Rocconi, E. 2009. 'Il suono musicale tra età ellenistica ed età imperiale'. In *La Musa dimenticata*, edited by M. C. Martinelli, F. Pelosi and C. Pernigotti. 191–204. Pisa: Edizioni della Normale.

Rocconi, E. 2012. 'The Aesthetic Value of Music in Platonic Thought'. In *Aesthetic Value in Classical Antiquity*, edited by I. Sluiter and R. M. Rosen. 113–132. Leiden: Brill.

Rocconi, E. 2016. 'The Music of the *Laws* and the Laws of Music'. *Greek and Roman Musical Studies* 4: 71–89.

Roochnik, D. 2001. 'The Deathbed Dream of Reason: Socrates' Dream in the Phaedo'. *Arethusa* 34: 239–258.

Rosenmeyer, T. G. 1998. 'Name-Setting and Name-Using: Elements of Socratic Foundationalism in Plato's *Cratylus*'. *Ancient Philosophy* 18: 41–60.

Rowe, C. 2007a. 'Interpreting Plato'. In *A Companion to Plato*, edited by H. H. Benson. 13–24. Oxford: Wiley-Blackwell.

Rowe, C. J. 2007b. *Plato and the Art of Philosophical Writing*. Cambridge: Cambridge University Press.

Rowell, L. 1979. 'Aristoxenus on Rhythm'. *Journal of Music Theory* 23: 63–79.

Sansone, D. 2018. 'Stylistic Characterization in Plato: Nicias, Alcibiades, and Laches'. *Greek, Roman, and Byzantine Studies* 58: 156–176.

Sayre, K. M. 1995. *Plato's Literary Garden: How to Read a Platonic Dialogue*. Notre Dame: University of Notre Dame Press.

Schaeffer, P. 2017. *Treatise on Musical Objects: An Essay Across Disciplines*. Translated by C. North and J. Dack. Berkeley: University of California Press.

Schafer, R. M. 1994. *The Soundscape: Our Sonic Environment and the Tuning of the World*. Rochester, VT: Destiny.

Schofield, M. 2010. 'Music All Pow'rful'. In *Plato's Republic: A Critical Guide*, edited by M. McPherran. 229–247. Cambridge: Cambridge University Press.

Schulze, H. 2018. *The Sonic Persona: An Anthropology of Sound*. New York: Bloomsbury Academic.

Schwartz, H. 2011. *Making Noise: From Babel to the Big Bang and Beyond*. Boston: Zone.

Scodel, H. R. 1987. *Diaeresis and Myth in Plato's Statesman*. Göttingen: Vandenhoeck & Ruprecht.

Scodel, R. 2001. 'The Poet's Career, the Rise of Tragedy, and Athenian Cultural Hegemony'. In *Gab es das griechische Wundes?*, edited by D. Papenfuss and V. Strocka. 215–225. Mainz: von Zabern.

Scruton, R. 1987. 'Analytical Philosophy and the Meaning of Music'. *The Journal of Aesthetics and Art Criticism* 46: 169–176.

Scruton, R. 1999. *The Aesthetics of Music*. Oxford: Oxford University Press.

Seaford, R. 1976. 'On the Origins of Satyric Drama'. *Maia* 28: 209–221.

Sedley, D. N. 2003. *Plato's Cratylus*. Cambridge: Cambridge University Press.

Sicking, C. M. J. 1998. 'Theophrastus on the Nature of Music'. In *Theophrastus. Reappraising the Sources*, edited by J. M. van Ophuijsen and M. van Raalte. 93–142. New Brunswick, NJ: Transaction.

Silverman, A. 1990. 'Plato on Perception and "Commons"'. *Classical Quarterly* 40: 148–175.

Silverman, A. 2001. 'The End of the *Cratylus*: Limning the World'. *Ancient Philosophy* 21: 25–43.

Silverman, A. 2010. 'Philosopher-kings and Craftsman-gods'. In *One Book, The Whole Universe*, edited by R. D. Mohr and B. M. Sattler. 55–67. Las Vegas: Parmenides Publications.

Small, C. 1998. *Musicking: The Meanings of Performing and Listening.* Hanover: University Press of New England.

Smith, I. 2008. 'False Names, Demonstratives and the Refutation of Linguistic Naturalism in Plato's *Cratylus* 427d1–431c3'. *Phronesis* 53: 125–151.

Steiner, D. 2011. 'Dancing with the Stars: *Choreia* in the Third Stasimon of Euripides' *Helen*'. *Classical Philology* 104: 299–323.

Sterne, J. 2003. *The Audible Past: Cultural Origins of Sound Reproduction.* Chapel Hill: Duke University Press.

Sterne, J. 2012. *The Sound Studies Reader.* New York: Routledge.

Stewart, R. S. 1989. 'The Epistemological Function of Platonic Myth'. *Philosophy and Rhetoric* 22: 260–280.

Stokes, M. C. 1986. *Plato's Socratic Conversations: Drama and Dialectic in Three Dialogues.* London: Athlone Press.

Stuttard, D. 2018. *Nemesis: Alcibiades and the Fall of Athens.* Cambridge, MA: Harvard University Press.

Tarrant, H. 1990. 'Myth as a Tool of Persuasion in Plato'. *Antichthon* 24: 19–31.

Tarrant, H. 1993. *Thrasyllan Platonism.* Ithaca, NY: Cornell University Press.

Tarrant, H. 2013. 'Socrates' Other Voices: *Euthyphro* in the *Cratylus*'. *Revue de métaphysique et de morale* 80: 507–523.

Taylor, A. E. 1928. *A Commentary on Plato's Timaeus.* Oxford: Oxford University Press.

Thomas, C. J. 2008. 'Inquiry Without Names in Plato's *Cratylus*'. *Journal of the History of Philosophy* 46: 341–364.

Toner, J., and C. Classen, eds. 2014. *A Cultural History of the Senses.* 6 vols. London: Bloomsbury.

Towey, A. 1991. 'Aristotle and Alexander on Hearing and Instantaneous Change: A Dilemma in Aristotle's Account of Hearing'. In *The Second Sense*, edited by C. Burnett, M. Fend and P. Gouk. 7–18. London: The Warburg Institute.

Trivigno, F. V. 2012. 'Etymology and the Power of Names in Plato's *Cratylus*'. *Ancient Philosophy* 32: 35–75.

Vahtikari, V. 2014. *Tragedy Performances Outside Athens in the Late Fifth and the Fourth Centuries BC.* Helsinki: Foundation of the Finnish Institute at Athens.

Wallace, R. W. 1991. 'Damone de Oa ed i suoi successori: un' analisi delle fonti'. In *Harmonia Mundi*, edited by R. W. Wallace and B. MacLachlan. 30–53. Rome: Ateneo.

Wallace, R. W. 2004. 'Damon of Oa: A Music Theorist Ostracized?' In *Music and the Muses: the Culture of Mousikē in the Classical Athenian City*, edited by P. Wilson and P. Murray. 249–268. Oxford: Oxford University Press.

Wallace, R. W. 2015. *Reconstructing Damon: Music, Wisdom Teaching, and Politics in Perikles' Athens.* Oxford: Oxford University Press.

Wehrli, F. 1944. *Die Schule des Aristoteles*. Basel: B. Schwabe.

Weil, H., and T. Reinach, eds. 1900. *'Plutarque,' De la musique*. Paris: Leroux.

Weiss, N. A. 2018. *The Music of Tragedy: Performance and Imagination in Euripidean Theater*. Oakland, CA: University of California Press.

Weiss, R. 2005. 'The Strategic Use of Myth in the *Protagoras* and *Meno*'. *Interpretation* 33: 133–152.

Werner, D. S. 2012. *Myth and Philosophy in Plato's Phaedrus*. Cambridge: Cambridge University Press.

Wersinger, A. G. 2006. 'Un élément musical inaperçu dans le Mythe d'Er: l'hymne des Moires et l'heptacorde inversé'. In *Musique & Antiquité: actes du colloque d'Amiens, 25–26 octobre 2004*, edited by O. Mortier-Waldschmidt. 147–164. Paris: Les Belles Lettres.

West, M. L. 1982. *Greek Metre*. Oxford: Oxford University Press.

West, M. L. 1992. *Ancient Greek Music*. Oxford: Oxford University Press.

Westerink, L. G., ed. 1956. *Anonymous Prolegomena to Platonic Philosophy*. 2nd edn. Amsterdam: North Holland Publishing.

Williams, B. 1994. 'Cratylus' Theory of Names and its Refutation'. In *Language*, edited by S. Everson. 28–36. Cambridge: Cambridge University Press.

Wilson, P. 1999. 'The *Aulos* in Athens'. In *Performance Culture and Athenian Democracy*, edited by S. Goldhill and S. Osborne. 58–95. Cambridge: Cambridge University Press.

Wilson, P. 2000. *The Athenian Institution of the Khoregia: the Chorus, the City, and the Stage*. Cambridge: Cambridge University Press.

Wilson, P. 2002. 'The Musicians among the Actors'. In *Greek and Roman Actors*, edited by E. Hall and P. Easterling. 39–69. Cambridge: Cambridge University Press.

Winnington-Ingram, R. P. 1928. 'The Spondeion Scale. Pseudo-Plutarch *de Musica*, 1134f–1135b and 1137b–d'. *Classical Quarterly* 22: 83–91.

Woerther, F. 2007. *L'èthos Aristotélicien: genèse d'une notion rhétorique*. Paris: Vrin.

Woerther, F. 2008. 'Music and the Education of the Soul in Plato and Aristotle: Homoeopathy and the Formation of Character'. *Classical Quarterly* 58: 89–103.

Wolfsdorf, D. 2013. *Pleasure in Ancient Greek Philosophy*. New York: Cambridge University Press.

Wolfsdorf, D. 2014. 'Timaeus' Explanation of Sense-Perceptual Pleasure'. *The Journal of Hellenic Studies* 134: 120–135.

Wood, A. 2007. 'Names and "Cutting Being at the Joints" in the *Cratylus*'. *Dionysius* 25: 21–31.

Wright, O. 1978. *The Modal System of Arab and Persian Music, A.D. 1250–1300*. Oxford: Oxford University Press.

Xenocrates. 1982. *Frammenti*. Edited by M. Isnardi Parente. Naples: Bibliopolis.

Zaslavsky, R. 1981. *Platonic Myth and Platonic Writing*. Washington, DC: University Press of America.

Zeyl, D. J. 2000. *Plato: Timaeus*. Indianapolis, In.: Hackett.

Zhmud, L. 2012. *Pythagoras and the Early Pythagoreans*. Oxford: Oxford University Press.

Ziegler, K., and M. Pohlenz. 1953. *Plutarch: De Musica*. Leipzig: Teubner.

Zuckerkandl, V. 1956. *Sound and Symbol: Music and the External World*. Princeton, NJ: Princeton University Press.

Index

Agathon 26
agōgē 135, 137–138, 151–153
Alcibiades 48
Anaxagoras 75
Anaximander 43
Anonyma Bellermaniana de musica scripta 138–139
Archelaos 75
Archytas 8, 44, 76, 171 n.11, 176 n.43, 176 n.59, 183 n.118
Aristides Quintilianus
    1.9 165 n.46
    1.12 134–138, 141–142
    3.20 44–45
    3.103 44–45
Aristophanes 26, 167 n.9
Aristotle
    nature 94, 179 n.24
    potentiality 107–108
    time 131
    sound and hearing 98–101, 180 n.49
    units of measurement 118
    An. Post.
        100a-c 96
    De an.
        417a.15-21 99
        419a.32-420b.5 98
        424a.18-25 99
    De caelo
        2.9 43–44
    De gen.
        787a.5-23 99
    Mem.
        452b23-453a3 131
    Metaph.
        1052b.15-1053a.23 118
    Ph.
        192b.13-15 94
        219a.32–220a.21 131
    Poet.
        1449a.14-19 27
    Post. An.
        71b.22-72a.25 100
        99b.36-100a.4 100, 128
Aristoxenus
    beauty, associated with enharmonic tunings 148
    continuity 111–112
    harmonic theory not independent of the rest of music 140
    influence on later music pedagogy 8, 164 n.26
    influence on later music theory 7
    materiality of sound, irrelevance to 94–95
    musical history 146–153
    potentiality 107–110
    relation to Plato 5–6, 143–144, 164 n.14
    rhythm 130–133
    theatre music 148–151
    theory and practice 120–123, 182 n.96
    time binding 11, 127, Chapter 5
    works and career 93–94
    Harm.
        1.4 94
        1.5 123
        1.7-8 141
        1.9 95
        1.18 94, 112
        1.23 146–147
        1.25 121–122
        1.27 111
        1.29 138
        2.32 95, 140
        2.33 114, 120, 147
        2.33-34 129
        2.36.10-16 107
        2.38-39 128
        2.39-40 14
        2.39-41 120
        2.43-44 95
        2.47-48 109, 110

Index

2.48 140–141
2.54 112
2.54-55 113
2.57-58 114–119
3.69.1-11 110
Rhythm. 130–133
2.3-6 130–131
2.16 131
2.20-21 133
2.30-35 133
Fragmenta Neapolitana 10–12 133
Fr. 6 Wehrli 152
Fr. 70 Wehrli 148
Fr. 76 Wehrli 151
Fr. 81 Wehrli 149–150
Fr. 82 Wehrli 143–144
Fr. 83 Wehrli 136–137
Fr. 84 Wehrli 141
Fr. 124 Wehrli 149
auditory culture 1, 2, 20–21, 89
Auloi
   rejected by Alcibiades 48

bass solo, bartender behavior during 165
beauty *see under* Aristoxenus
Becker, Howard 9
Belfiore, Elizabeth 50–51
Berger, Carol 12
body techniques *see* Techniques of the body
Brann, Eva 35, 38
Burkhert, Walter 45

chromatic *see under* genus
Cicero
   Resp.
      6.18-19 44
Cleonides 14, 134

Damon 8
De audibilibus 101–102
Democritus 75–76
Derrida, Jacques 4
Diatonic *see under* genus
Diogenes Laertius
   3.56 27

education 2, 80
empeiria ('experience') 96

Enharmonic *see under* genus
Equal Temperament 15–16
Ethos 20, 139–140, 146–147, 154–156, 187 n.59
Etymology 59–60
Euripides 26
   Hippolytus an important structuring element in Plato's *Phaedrus* 51–52

Foucault, Michel 4, 13
functional differentiation 10

Gadamer, Hans-Georg 13, 35
genus
   enharmonic 18–19, 107–108, 110, 136–137, 141–143, 146–148, 190 n.87
   chromatic 18–19, 110, 119, 121–122, 136, 139–140, 147, 148
   diatonic 18–19, 68, 110, 136–137, 141
Glaucus of Rhegium 190 n.104
Gorgias 150

Hadot, Pierre 3
harmonia ('tuning') 15
   see also genus
hearing, theories of 74–77, 97–106
Heraclides Ponticus 143, 191 n.114
Hippocrates *On Ancient Medicine* 117–118
historicism 13

Iser, Wolfgang 35

Kane, Brian 2
Korzybski, Alfred 10
Koselleck, Reinhart 127
Kuhn, Thomas 13

Langer, Suzanne 125–126, 160
Lasus of Hermione 8, 122, 150–151
listening 1, 2
Luhmann, Niklas 10

Macrobius
   In Somn. 2.4.15 44
Marsyas 47–48
mathematical musicology 16, 95, 116–117

Mauss, Marcel 2
melos ('song') 15
meloidia 20
melopoeia 20, 134-139, 166 n.49
memory 128-129
metron ('standard of measurement') 117-118
mode *see* scale species
movement
    see reading
    babies, movement of 80
    circular movement is best 79
    cosmic movement 43-44, 66, 70
    harmonics and movement 32
    knowledge impossible if movement dominates 31
    life defined by movement 79
    music associated with 11-12, 84
    perception based on 60, 71
    politics an attempt to regulate, 79, 80, 82, 84
    psychic movement 35, 36, 38, 57, 72-73
    soul a capacity for self-movement 79
    sound based on movement, 74-79, 95
    therapy, movement as 81
music of the spheres 8, 43-44
music theory 6-7
    and Greek philosophy 8-10
musical autonomy 96
musicking 9-10

nature 94, 96, 179 n.24, 179 n.26
nome, *see nomos*
nomos 39, 65, 82, 142, 144, 170 n.66, 175 n.25, 189 n.74, 189 n.87, 190 n.104

Olympiodorus 28
Olympus 136-137, 142

Patočka, Jan 4
perception 6, 71-72, 95
    order in perception 96
Petteia 135-137
Philolaus 8, 43
Plato 3, 5
    allegory of the cave 33-34
    gestural rhetoric 36
    musical training 25-26

myths and likenesses 33-34
reading as erogonomic activity 35-38, 40, 79
speaker-change in his texts 40, 170 n.68
swans as metaphor for his writing 26, 29
texts as control mechanisms for psychic training 6, 89, *passim*
teaching by refusing to teach 34-35
time binding 11
tragedy 25-27, 169 n.58
writing, comparable to music 38-39, 86-87, 169 n.58
writing, hestitations about 29-30, 52-54
writing, variety of 54-55
Cra. 59-62
    411b-c 60
    426d-427b 60
    440a-b 30-31
Ep.
    7.341c 29-30
Ion
    533d-534a 55-56
Leg. 79-89
    movement, importance in 79-84
    653d-e 80
    659d 80
    669b-670e 84-86
    691a 39
    700a-701b 5
    722d-e 39, 81-82
    788a-c 81
    791a 81
    802c-d 82-83
    811c-e 39, 86
    817b 39
Phaedr. 49-55
    235c-d 49
    242d-e 49
    253e 50
    275d-278e 29, 52-53
Phd.
    60d-61c 39
Phlb.
    17b-e 87
    25e-26a 87
    55e-56a 88
    64d-e 87
Prot.
    326a-b 38

Resp.
   Movement of the argument 38
   388a-c 5
   394e-397b 56–57
   397a 53
   397b-402d 5
   398e-399c 52
   399c-e 53
   402c 53–54
   514a-517a 33–34
   530d-531c 32
   591c-d 39
   597a-605b 56
   616d-617b 43–46
   617a-d 39
Soph.
   253b 40
Symp.
   210a-211d 48
   215e-216a 47–48
Ti. 62–79
   movement in 64
   19b-c 64
   27d-28c 62
   29b-29d 63–64
   29d 65
   29f-30d 65
   32a-33b 66
   35b-36d 66–68
   37b 44
   42a-43c 70–72
   47b-c 73
   47c-e 73
   48a-e 74
   67b 75
   80a-c 77
   90c-d 78
Tht.
   152a-171c 31–32
"Plutarch" *De musica*
   Portions attributable to Aristoxenus 188 n.65
   1134e 136
   1135c 148
   1135d 148
   1136c 144
   1136d 149–150
   1136e-1137a 143
   1141c 150
   1142b 151
   1142d 192
   1142e 147
   1142f 141
   1143b-1143d 141–142
   1143f-1144b 145
   1144a 141
   1145a 148–149
Proclus
   In R. 2.238-9 Kröll 45–46
Ptolemy *Harm.* 3.8-15 44
Pythagoras 169 n.45

Rancière, Jacques 13–14
Rapp, Jennifer 36
reading
   as movement 35–36, 40, 57
rhythm 130–133
   an abstraction 132

scale species 19–20
Schaeffer, Pierre 42
sirens 45–46
Small, Christopher 9
Socrates
   endorsed and disavowed 46
   influence on Plato 26
   satyr, compared to 47, 50–51
   siren, compared to 47
   styles of communication 46
sound vs. hearing 97–106
Sterne, Jonathan 1, 2, 89
Sun Ra 161

techniques of the body 3
Terpander 148
tetrachord 16–18
Theon of Smyrna
   146.8 45
Theophrastus 102–106
time binding 10–11
time in music 12, 125–156, 185 n.14
tragedy 25–26, 83
tune 20, 134–139

Xenocrates 97–98

Zuckerkandl, Victor 12, 126–127

www.ingramcontent.com/pod-product-compliance
Lightning Source LLC
Chambersburg PA
CBHW052040300426
44117CB00012B/1908